THE *Holy* SPIRIT

His Identity, Mission, and Ministry

ROBERT L. MILLET

DESERET
BOOK

Salt Lake City, Utah

ALSO BY ROBERT L. MILLET

The Atoning One

Whatever Happened to Faith?

Precept upon Precept

Men of Covenant

Living in the Millennium

Living in the Eleventh Hour

Lehi's Dream

Making Sense of the Book of Revelation

Talking with God

Men of Influence

Holding Fast

Men of Valor

What Happened to the Cross?

Are We There Yet?

Getting at the Truth

Grace Works

When a Child Wanders

Quotations on pp. v–vi can be found at:

Joseph Smith, "Gift of the Holy Ghost," *Times and Seasons*, vol. 3, no. 16 (15 June 1842): 823.

Brigham Young, in *Journal of Discourses*, 12:104.

John Taylor, in *Journal of Discourses*, 13:373.

Russell M. Nelson, "Revelation for the Church, Revelation for Our Lives," *Ensign*, May 2018, 96.

Library of Congress Cataloging-in-Publication Data

Names: Millet, Robert L., author.

Title: The Holy Spirit : his identity, mission, and ministry / Robert L. Millet.

Description: Salt Lake City, Utah : Deseret Book, [2019] | Includes bibliographical references and index.

Identifiers: LCCN 2019014237 | ISBN 9781629729787 (hardbound : alk. paper)

Subjects: LCSH: Holy Spirit. | Spiritual life—The Church of Jesus Christ of Latter-day Saints. | Spiritual life—Mormon Church. | The Church of Jesus Christ of Latter-day Saints— Doctrines. | Mormon Church—Doctrines.

Classification: LCC BX8643.H63 M55 2019 | DDC 231/.3—dc23

LC record available at https://lccn.loc.gov/2019014237

Printed in the United States of America

Publishers Printing, Salt Lake City, UT

10   9   8   7   6   5   4   3   2   1

WE BELIEVE IN THE GIFT OF THE HOLY GHOST being enjoyed now, as much as it was in the Apostles' days. . . . We believe that the holy men of old spake as they were moved by the Holy Ghost, and that holy men in these days speak by the same principle.

—JOSEPH SMITH

THERE IS NO DOUBT, if a person lives according to the revelations given to God's people, he may have the Spirit of the Lord to signify to him His will, and to guide and to direct him in the discharge of his duties, in his temporal as well as his spiritual exercises. I am satisfied, however, that in this respect, we live far beneath our privileges.

—BRIGHAM YOUNG

I DO NOT CARE HOW LEARNED a man may be, or how extensively he may have traveled. I do not care what his talent, intellect, or genius may be, at what college he may have studied, how comprehensive his views or what his judgment may be on other matters, he cannot understand certain things without the Spirit of God.

—JOHN TAYLOR

Our Savior and Redeemer, Jesus Christ, will perform some of His mightiest works between now and when He comes again. We will see miraculous indications that God the Father and His Son, Jesus Christ, preside over this Church in majesty and glory. But in coming days, it will not be possible to survive spiritually without the guiding, directing, comforting, and constant influence of the Holy Ghost. My beloved brothers and sisters, I plead with you to increase your spiritual capacity to receive revelation.

—Russell M. Nelson

CONTENTS

Preface vii

Acknowledgments x

Introduction: No Greater Gift 1

PART I
The Personage and the Gift

1   Who Is the Holy Ghost? 9

2   Christ and the Spirit: Partners in Redemption 20

3   Filling the Immensity of Space 33

4   An Abundant Outpouring 43

5   The Upward Reach for the Spirit 55

PART II
Knowledge That Protects and Confirms

6   Discerning True and False Spirits 71

7   Quenching the Spirit 84

8   Empowered and Instructed in Prayer 110

9   Knowing and Knowing That We Know 123

PART III
Manifesting His Will

10   Matters Only God Can Make Known 141

11   Avenues of Divine Guidance 159

12 The Spirit Works through Mortals 176

13 Speaking with the Tongue of Angels 193

PART IV
Changed, Renewed, and Purified

14 Entrance into the Royal Family of Jesus Christ 211

15 Transformation and Deep Conversion 228

16 Laying Hold on Every Good Gift 244

17 Pardoned and Purified 257

18 He Will Seal Us His 271

19 Sweet Communion and Constant Companionship. 284

Conclusion: The Spirit—Forever Worthy of Our Trust 297

Sources Cited. 307

Scripture Index 315

Subject Index. 319

PREFACE

The Holy Spirit is in many ways the breath of life to the Church of Jesus Christ. This book is an effort to better understand and appreciate how the third member of the Godhead is inextricably linked to every facet of the Christian faith. Indeed, one would be hard pressed to find something with which the Saints of God labor in the work of the ministry in which the Spirit is not involved. This has not been an easy book to write, but it has proven to be one of the most intellectually stimulating and spiritually uplifting projects I have undertaken. One of the challenges of writing a book of this kind is delimitation, the admission that I simply cannot cover every facet of the topic. For that I apologize. Having said that, I hasten to add that I have tried to be as comprehensive as possible so that this work might serve as a valuable resource on this crucial gospel topic.

Several years ago, while serving as a stake president, I attended a training meeting for all the stake presidents in our area. One of the Church leaders who addressed us was President Russell M. Nelson, then a member of the Quorum of the Twelve Apostles. He spoke at some length about Christ our Savior, indicating that he wanted to discuss with us both the mission and the ministry of Jesus. I had never considered that there was a distinction between those two words and had for many years used them interchangeably. President Nelson pointed out, however, that the *mission* of Jesus Christ was *His alone,* namely the atoning work performed in Gethsemane and on Golgotha and the triumphant climax of his work that we know to be the Resurrection, His glorious rise from the dead into immortality. No other person, President Nelson pointed out, could have suffered for the sins of the world.[1] Only the sinless Son of Man had the power to do that. President Nelson then explained that Jesus's *ministry* pertained to his life, including his everyday tender encounters with individuals.[2] These are deeds, President Nelson declared, that each one of us can do as well. It is the way that the prophets have charged us to minister to our brothers and sisters.

In a similar manner and in that spirit, we will speak here of the *identity* of the Holy Ghost (who he is and what his position is within the Godhead); the *mission* of the third member of that divine Presidency (how and by what means he operates, prompts, inspires, sanctifies, and seals); and the *ministry* of the Holy Ghost (how he deals with each one of us individually, tutors us tenderly, and leads us to the Father and the Son): in short, how he ministers to all who choose to live in such a manner as to enjoy his presence and influence.

In this work I have sought to prepare a sound doctrinal work but also to follow Nephi's example to "liken all scriptures" unto ourselves (1 Nephi 19:24). I have therefore included stories or illustrations, either from my own experience or that of Church leaders that can serve as applications of the doctrine and principles discussed. My hope is that this approach will prove beneficial to you, the reader. To be sure, I am a staunch believer in the groundbreaking insight of President Boyd K. Packer: "True doctrine, understood, changes attitudes and behavior."[3] Decades of teaching the gospel of Jesus Christ have also impressed upon me the importance of instruction being *relevant* to listeners, delivered in such a way that those who hear the message not only better

---

1. *Teachings of Russell M. Nelson*, 161.
2. *Teachings of Russell M. Nelson*, 162.
3. "Little Children," *Ensign*, November 1986, 17.

understand the doctrine or principle taught but also see very clearly how it applies and relates to them. In this manner, then, the doctrinal message will find a permanent place in the listener's *mind* and *heart*.

More than any other work I have written, this one has caused me to search my soul, examine my motives, and purify my thoughts and actions. Why? Because it is about the third member of the Godhead. It is a book that will not communicate what the Lord wants understood and felt unless the Spirit of God accompanies it. I will be grateful if, by reading this volume, my sisters and brothers of the faith gain an expanded and broadened perspective on the work of the Spirit. I will be particularly thankful if readers come away more deeply desirous to seek the Spirit, live in a manner to be guided by that Spirit, and begin to enjoy, perhaps as never before, its many gifts and fruit.

I have sought earnestly to be in harmony with holy scripture and the teachings of apostles and prophets regarding the Person and work of the Holy Ghost and not to go beyond what is stated there. I have especially searched through and reflected carefully on the remarks of the Brethren, so as to represent them properly and accurately. Having said that, I point out that this work is a private endeavor and not an official publication of The Church of Jesus Christ of Latter-day Saints nor of Brigham Young University, where I spent most of my professional life.

With Nephi, son of Lehi, I bear witness that the Holy Spirit is "the gift of God unto all those who diligently seek [the Son of God]. . . . For he that diligently seeketh shall find; and the mysteries of God shall be unfolded unto them, by the power of the Holy Ghost, as well in these times as in times of old, and as well in times of old as in times to come; wherefore, the course of the Lord is one eternal round" (1 Nephi 10:17–19). My sincere hope is that this exploration of the life, work, mission, and ministry of the Holy Ghost will prove rewarding and soul-satisfying to you and that the same Spirit that rested upon Adam and Enoch and Noah and Abraham, upon Abinadi and Alma and Samuel and Moroni, will rest upon you and yours now and always.

ACKNOWLEDGMENTS

First of all, I acknowledge my friend and colleague Von Memory, who painstakingly read and reread the manuscript and offered cautions, corrections, and thoughtful suggestions. This is simply a better book because of Von's gospel knowledge and his wise recommendations.

In the preparation of this work I am appreciative of my friends and associates at Deseret Book Company. I offer special thanks to Lisa Roper, product director, who helped to move this project along from concept to finished product. I also express special appreciation to my dear friend, Suzanne Brady, whose doctrinal understanding and keen editorial skills have been a blessing to me and my work for decades.

As is the case with anything I undertake that is worthwhile, I owe a special debt of gratitude, appreciation, and love to my wife, Shauna. She, like Joseph of old, is "one in whom the Spirit of God is" (Genesis 41:38), my eternal example and model of how to receive and respond to the Spirit's divine guidance.

Introduction

NO GREATER GIFT

⁓

*I*n December 1839 the Prophet Joseph Smith and Elias Higbee traveled to Washington, D.C., to seek redress from the government for the losses suffered by the persecuted and beleaguered Latter-day Saints. In their meeting with President Martin Van Buren, Joseph recorded that the president "interrogated us wherein we differed in our religion from the other religions of the day."[1] If you had been in the room and been asked to respond to President Van Buren's question, how would you have answered?

Perhaps you would have begun by explaining that Latter-day Saints believe that in the year 1820 God the Eternal Father and his Son Jesus Christ appeared in person in a grove in upstate New York to initiate a final gospel dispensation. Or you might have opened your copy of the Book of Mormon and read selected passages, emphasizing that you were reading from a sacred scriptural record kept by an ancient American branch of Israel. You might have emphasized that your religion teaches of a premortal existence, that all persons lived with God in the spirit before their mortal birth. Or maybe you would have explained how the vision of the glories (Doctrine and Covenants 76) is a scriptural commentary on the Savior's words that "in my Father's house

---

1. *Joseph Smith* [manual], 97.

are many mansions" (John 14:2). Any of those answers would have been correct; all of those doctrinal teachings are significant features of the restored gospel, perspectives that are distinctive from that which is found within more traditional Christianity.

And yet, the Prophet of the Restoration chose to give another answer altogether. "Brother Joseph said we differed in mode of baptism, and the gift of the Holy Ghost by the laying on of hands. We considered that *all other considerations were contained in the gift of the Holy Ghost.*"[2] Joseph's statement is a comprehensive reply that gets to the heart of the gospel of Jesus Christ. Suppose we had the teachings, covenants, ordinances, organizational structure, apostolic leadership, and missionary system of the current Church and yet there was no gift of the Holy Ghost? What then? What good are the teachings or doctrines if there is no Spirit to bring clarity or conviction to the souls of individuals? What good are the covenants and ordinances if there is no Holy Ghost acting as the Holy Spirit of Promise to ratify and approve and make binding those rites? And what possible good could come from sending tens of thousands of young men and women and experienced couples to all parts of the globe if there was no way by which listeners could come to know that the message of the restored gospel is from God and it is true?

Reflect for a moment on the prayers offered last Sunday in your sacrament meeting, Sunday School, or priesthood or Relief Society meeting. With all that we might appropriately pray for—the leaders of the Church, the leaders of nations, peace in the world, the full-time missionaries and members in the military, the rising generation of Latter-day Saints, the sick and afflicted within our congregation—with all of those and many more who need our prayers, we always feel the need to say something like the following: "Father, please bless us with thy Spirit," or "Please send thy Spirit to be with us," or "Please bless those

---

2. *Joseph Smith* [manual], 97; emphasis added.

who speak to us that they may be led by the power of thy Spirit and that we may receive by that same Spirit." It would be strange indeed to try to imagine any gathering, any assembly of true followers of the Lord Jesus Christ, wherein someone did *not* petition our Father in Heaven for the comfort, peace, inspiration, and guidance of the Holy Ghost.

We know from experience that it is only when the Holy Spirit is with us, in our midst, that true learning and spiritual growth can take place. Ponder on this for a moment. We are asking our Heavenly Father, the Almighty Elohim, for a member of the Godhead, the third member, to accompany us, dwell with us, teach us, reprove us, and correct us. It is no wonder that our Savior, only hours before the ordeals of Gethsemane and the cross, should explain to his beloved apostles: "I tell you the truth; it is expedient for you that I go away: for if I go not away, the Comforter will not come unto you; but if I depart, I will send him unto you" (John 16:7). No, Jesus Christ himself could not stay on earth throughout all time, but he could send another in his place, another Comforter. That Comforter would "teach [us] all things, and bring all things to [our] remembrance" (John 14:26). He would open the eyes of persons who had long dwelt in the regions of darkness, enlighten the understanding of those who had wandered in error and confusion, and sanctify the minds and hearts of penitent souls who had come unto Christ and repented of their sins.

While serving as a bishop decades ago, it was my sobering task to work closely with a member of the ward who had, because of a very serious moral transgression, been excommunicated from the Church. We met frequently for many months, and in each interview I attempted to express to him the love of the Lord as well as my own affection for him, to assist and walk with him through the painful but important process of repentance, and to extend to him regularly the hope for complete forgiveness and restoration of temple blessings. Early in the process, in about our second meeting, he made a comment that moved me deeply. With tears in his eyes he said, "Bishop, I never knew how much light I had until I had lost it." Then he added poignantly, "It's so dark out here!" It wasn't just his membership in the Church that he missed so desperately, nor even the association of the faithful members. It was the light, life, and liberating strength that come only through the power of God's Spirit. This brother had forfeited a precious gift, a priceless Companion, and he worked and prayed tenaciously until those consummate gifts were once again part of his life.

The late Stephen R. Covey once made a profound observation: "I believe sometimes that as Latter-day Saints we are like fish who discover water last. We are so immersed in the element that we are unaware of its presence. We have been immersed in the revelations of the Lord in this dispensation. No dispensation can compare to this one." Brother Covey reminded students that "it's possible to be given a gift and receive not that gift."[3]

For that very reason, President Brigham Young called the Latter-day Saints to higher ground: "There is no doubt, if a person lives according to the revelations given to God's people, he may have the Spirit of the Lord to signify to him His will, and to guide and to direct him in the discharge of his duties, in his temporal as well as his spiritual exercises. I am satisfied, however, that in this respect, *we live far beneath our privileges.*"[4]

President Wilford Woodruff put things into perspective when he taught that the gift of the Holy Ghost "is the greatest gift that can be bestowed upon man."[5] More recently, President Russell M. Nelson declared: "One of the things the Spirit has repeatedly impressed upon my mind . . . is how willing the Lord is to reveal His mind and will. The privilege of receiving revelation is one of the greatest gifts of God to His children."[6]

---

3. "Educated Conscience," 131.
4. In *Journal of Discourses,* 12:104; emphasis added.
5. *Wilford Woodruff* [manual], 49.
6. "Revelation for the Church, Revelation for Our Lives," *Ensign,* May 2018, 94.

Latter-day Saints believe that some form of the Church of Jesus Christ has been on earth from the days of Adam and Eve; that prophets and seers have, through the generations, been raised up to deliver the mind of God; that priesthood powers and keys have been revealed to administer the gospel of Jesus Christ; and that the Holy Ghost has been conferred upon individuals throughout recorded time in order that they might be inspired, comforted, strengthened, warned, sanctified, and sealed up unto eternal life. The Prophet of the Restoration thus declared: "We believe in the gift of the Holy Ghost being enjoyed now, as much as it was in the Apostles' days. . . . We believe that the holy men of old spake as they were moved by the Holy Ghost, and that holy men in these days speak by the same principle."[7]

As the years go by, and as the pain and pressures of life drive me to my knees more frequently, I appreciate more fully just how significant the words of the Prophet Joseph Smith are. The grand distinction between the Latter-day Saints and other men and women of good will is indeed the gift of the Holy Ghost—that precious, proffered gift that can come to us only through the laying on of hands by those holding the Melchizedek Priesthood. That divine conferral is the difference, an ordinance that makes all the difference, in how we as Latter-day Saints perceive our mortal experience; speak and teach and testify; face and deal with the inevitable tragedies and traumas of mortality; receive and are true and faithful to sacred, saving covenants and ordinances; and anticipate life everlasting in the world to come.

---

7. *Joseph Smith* [manual], 97.

PART I

The Personage and the Gift

Chapter 1

WHO IS THE HOLY GHOST?

s is the case with the ministry of the Father and the Son, the ministry of the Holy Ghost did not begin in this second estate. Joseph Smith the Prophet declared that "everlasting covenant was made between three personages before the organization of this earth and relates to their dispensation of things to men on the earth. These personages . . . are called God the first, the Creator; God the second, the Redeemer; and God the third, the Witness or Testator."[1]

THROUGH RESTORATION LENSES

Many within Christendom today believe that the third member of the Godhead, the Holy Ghost, or Holy Spirit, first entered salvation history in the meridian of time, after the Savior's death and resurrection. The Gospel of Mark begins the story as follows: "And John [the Baptist] . . . preached, saying, There cometh one mightier than I after me, the latchet of whose shoes I am not worthy to stoop down and unloose. I indeed have baptized you with water: but *he shall not only baptize you with water, but with fire, and the Holy Ghost*" (JST, Mark 1:6–8; emphasis added). This prophetic declaration of John the Forerunner was fulfilled, many understand, when, some fifty days after

1. *Joseph Smith* [manual], 42.

the crucifixion of the Savior (Pentecost), the Spirit of God was poured out upon a large group of people in a most unusual manner.

Luke records that "there came a sound from heaven as of a rushing mighty wind, and it filled all the house where they were sitting. And there appeared unto them cloven tongues of fire, as it sat upon each of them. And they were all filled with the Holy Ghost, and began to speak with other tongues, as the Spirit gave them utterance" (Acts 2:2–4). Or, as rendered in other translations, "flames like tongues of fire distributed among them" (Revised English Bible) or "tongues of fire that separated and came to rest on each of them" (New International Version). This was the day of Pentecost, the season of the first fruits, believed to be the time when Moses received the Ten Commandments on Mount Sinai. Latter-day Saints are particularly interested in this glorious occasion, since a similar pentecostal outpouring took place in Kirtland, Ohio, in 1836 at the time of the dedication of the first temple in this dispensation (Doctrine and Covenants 110).

Latter-day Saints do not believe, however, that the day of Pentecost was the first time the Holy Ghost was made manifest among God's children. We know, for example, of occasions in the Old Testament when the Spirit was manifested. One is described in the book of Numbers. Jehovah instructed Moses to gather together seventy of the elders of Israel and take them to the tabernacle, the portable temple. The Lord explained that He would come down and speak with Moses and then "take of the spirit which is upon thee, and . . . put it upon them; and they shall bear the burden of the people with thee, that thou bear it not thyself alone." Jehovah later "took of the spirit that was upon [Moses], and gave it unto the seventy elders: and it came to pass that, when the spirit rested upon them, they prophesied, and did not cease" (Numbers 11:16–17).

The spirit of prophecy began to spread, and Joshua, Moses's trusted assistant, said to the Lawgiver, "My lord Moses, forbid them." Then comes one of the most inspiring and instructive passages in scripture:

"And Moses said unto [Joshua], enviest thou for my sake?" That is, "Do you think this troubles me? Do you suppose I am offended? Do you fear that someone will take my job?" There follows this timeless pronouncement from Moses: "Would God that *all the Lord's people were prophets,* and that *the Lord would put his spirit upon them!*" (Numbers 11: 24–29; emphasis added). We could recite multiple examples in the Old Testament of the Spirit inspiring, directing, and empowering the Lord's faithful people. The apostle Peter summed it up by pointing out that "no prophecy of the scripture is of any private interpretation. For the prophecy came not in old time by the will of man: but *holy men of God spake as they were moved by the Holy Ghost*" (2 Peter 1:20–21; emphasis added).

The Church of Jesus Christ of Latter-day Saints boldly speaks of what might be called Christ's eternal gospel, the singularly significant truth that Christian prophets have taught Christian doctrine and administered Christian ordinances since the time of our first parents in Eden. Adam and Eve were taught the gospel and were thus earth's first Christians. They prayed to the Father in the name of the Son, repented of their sins, were baptized by immersion, received the gift of the Holy Ghost, entered into the order of the Son of God by receiving the priesthood, and were married for eternity. They knew, and they taught their children and their grandchildren, the plan of salvation and that their redemption would be wrought through the shedding of the blood of the Son of Man (Moses 5:1–9; 6:51–68).[2]

---

2. President Ezra Taft Benson explained that "Adam and his posterity were commanded by God to be baptized, to receive the Holy Ghost, and to enter into the order of the Son of God. To enter into the order of the Son of God is the equivalent today of entering into the fulness of the Melchizedek Priesthood, which is only received in the house of the Lord. . . . Today we would say they went to the House of the Lord and received their blessings. . . . This order is otherwise described in modern revelation as an order of family government where a man and woman enter into a covenant with God—just as did Adam and Eve—to be sealed for eternity, to have posterity, and to do the will and work of God throughout their mortality" ("What I Hope You Will Teach Your Children about the Temple," *Ensign,* August 1985, 8–9).

What was true of our first parents was likewise true of Abel, Seth, Enoch, Melchizedek, and Abraham. They had the gospel. They knew the Lord, taught his doctrine, and officiated as his authorized administrators in his earthly kingdom. Isaac, Jacob (Israel), Joseph, Ephraim, and all the patriarchs enjoyed personal revelation and communion with Jehovah, the God of the Old Testament. Samuel, Nathan, and others from Isaiah to Malachi in the Old World and from Lehi to Moroni in the New—all these prophets held the Melchizedek Priesthood.[3]

"Now taking it for granted that the scriptures say what they mean, and mean what they say," Joseph Smith pointed out, "we have sufficient grounds to go on and prove from the Bible that the gospel has always been the same; the ordinances to fulfill its requirements, the same; and the officers to officiate, the same; and the signs and fruits resulting from the promises, the same."[4]

THE PERSONAGE OF THE HOLY GHOST

What do we understand about the Personage we know as the Holy Ghost, the third member of the Godhead? Elder Bruce R. McConkie taught: "Prophets and saints in all dispensations have seen the Lord Jesus Christ in both the dreams of the night and the visions of the day, and also face to face as a man looketh upon and speaketh with his friends. Some have even been privileged to see the Father also. But with the Holy Ghost it is otherwise. His voice is heard; his influence is felt; his presence is manifest—but his person is kept hidden from view in all but rare instances."[5]

1. The Holy Ghost is a male spirit personage, a spirit son of God the Father. In a sermon delivered in 1857, President Heber C. Kimball

---

3. *Joseph Smith* [manual], 109.
4. *Joseph Smith* [manual], 93.
5. *New Witness for the Articles of Faith*, 254.

stated: "The Holy Ghost is a man; he is one of the sons of our Father and our God; and he is that man that stood next to Jesus Christ, just as I stand by Brother Brigham."[6]

This being is known by such name-titles as the Holy Ghost, the Holy Spirit, the Spirit of God, the Spirit of Truth, the Comforter, the Witness or Testator, Revelator, Sanctifier, Sealer, and the Holy Spirit of Promise. Joseph Smith delivered to the Saints in Ramus, Illinois, significant doctrinal items of instruction on 2 April 1843: "The Father has a body of flesh and bones as tangible as man's; the Son also; but the Holy Ghost has not a body of flesh and bones, but is a personage of Spirit" (Doctrine and Covenants 130:22).

We may infer, therefore, that he will eventually receive a physical body, like every other son and daughter of the Father who was faithful in the first estate. On 16 June 1844, only nine days before the martyrdom, George Laub, an early member of the Church whose journal is an important contemporary source of some of the teachings of Joseph Smith, recorded that the Prophet Joseph taught that while the Father, Son, and Holy Ghost are one, or agree in one, "the Holy Ghost is yet a spiritual body and waiting to take to himself a body, as the Savior did or as God [the Father] did."[7]

2. He has form, shape, and occupies space. For a time during his grand panoramic vision, Nephi was tutored by the Spirit. He had seen the tree of life and desired to know what it represented, "for I spake unto him as a man speaketh; for *I beheld that he was in the form of a man; yet nevertheless I knew that it was the Spirit of the Lord;* and he spake unto me as a man speaketh with another" (1 Nephi 11:11; emphasis added). Over the years, persons reading the Book of Mormon

---

6. In *Journal of Discourses,* 5:179.

7. *Words of Joseph Smith,* 382. Franklin D. Richards recorded under date of 27 August 1843 that the Prophet Joseph said, "The Holy Ghost is now in a state of probation which if he should perform in righteousness he may pass through the same or a similar course of things that the Son has" (*Words of Joseph Smith,* 245).

have wondered whether "Spirit of the Lord" refers to Jehovah, the premortal Christ, or the Holy Ghost. How would we know? One approach is to read every reference in the Book of Mormon where the phrase "Spirit of the Lord" is used. When we do so, we discover that this title is used about forty times in the Book of Mormon, and in every case it is quite clear that the being referenced is the Holy Ghost, or in a few cases, the Light of Christ. Not one of the references seems to apply to Jehovah himself. Elder James E. Talmage stated: "That the Spirit of the Lord is capable of manifesting Himself in the form and figure of man, is indicated by the wonderful interview between the Spirit and Nephi, in which He revealed Himself to the prophet, questioned him concerning his desires and belief, instructed him in the things of God, speaking face to face with the man."[8]

Having taught the members of the Church in Ramus, Illinois, that the Holy Ghost does not have a body, as do the first and second members of the Godhead, Joseph added, "Were it not so, the Holy Ghost could not dwell in us" (Doctrine and Covenants 130:22). This statement requires some clarification, for the Holy Ghost, like the Father and the Son, can be in only one place at a time. Or, as President Joseph Fielding Smith noted, "As a Spirit personage the Holy Ghost has size and dimensions. He does not fill the immensity of space [as does the Light of Christ or the Spirit of Jesus Christ], and cannot be everywhere present in person at the same time."[9] William Clayton recorded the following statement by the Prophet on 2 April 1843: "The Holy Ghost is a personage, and a person cannot have the personage of the Holy Ghost in his heart."[10] "No member of the Godhead dwells in us in the literal sense of the word," Elder McConkie wrote, "but all of them dwell in us figuratively to the extent that we are like them. If

---

8. *Articles of Faith*, 144; see also Romney, "The Holy Ghost," *Ensign*, May 1974, 90–95.

9. *Doctrines of Salvation*, 1:38.

10. *Words of Joseph Smith*, 170.

we have 'the mind of Christ' (1 Corinthians 2:16), which we receive by the power of the Holy Ghost, then Christ dwells in us. If the love of God abides in our souls, which love is a gift of God that comes by the power of the Holy Ghost, then God dwells in us. In some way beyond our comprehension, all of this is possible by the power of the Holy Ghost."[11] The Prophet Joseph taught: "A man may receive the Holy Ghost, and it may descend upon him and not tarry with him" (Doctrine and Covenants 130:23). We will discuss later the principle that the Spirit on some occasions may not tarry with individuals.

"Jesus, when he was baptized, went up straightway out of the water; and John saw, and lo, the heavens were opened unto him, and he saw the Spirit of God descending like a dove and lighting upon Jesus. And lo, he heard a voice from heaven, saying, This is my beloved Son, in whom I am well pleased. Hear ye him" (JST, Matthew 3:45–46). Luke's account of the same event may confuse some readers: "Now when all the people were baptized, it came to pass that Jesus also came unto John; and being baptized of him, and praying, the heaven was opened; and the Holy Ghost descended, in bodily shape like a dove, upon him; and a voice came from heaven, which said, Thou art my beloved Son, in thee I am well pleased" (JST, Luke 3:28–29).

One could easily read these two accounts, especially Luke's, and conclude that the Holy Ghost—remember, he is a male spirit personage—was somehow transformed into a dove. President Brigham Young, in speaking of this New Testament moment, clarified that "the Holy Ghost, in the form of a dove, it is said, rested upon him. This is not exactly the fact, though a natural dove descended and rested on the head of the Lord Jesus, in witness that God had accepted the offering of His Son. But the dove was not the Holy Ghost, but the sign that the Holy Ghost was given to him."[12]

---

11. *New Witness for the Articles of Faith*, 271–72.
12. In *Journal of Discourses*, 14:96. That Brother Brigham was a serious

3. As a member of the Godhead, the Holy Ghost possesses all attributes, qualities, and divine characteristics in perfection. Indeed, he is God (Acts 5:3–4). Modern revelation affirms that "the Comforter knoweth all things" (Doctrine and Covenants 42:17). Among the various titles and functions of the Holy Ghost are "the record of heaven; the Comforter; the peaceable things of immortal glory; the truth of all things; that which quickeneth all things, which maketh alive all things; that which knoweth all things, and hath all power according to wisdom, mercy, truth, justice, and judgment" (Moses 6:61). He is not only the representative and witness of the Father and Son, but he is also *one in mind* with them. We learn in the *Lectures on Faith* that "these three are one; or, in other words, these three constitute the great, matchless, governing and supreme, power over all things; . . . and these three constitute the Godhead, and are one."[13]

Even though Latter-day Saints believe in three members of the Godhead—three distinct persons, three distinct beings, three Gods—yet we consider ourselves to be monotheistic, meaning that we believe in one God—one divine Godhead, one supreme Presidency. The Book of Mormon and the Doctrine and Covenants both teach that the Father, the Son, and the Holy Ghost are one God. Consider the following passages:

"And now, behold, my beloved brethren, this is the way [the doctrine of Christ]; and there is none other way nor name given under heaven whereby man can be saved in the kingdom of God. And now, behold, this is the doctrine of Christ, and the only and true doctrine of the Father, and of the Son, and of the Holy Ghost, *which is one God, without end*" (2 Nephi 31:21; emphasis added).

In the resurrection, everything will "be restored to its perfect frame, as it is now, or in the body, and shall be brought and be arraigned

---

student of Joseph Smith is clear from the Prophet's statement on this matter (*Joseph Smith* [manual], 81).

13. *Lectures on Faith*, 60.

before the bar of Christ the Son, and God the Father, and the Holy Spirit, *which is one Eternal God,* to be judged according to their works, whether they be good or whether they be evil" (Alma 11:44; emphasis added).

"And after this manner shall ye baptize in my name; for behold, verily I say unto you, that *the Father, and the Son, and the Holy Ghost are one;* and I am in the Father, and the Father in me, and the Father and I are one" (3 Nephi 11:27; emphasis added; see also v. 36).

Those who are found guiltless at the judgment bar will "dwell in the presence of God in his kingdom, to sing ceaseless praises with the choirs above, unto the Father, and unto the Son, and unto the Holy Ghost, *which are one God,* in a state of happiness which hath no end" (Mormon 7:7; emphasis added).

The Holy Ghost "beareth record of the Father and of the Son; which *Father, Son, and Holy Ghost are one God,* infinite and eternal, without end" (Doctrine and Covenants 20:27–28; emphasis added).

In short, we Latter-day Saints declare to the world that there are three members of the Godhead—the Father, the Son, and the Holy Ghost. Each member of the Godhead possesses all of the attributes and qualities of godliness in perfection. The love and unity between the members of the Godhead is of such magnitude that we can rightfully refer to them as *one God.* At the Last Supper, Christ declared to his apostles: "Howbeit when he, the Spirit of truth, is come, he will guide you into all truth: for he shall not speak of himself; but whatsoever he shall hear [presumably from the Father and Son], that shall he speak: and he will shew you things to come. He shall glorify me: for he shall receive of mine, and shall shew it unto you" (John 16:13–14).

Given the perfect unity between the three members of the Godhead, do we as Latter-day Saints worship the Holy Ghost? Is any facet of our worship directed specifically to the Spirit? He is the third member of the Godhead, the messenger and representative of the Father and Son, the one who bears witness of both. The Holy Spirit is one with the Father and the Son and possesses the qualities and attributes they do. There is evidence in holy writ that the Holy Ghost is God (Acts 5:3, 4, 9), but no scripture or prophetic statement suggests we should worship him or pray to him. I am aware that many of our more conservative Protestant brothers and sisters pray to the Holy Spirit, but that practice is not a part of the restored gospel.

4. His person must not be confused with his powers and influence. Once again from Elder Talmage: "Much of the confusion existing in human conceptions concerning the nature of the Holy Ghost arises from *the common failure to segregate His person and powers.* Plainly, such expressions as being filled with the Holy Ghost, and His falling upon persons, have reference to the powers and influences that emanate from God, and which are characteristic of Him; for the Holy Ghost may in this way operate simultaneously upon many persons even though they be widely separated, whereas the actual person of the Holy Ghost cannot be in more than one place at a time. . . . The Holy Ghost may be regarded as the minister of the Godhead, carrying into effect the decision of the Supreme Council."[14]

Latter-day Saints have an understanding concerning the vital and distinctive roles of the third member of the Godhead that is not to be found in either Christian or non-Christian faiths throughout the world. A magnificent feature of our Heavenly Father's plan of salvation, his great plan of happiness, is that each of the children of God comes to earth, takes a physical body, has the knowledge and understanding of life in our first estate erased temporarily from our minds, and learns to walk by faith.

Even though we have left the immediate presence of the Father and the Son and assumed our second estate in a telestial and fallen world,

---

14. *Articles of Faith,* 145; emphasis added.

we are not left on our own; we are not bereft of the opportunity of having God close at hand. The Holy Ghost is that spirit personage sent principally to assist each of us to recognize the gospel message when we hear it and then to come unto Christ by covenant. His assignment is to prepare all human beings to receive joy and happiness here and life eternal in the world to come. The Holy Spirit will certify to our minds and hearts that which is true and good and uplifting. He has been given by the Father and the Son the mission to teach, to clarify, to illuminate. The Holy Ghost also cleanses, purifies, and prepares each child of the Father to qualify for reentrance into the royal family of God. Having the Spirit is indeed a supernal gift, a precious privilege. God be thanked for this remarkable gift!

Chapter 2

CHRIST AND THE SPIRIT: PARTNERS IN REDEMPTION

One often-quoted passage of scripture within our standard works is that broad distillation of his purpose that God spoke to Moses: "This is my work and my glory—to bring to pass the immortality and eternal life of man" (Moses 1:39). This one verse summarizes and comprehends the depth and breadth and height of the plan of salvation. The Father, the Son, and the Holy Ghost are focused, even riveted, upon the accomplishment of that grand purpose for all the sons and daughters of God.

The scriptures also attest that the work of redemption, the labor of salvation, is an endeavor undertaken by all three members of the Godhead. In speaking of the Savior's atoning suffering, for example, Roman Catholic scholar Richard John Neuhaus noted: "It is not an angry Father punishing an innocent Son, with the Spirit on the sidelines helplessly watching. No, it is the Father, Son and Spirit conspiring together to save us from ourselves."[1]

Let us consider how the saving work of Jesus Christ and the Holy Ghost, the second and third members of the Godhead, is everlastingly linked.

---

1. *Death on a Friday Afternoon*, 221.

THE CREATION

As we have previously noted, Joseph Smith explained: "Everlasting covenant was made between three personages before the organization of this earth and relates to their dispensation of things to men on the earth. These personages . . . are called God the first, the Creator; God the second, the Redeemer; and God the third, the Witness or Testator."[2] In one part of his sermon at the funeral of King Follett, the Prophet turned his attention to the premortal preparations for the Creation. "In the beginning," Joseph explained, "the head of the Gods called a council of the Gods; and they came together and concocted a plan to create the world and people it."[3] Though Joseph did not state specifically who "the Gods" were who were brought forth by the head of the Gods (no doubt our Heavenly Father was the Head), Jesus Christ would surely have been in attendance and an active participant in planning for worlds that he himself would give his life to save and redeem. One would suppose that the Holy Ghost was also one of "the Gods" who made the necessary preparations for the Creation.

John the Beloved wrote in his Gospel: "In the beginning was the Word, and the Word was with God, and the Word was God. The same was in the beginning with God. *All things were made by him; and without him was not anything made that was made*" (John 1:1–3; emphasis added; see also Doctrine and Covenants 93:6–18). It is clear from holy scripture that God the Father "created all things by Jesus Christ" (Ephesians 3:9). In the Book of Mormon Amulek refers to the Redeemer as "the very Eternal Father of heaven and of earth, and all things which in them are" (Alma 11:39). In addition to Jesus himself (3 Nephi 9:15), the prophets Nephi (2 Nephi 25:12) and King Benjamin (Mosiah 3:8) teach the same truth.

In Hebrews 1:1–2 we read that God the Father appointed Jesus

2. *Joseph Smith* [manual], 42.

3. *Words of Joseph Smith*, 341; see also 345, 351, 358.

Christ heir of all things, by whom the worlds were made. We learn also from God's words to Moses that the Creation took place by "*the word of my power . . . which is mine Only Begotten Son,* who is full of grace and truth. And worlds without number have I created; and I also created them for mine own purpose; and by the Son I created them, which is mine Only Begotten" (Moses 1:32–33; emphasis added). Also in the book of Moses, we learn from Enoch that "were it possible that man could number the particles of the earth, yea, millions of earths like this, it would not be a beginning to the number of thy creations" (Moses 7:30).

In a revelation given to Joseph Smith in September 1830, the Lord explained that "all my judgments are not given unto men; and as the words have gone forth out of my mouth even so shall they be fulfilled, that the first shall be last, and that the last shall be first in all things *whatsoever I have created by the word of my power, which is the power of my Spirit.* For *by the power of my Spirit created I them*" (Doctrine and Covenants 29:30–31; emphasis added). Note that here "the word of my power," that power by which the Creation was accomplished, is in fact "the power of my Spirit."

It seems reasonable to conclude that the Savior and his associates in the work of Creation—which, as we have indicated, must have included the Holy Ghost—drew upon that light "which is in all things, which giveth life to all things, which is the law by which all things are governed, even the power of God who sitteth upon his throne" (Doctrine and Covenants 88:13). Thus the Light of Christ is a creative power, the means by which the laws that govern the planets and provide order in the cosmos were put in place.

JESUS CHRIST SENDS THE HOLY SPIRIT

In the meridian of time in the Old World, the Father could not send the Spirit as a constant companion to the Saints of that day until after Jesus had suffered, died, and been resurrected (JST, John

7:37–39). "It may seem strange to some who may not have reflected on this matter fully," President Joseph F. Smith observed, "that the disciples of Christ were without the gift of the Holy Ghost until after his resurrection. But so it is written. . . . While Jesus was with them he was their light and their inspiration. They followed him by sight, and felt the majestic power of his presence, and when these were gone they returned to their nets and to their various occupations and to their homes. Then after the Savior's rise from the tomb, on the Day of Pentecost, the gift of the Holy Ghost was sent in great power."[4]

A most fascinating period of Christian history is the centuries following the council of Nicaea in A.D. 325. The earliest versions of the Nicene Creed stated that the Holy Ghost was sent forth "from the Father." More than two hundred years later, in A.D. 589 at the council of Toledo, the Western branch of the Christian Church (which would come to be known as the Roman Catholic Church) insisted that the creed be amended to include the Latin word *filioque,* which means "and from the Son." Thus the amended creed declared that the Holy Spirit proceeded "from the Father and the Son."

Why would the Western Church insist on that addition? It has to do with the doctrine that was put in place at the council at Nicaea that the Father and the Son are coeternal, that there was never a time when the Father existed that the Son did not also exist, and that they are equal in might and majesty and power. The leaders from the West

---

4. *Gospel Doctrine*, 20. President George Albert Smith taught that "when the disciples of the Savior were with him they admired him not knowing how great he really was, but not until the power of the Holy Ghost came upon them, not until they had the baptism of fire were they able to face the problems and endure the persecutions that almost made life unendurable. When the inspiration of the Almighty gave them understanding they knew they were living [an] eternal life, and if they proved faithful they knew that when they laid their bodies down in death they would be raised from the tomb to glory and immortality. That was the result of the inspiration of the Spirit of God that came upon them, the inspiration of the Almighty that gave them understanding" (*George Albert Smith* [manual], 119).

explained that to say simply that the Spirit proceeded *only* from the Father was to imply that the Father had a power or right that the Son did not, which they could not accept. And so the Western Church accepted this doctrinal alteration. The Eastern Church (later known as the Eastern Orthodox Church) felt it inappropriate to amend the Nicene Creed. This difference of opinion was a significant factor in the final division of the two factions in A.D. 1054. We have already established that God the second and God the third are subordinate to God the first, the Father. I mention this rather complex issue in Christian history to give readers a sense of the difficult path the doctrine of the Holy Spirit would travel after the deaths of the apostles and the loss of apostolic priesthood power and doctrinal oversight.

From the Prophet Joseph's inspired translation of the Bible, we know that Jesus baptized people by water and by the Holy Ghost (JST, Mark 1:5–6). We see this practice in both the Book of Mormon and the Doctrine and Covenants. As the risen Lord began his sermon to the multitude gathered at Bountiful (a sermon similar to the Sermon on the Mount in Galilee, recorded in Matthew 5–7), he gave what might be called a preliminary beatitude: "Blessed are ye if ye shall give heed unto the words of these twelve whom I have chosen from among you to minister unto you, and to be your servants [the twelve Nephite apostles[5]]; and unto them I have given power that they may baptize you with water; and *after that ye are baptized with water, behold, I will baptize you with fire and with the Holy Ghost;* therefore blessed are ye if ye shall believe in me and be baptized, after that ye have seen me and know that I am" (3 Nephi 12:1; emphasis added).

In a revelation given to Ezra Thayer and Northrup Sweet, the Lord spoke through the Prophet Joseph Smith: "Ye shall remember the church articles and covenants to keep them. And whoso having faith

---

5. That the Nephite twelve were indeed apostles is taught in Moroni 2:2, in the Wentworth Letter (*Joseph Smith* [manual], 445), and by Elder Parley P. Pratt, *Key to the Science of Theology,* 31.

you shall confirm in my church, by the laying on of the hands, and *I will bestow the gift of the Holy Ghost* upon them" (Doctrine and Covenants 33:14–15; emphasis added). Note that Brothers Thayer and Sweet were to perform the ordinance—lay their hands upon the head of the newly baptized person and confirm him or her a member of the Church of Jesus Christ—but it was Jesus Christ himself who would send the Spirit.

JESUS AND THE FULNESS OF THE SPIRIT

Jesus Christ had a dual inheritance. First, he was the son of Mary, and from her he inherited *mortality,* the flesh, including the capacity to die. Jesus needed to be mortal to understand and appreciate the challenges of being a human being. Indeed, "in all things it behoved him to be made like unto his brethren" (Hebrews 2:17). He went out into a fallen world and day by day encountered pain, affliction, temptation, infirmity, and weakness, "that his bowels may be filled with mercy, according to the flesh, that he may know according to the flesh how to succor his people according to their infirmities" (Alma 7:11–12). Second, Jesus was the Son of God, the Almighty Elohim, and from the Father he inherited *immortality,* the capacity and power to live forever.

This coinheritance was absolutely necessary. It was essential that he should "suffer temptations, and pain of body, hunger, thirst, and fatigue, *even more than man can suffer,* except it be unto death" (Mosiah 3:7; emphasis added). Truly, Jesus of Nazareth was a man, but he was so much more than a man. Had that not been the case, he could not have endured the anguish and excruciating suffering that took place in the Garden of Gethsemane and again on the cross of Calvary. Had that not been the case, he could not have the power to forgive sin and make "new creatures" of those who come to him in faith (2 Corinthians 5:17; Galatians 6:15; Colossians 3:5; Mosiah 27:26).

During the Passover season Jesus taught a profound truth about himself: "For as the Father hath life in himself; so hath he given to the Son to have life in himself; and hath given him authority to execute judgment also, because he is the Son of man" (John 5:26–27), that is, the "Son of Man of Holiness," God the Eternal Father (Moses 7:35). Had he not had this kind and quality of life within him—a power he received from the Father (see John 10:17–18)—he could not have raised himself from the tomb. Lehi instructed his son Jacob on how vital it was for the Nephites to be taught the great plan of redemption "that they may know that there is no flesh that can dwell in the presence of God, save it be through the merits, and mercy, and grace of the Holy Messiah"—and now, please focus on what follows—"who layeth down his life according to the flesh [his mortal inheritance], and *taketh it again by the power of the Spirit* [his immortal inheritance], that he may bring to pass the resurrection of the dead, being the first that should rise" (2 Nephi 2:8; emphasis added).

One of the reasons that Jesus Christ could extend a divine lifeline to you and me is that he was sinless. Because he had never taken a moral detour, had never taken a backward step into transgression, it could be said of him that he owed absolutely nothing to the law of justice; justice could make no demands upon him. The Spirit of God that was always with him could not have remained with him as a constant companion, an ever-present associate, had he not stood wholly innocent before the law. That is, because Jesus never sinned, he had never forfeited the influence of the Spirit. We know that when we sin, we lose a portion of the Holy Spirit (Alma 34:35; Doctrine and Covenants 19:20), which returns to us when we appropriate the Savior's Atonement through genuine, heartfelt repentance (Mosiah 4:1–3).

In speaking to students at a Brigham Young University fireside, Elder Bruce R. McConkie stated: "We have to become perfect to be saved in the celestial kingdom. But nobody becomes perfect in this life. Only the Lord Jesus attained that state, and *he had an advantage that none of us has. He was the Son of God, and he came into this life with a spiritual capacity and a talent and an inheritance that exceeded beyond all comprehension what any of the rest of us was born with.*"[6] In short, Jesus was in many ways just as we are. And yet he possessed innate powers, divine attributes, and heavenly qualities that no other mortal being possessed. Jesus himself said: "For he whom God hath sent [speaking of himself] speaketh the words of God: for God giveth him not *the Spirit* by measure, for he [the Spirit] *dwelleth in him, even the fulness*" (JST, John 3:34; emphasis added). Joseph Smith taught: "Where is the man that is free from vanity? None ever were perfect but Jesus; and why was He perfect? Because He was the Son of God, and *had the fullness of the Spirit,* and greater power than any man."[7]

What did the Prophet Joseph mean when he declared that Jesus "had the fullness of the Spirit, and greater power than any man"? As we have indicated, Jesus inherited from our Eternal Father the powers of immortality, the capacity to live forever. In addition, he was especially sensitive to the Spirit because of his sinlessness. Sin not only corrupts the mind and heart but also takes a toll on the physical body (1 Corinthians 11:26–27, 29–30; Alma 14:6; 15:3).

Consider that unrepented sin sows the seeds of death. Would not the opposite situation be that sinlessness results in a person being wholly and perfectly alive? Mormon wrote that the three translated Nephites were "sanctified in the flesh, that they were holy, and that the powers of earth could not hold them" (3 Nephi 28:39). President Brigham Young said regarding the near omnipresence of sin, "Do not suppose that we shall ever in the flesh be free from temptations to sin. . . . *Were it possible for a person to attain to this degree of perfection in the flesh, he could not die* neither remain in a world where sin predominates. . . . I think we shall more or less feel the effects of sin so long as we live, and finally have to pass the ordeals of death."[8]

---

6. "Jesus Christ and Him Crucified," 399; emphasis added.
7. *Joseph Smith* [manual], 53; emphasis added.
8. In *Journal of Discourses,* 10:173; emphasis added.

JESUS SUFFERS A LOSS OF THE SPIRIT

The immediate consequence of sin is withdrawal of the Spirit (Mosiah 2:36; Alma 34:35; Doctrine and Covenants 19:20). In taking upon himself the effects of the sins of all humankind, our Lord was thus exposed to the awful (and to Jesus, unusual) withdrawal of the Spirit that had been his constant companion from the beginning. Had Jesus sinned? No. Not at all. Did he deserve to suffer as he did? Absolutely not. In becoming our divine Substitute, however, our stand-in for sin, the Savior became, as it were, the great sinner. He suffered as though he were the guilty party (2 Corinthians 5:21; Galatians 3:13).

In speaking of the atoning mission of our Master, President Brigham Young explained: "The Father withdrew His spirit from His Son, at the time he was to be crucified." Thus "when the crisis came for him to offer up his life, the Father withdrew Himself, withdrew His Spirit. . . . That is what made him sweat blood. If he had had the power of God upon him, he would not have sweat blood."[9] Christ descended below all things (Ephesians 4:8–10; Doctrine and Covenants 88:6). The Redeemer has thus "trodden the wine-press alone, even the wine-press of the fierceness of the wrath of Almighty God" (Doctrine and Covenants 76:107; see also Isaiah 63:3; Doctrine and Covenants 88:106; 133:50).

LIFE IN CHRIST

Every Christian knows that Jesus came into the world to *die for us,* to offer himself as a willing sacrifice for the sins of humanity. He suffered unimaginable anguish and pain in Gethsemane, and that atoning suffering recurred and was brought to its conclusion on Golgotha. In the premortal council of heaven Jehovah had manifested that his eye was indeed single to the glory of God when he said simply, "Father, *thy will be*

---

9. In *Journal of Discourses,* 3:206. Elder Jeffrey R. Holland taught that although the Father's Spirit was withdrawn from Christ, the Father was never closer to his Son than during the hours of the Savior's Atonement ("None Were with Him," *Ensign,* May 2009, 87–88).

done, and the glory be thine forever" (Moses 4:2; emphasis added). That same Jehovah, who was now Jesus Christ, hung on the cross, and "when he had cried again with a loud voice, saying, Father, it is finished, *thy will is done,* yielded up the ghost" (JST, Matthew 27:54; emphasis added).

What is less understood by disciples of Jesus is that our Lord also came to earth *to live in us.* One of the most essential ways he comes to live in us is by providing light and life for us when we have managed to repent and put to death the old man or woman of sin (Romans 6:6). Having served as a bishop and a stake president, I have been asked more than once by persons who had been guilty of serious transgression and were on the road to forgiveness, "How can I know when I have been forgiven? When can I stop asking for forgiveness for this particular sin?"

Those are not only practical questions but very important and timely ones. In every case I asked the person to open his or her copy of the Book of Mormon, turn to Mosiah 4, and read silently the first three verses, looking particularly at verse 3. Then I asked, "How can you know when you are forgiven? What do we learn from verse 3?"

Mormon states, "And it came to pass that after they had spoken these words [their plea for mercy through the Savior's Atonement] the Spirit of the Lord came upon them, and they were filled with joy, having received a remission of their sins, and having peace of conscience, because of the exceeding faith which they had in Jesus Christ" (Mosiah 4:3).

Right away they would say, "I'll feel joy."

"Anything else?" I would ask.

"Oh, yes," they would reply. "I will feel a peace of conscience."

I would ask if there is any other way that they can recognize when they have received a remission of their sins. It is surprising how many missed what is actually the first evidence mentioned: "The Spirit of the Lord came upon them." The principle is quite simple: If it is true that the Holy Spirit cannot dwell in us if we are unclean, what does it mean when we begin to feel and experience the Spirit once again in our lives?

We are no longer unclean. Our sins have been forgiven. In short, the presence of the Spirit is a signal, a sign, to us that we are spiritually on course, on the covenant path.

The apostle Paul set forth a profound truth when he wrote, "I am crucified with Christ: *nevertheless I live; yet not I, but Christ liveth in me*" (Galatians 2:20; emphasis added). Christ lived in Paul by means of that dynamic, living influence we know as the power of the Holy Spirit. Paul's motivation to become a holy man was not self-generated, did not come to pass simply from sheer grit and will power; rather, his passion to do good and be his best was driven by the Spirit. His capacity to teach and testify in a manner that people simply could not ignore his message did not derive merely from his rabbinic training, his study with Gamaliel; like his Master, Paul spoke as one having authority from God by means of the true Teacher, the Holy Ghost.

Paul used one particular expression more than 150 times in his epistles. In some form or another, Paul wrote of the need for true believers to be "in Christ." Perhaps the most well-known example is from his second letter to the Corinthians. The apostle declared, "Therefore if any man be in Christ, he is a new creature: old things are passed away; behold, all things are become new" (2 Corinthians 5:17). The apostle John taught this same doctrine when he wrote, "Whoso keepeth his word, in him verily is the love of God perfected: hereby know we that we are in him" (1 John 2:5). In short, "hereby know we that we dwell in him, and he in us, because he hath given us of his Spirit" (1 John 4:13; see also v. 15; John 6:56; 17:20–21). In latter-day revelation the Savior spoke of his oneness with the Father as well as the means whereby his followers could be one with them: "And the Father and I are one. I am in the Father and the Father in me; and inasmuch as ye have received me, ye are in me and I in you" (Doctrine and Covenants 50:43).

When we kneel in prayer and plead for the Lord's Spirit to guide and empower our Relief Society or priesthood or Sunday School lesson, we are in essence asking to be tuned in to the Lord's way of thinking and feeling, to his way of expressing things. When we feel moved upon to sit down and counsel with a child or grandchild who is going through a difficult time, we may find that counsel going in a direction we never would have supposed it would. On that occasion we are entering the divine realm and find ourselves offering advice that is well beyond our own experience or knowledge; we are loving deeply and counseling wisely, just as the wonderful Counselor would if he were there (Isaiah 9:6).

When shy, perhaps rather backward and thoroughly inexperienced young men and women are called to serve as full-time missionaries for The Church of Jesus Christ of Latter-day Saints, they may feel incapable of addressing strangers, of bearing testimony of that about which they are not fully convinced, of conquering a foreign language, or of having the physical energy to work for ten to twelve hours per day. They enter the Missionary Training Center, are caught up in the glorious Spirit that fills that facility, and arrive in the mission field only weeks later enthusiastic, excited, and spiritually empowered. It seems that on every street corner they greet busy people, people about whom they know little or nothing, and yet, in a strange but wonderful way, they are overcome with love for these people. They have begun to be captained by Christ, led and directed and motivated by the Holy Spirit of God. They have begun a *life in Christ*.

Latter-day Saint philosopher Adam Miller explained beautifully that being "in Christ" is like being "in love": "Something changes when you are in love. It's not just that a new person is added to your life, one person among many. It's that this new person changes for you what it means to be alive. Life is no longer just lived. Now, life is lived *in* love. You may keep the same job, have the same friends, and eat the same food, but something basic about why you do these things, or even how you do them, will have changed. . . . In love, life as a whole feels different. You see what you didn't use to see. You hear what you didn't use to hear. You care for things you'd ignored. You become capable of doing things that, last week, you weren't able to do." Brother Miller said further, "Life in Christ is like this. In Christ, the way I live—my manner of living—is changed from the inside out. Like being in love, living in Christ changes what it means to be alive."[10]

The three members of the Godhead are wholly united in bringing to pass our immortality and eternal life. Perhaps nothing illustrates this purpose more beautifully than the manner in which the second and third members of this divine Presidency accomplish the reclamation of individual souls and the renovation of society. From creation through redemption and into a new kind of life—a life not just focused upon but given over to the Lord Jesus Christ—the Redeemer and the Witness, or Testator, work hand in hand. The repentant children of God are forgiven, cleansed, redeemed, and exalted because Jesus Christ volunteered to ransom fallen humanity from sin and death and because the Holy Ghost becomes the medium, the means, by which those mighty changes take place (Mosiah 5:2). Indeed, Presiding Bishop Gérald Caussé referred to the Holy Ghost as "the agent of the Atonement."[11]

John the Beloved reminds us that "it is the Spirit that beareth witness, because the Spirit is truth. For there are three that bear record in heaven, the Father, the Word, and the Holy Ghost: and these three are one" (1 John 5:6–7). It is that supernal oneness, that unbreakable unity, for which we as the children of God strive, for if we are one, we are his (Doctrine and Covenants 38:27).

---

10. *Early Resurrection*, 11–12.
11. "For When I Am Weak, Then Am I Strong," 6.

Chapter 3

FILLING THE
IMMENSITY OF SPACE

his then is the message which we have heard of [Christ], and declare unto you," John the Beloved wrote in his first epistle, "that God is light, and in him is no darkness at all" (1 John 1:5). We do not travel far in our study of John's Gospel before we read that Jesus Christ is "the true Light, which lighteth every man that cometh into the world" (John 1:9). Because Jehovah was the foreordained Redeemer and Savior of worlds (Doctrine and Covenants 76:22–24; Moses 1:32–35), the Lamb slain from the foundation of the world (Revelation 5:6; 13:8; Moses 7:47), the Father's plan became his by adoption: the gospel of God (Romans 1:1–3) is the gospel of Jesus Christ. Because the Father has invested his Beloved Son with his own attributes and powers (Mosiah 15:3; Doctrine and Covenants 93:4) and because the "Father of lights" (James 1:17) has ordained that Christ is the Light of lights and the Light of the world, those powers of life and light that we know as the power of God have come to be known as the Light of Christ, or the Spirit of Jesus Christ.

NATURAL AND REDEMPTIVE FUNCTIONS

Though there is but passing reference to the Light of Christ in the New Testament, the teachings of Restoration scripture abound in detail, assisting us to understand how and in what manner the Light of

Christ lights every person born into mortality. We come to know, first of all, that that light is a manifestation of the glory of God, a divine influence that fills the immensity of space and the means whereby God, a corporeal being who can be in only one place at a time, is nevertheless omnipresent.

The Light of Christ has what might be called both *natural* functions and *redemptive* functions. As to its natural functions, the revelation known as the Olive Leaf explains that "he that ascended up on high"—Jesus Christ—also "descended below all things, in that he comprehended all things, that he might be in all and through all things, the light of truth; which truth shineth. *This is the light of Christ.* As also [the Light of Christ] is in the sun, and the light of the sun, and the power thereof by which it was made. As also [this light] is in the moon, and is the light of the moon, and the power thereof by which it was made; as also the light of the stars, and the power thereof by which they were made; and the earth also, and the power thereof, even the earth upon which you stand." This light *"proceedeth forth from the presence of God to fill the immensity of space*—the *light* which is in all things, which giveth *life* to all things, which is the *law* by which all things are governed, even the *power* of God who sitteth upon his throne, who is in the bosom of eternity, who is in the midst of all things" (Doctrine and Covenants 88:6–13; emphasis added; compare Ephesians 4:8).

Elder Parley P. Pratt wrote that the Light of Christ "is, in its less refined existence, the physical light which reflects from the sun, moon, and stars, and other substances; and by reflection on the eye, makes visible the truths of the outward world." Then, in speaking of the redemptive or saving functions of the Light of Christ, he added: "It is, also, in its higher degrees, the intellectual light of our inward and spiritual organs, by which we *reason, discern, judge, compare, comprehend,* and *remember* the subjects within our reach. Its inspiration constitutes *instinct in animal life, reason in man, vision in the Prophets,* and is continually flowing from the Godhead throughout all his creations."[1]

In short, the same power that makes it possible for us to see with our physical eyes also makes it possible for us to see with our spiritual eyes. Discernment, the innate capacity to distinguish good from evil and the relevant from the irrelevant, also comes through this Spirit of Jesus Christ (Moroni 7:12–19). "And *the Spirit giveth light to every man that cometh into the world;* and the Spirit enlighteneth every man through the world, that hearkeneth to the voice of the Spirit." Further, those who are true to this Spirit within them—which includes their conscience and thus the canons of right and wrong and decency in society—will be led, either in this life or the next, to the higher light of the Holy Ghost that comes through the gospel covenant (Doctrine and Covenants 84:46–48; emphasis added).[2]

Elder Bruce R. McConkie wrote: "The light of Christ . . . is the agency of God's power and the law by which all things are governed. It is also the agency used by the Holy Ghost to manifest truth and dispense spiritual gifts to many people at one and the same time (Moroni 10:17). For instance, it is as though the Holy Ghost, who is a personage of spirit, was broadcasting all truth throughout the whole universe all the time, using the light of Christ as the agency by which the message is delivered. But only those who attune their souls to the Holy Spirit receive the available revelation. It is in this way that the person of the Holy Ghost makes his influence felt in the heart of every righteous person at one and the same time."[3]

Elder McConkie also observed that the Light of Christ "has neither shape nor form nor personality. It is not an entity nor a person nor a personage. It has no agency, does not act independently, and exists not

---

1. *Key to the Science of Theology,* 47; emphasis added.
2. See Smith, *Gospel Doctrine,* 67–68; McConkie, *New Witness for the Articles of Faith,* 260.
3. *New Witness for the Articles of Faith,* 70.

to act but to be acted upon. . . . It is the power of God who sitteth upon his throne. It may be that it is also priesthood and faith and omnipotence, for these too are the power of God."[4]

THE SPIRIT POURED OUT UPON ALL FLESH

The ancient prophet Joel is often referred to as one of the so-called minor prophets because his book is short. There is, however, nothing minor about one of Joel's marvelous prophecies: "And it shall come to pass afterward, that I will pour out my spirit upon all flesh; and your sons and your daughters shall prophesy, your old men shall dream dreams, your young men shall see visions: and also upon the servants and upon the handmaids in those days will I pour out my spirit" (Joel 2:28–29). We are aware of at least two fulfillments of this prophecy. The apostle Peter declared that what took place on the day of Pentecost was a fulfillment of Joel's prediction (Acts 2:14–18). When Moroni first appeared to Joseph Smith in September of 1823, he boldly quoted Joel's prophecy and declared that "this was not yet fulfilled, but was soon to be" (Joseph Smith–History 1:41). This is, of course, an illustration of a prophecy having multiple fulfillments.

The Spirit of God is certainly the driving influence behind the dissemination of eternal truth and the spiritual transformation of those who submit to the terms and conditions of the gospel of Jesus Christ. But what of others outside the faith? Would not this Spirit affect them?

President Joseph Fielding Smith, after having quoted the prophecy of Joel, explained: "Now, my brethren and sisters, I am not going to confine this prophecy to the members of the Church. The Lord said he would pour out his Spirit upon all flesh. That does not mean that upon all flesh the Holy Ghost should be sent, . . . but the Lord would pour out his blessings and his Spirit upon all people and use them to accomplish his purposes. . . .

4. *New Witness for the Articles of Faith*, 257–58.

"There has never been a step taken . . . , in discovery or invention, where the Spirit of the Lord (that is, the spirit of which Joel spoke, the Light of Christ, not the Holy Ghost!) was not the prevailing force, resting upon the individual, which caused him to make the discovery or the invention. . . . Nor did the Lord always use those who have faith, nor does he always do so today. He uses such minds as are pliable and can be turned in certain directions to accomplish his work, whether they believe in him or not."[5]

In short, the Light of Christ, or the Spirit of Jesus Christ, has been the spiritual impetus and driving force behind the rapid intellectual, scientific, and technological developments from the time of the Industrial Revolution through our own Information Age.

Elder B. H. Roberts offered the following insight on this principle: "God raises up wise men . . . of their own tongue and nationality, speaking to them through means that they can comprehend; not always giving a fulness of truth such as may be found in the fulness of the gospel of Jesus Christ; but always giving that measure of truth that the people are prepared to receive." The Church of Jesus Christ of Latter-day Saints thus declares that "all the great teachers are servants of God; among all nations and in all ages. . . . Wherever God finds a soul sufficiently enlightened and pure; one with whom his Spirit can communicate, lo! he makes of him a teacher of men. . . . While the path of sensuality and darkness may be that which most men tread, a few . . . have been led along the upward path; a few in all countries and generations have been wisdom seekers, or seekers of God."[6]

A MORAL MONITOR

Let's reflect for a moment on what we have just said. The Light of Christ, or Spirit of Jesus Christ, is a divine inheritance given to every

---

5. *Doctrines of Salvation,* 1:176–78; emphasis added.
6. *Defense of the Faith and the Saints,* 1:512–13.

mortal being; it is an innate sense of decency and propriety, an inner voice that assists us to discern good from evil, right from wrong. The prophet-editor Mormon taught his people in the synagogue that "the Spirit of Christ is given to every man, that he may know good from evil; wherefore, I show unto you the way to judge; for every thing which *inviteth to do good, and to persuade to believe in Christ,* is sent forth by the power and gift of Christ; wherefore ye may know with a perfect knowledge it is of God" (Moroni 7:16; emphasis added).

Parents, particularly Christian fathers and mothers, have been instructed to bring up their children "in the nurture and admonition of the Lord" (Ephesians 6:4; Enos 1:1), that is, "in the training and instruction of the Lord" (New International Version; English Standard Version), to "take them by the hand and lead them in the way of the Master."[7] In modern revelation parents are commanded to teach their children *to understand* the first principles and ordinances of the gospel, to pray, and to observe the Sabbath day (Doctrine and Covenants 68:25, 28–29).

In May 1833, one of the bishops of the Church and members of the First Presidency were firmly charged to "bring up your children in light and truth" and to "set in order your own house" (Doctrine and Covenants 93:40, 43). Such instruction would obviously entail counsel, cautions, and precautions, as well as proper direction regarding the standards of right and wrong and the laws in society that must be observed if order and peace are to be enjoyed. This instruction, linked to the inner promptings from deep within that we know as the Light of Christ, are the principal means by which an individual's *conscience* is formed.

Stephen R. Covey told a wonderful story many years ago about the power of conscience to change individuals and groups of people. "A university in Arizona . . . had what they called a 'Religion in Life Week,'" Brother Covey began. "I was invited to be a religious representative of our Church along with other representatives of other churches. The

---

7. Peterson, *The Message*, 2333.

second night there I was invited to speak to a sorority-fraternity exchange at the Chi Omega house on the subject of the new morality. I basically gave our Church's approach to it: that chastity is an eternal law, that the 'new morality' is really the old immorality, and so forth. I felt very alone because there seemed to be considerable difference in thinking. Two individuals were very articulate in expressing their opposition to my position. One, sitting in front, said basically, 'Well, I don't know. It seems to me that true, mature love gives more freedom than you're giving it.'

"I tried to reason and indicate what would happen if one were to take poison, even if he were unaware of it, and how also if one violated the law of chastity he would suffer great consequences. He argued against this, indicating that this didn't give the kind of freedom that a careful, mature, responsible love would give people. I prayed and remembered the scripture in Revelation, 'Behold, I stand at the door, and knock: if any man will hear my voice, and open the door, I will come in to him and will sup with him, and he with me' (Revelation 3:20). So I asked them, 'Would you listen for just a minute? Inwardly sense what might happen, what the real answer is to this question that we have tonight. I'll ask a question, and you be still and listen. I'll promise you, you will sense inwardly—you won't hear it in your ear—that what I've been speaking about is true on this principle of chastity.'

"They became still. Some of them were looking around to see who was going to take it seriously. And I really pressed the point: 'Just listen for one minute.' During that quiet minute I asked the question 'Now, is chastity, as I have explained it tonight, a true principle or not?' Then I paused. At the end of a full minute, I turned to the fellow who had been the spokesman in front and I asked him, 'My friend, in all honesty, what did you feel? What did you hear?' He said, 'What I heard is not what I've been saying.' I asked the other, 'What did you hear?' He said, 'I don't know. I just don't know any more.'

"One stood up in the back independently, spontaneously, on his own, and said, 'I want to say something to my fraternity brothers that

I've never said before. I believe in God.' And he sat down. A completely different spirit was present. It softened everybody."[8]

Brother Covey wrote of the profound effect of that moment of reflection, that time when young men and women were essentially asked to listen to their conscience: "A totally different spirit came to that group, a spirit that had distilled gradually and silently during that minute of silence. I believe it was the spirit of the Lord that they felt inside. It had some interesting effects upon them. For one thing, they became subdued and quiet and rather reverent from then on. For another, it communicated worth to them. They became less intellectual and defensive and more open and teachable."[9]

Closely linked to the education of *conscience,* which Stephen Covey just described, is the importance of the education of our *desires,* our hopes and dreams, those things we yearn and pine for. "The education then of our desires," President Joseph F. Smith explained, "is one of far-reaching importance to our happiness in life. . . .

"God's ways of educating our desires are, of course, always the most perfect. . . . And what is God's way? Everywhere in nature we are taught the lessons of *patience* and *waiting.* We want things a long time before we get them, and the fact that we wanted them a long time makes them all the more precious when they come."[10]

The Light of Christ, or the Spirit of Jesus Christ, is truly in and through all things; it is the means by which God is omnipresent. "Whither shall I go from thy Spirit," the Psalmist asked, "or whither shall I flee from thy presence? If I ascend up into heaven, thou art there: if I make my bed in hell, behold, thou art there" (Psalm 139:7–8).

8. "Educated Conscience," 134–35.
9. *Spiritual Roots of Human Relations,* 148.
10. *Gospel Doctrine,* 297.

In describing this light, or divine influence, Elder B. H. Roberts explained that this is how we "reconcile the personality of God with God's everywhereness. The Spirit that becomes *God immanent in the world* proceeds forth from the personal presence of God, . . . a presence from which you cannot flee, from which you cannot hide, in whose presence you must stand whether you will or no."[11]

Oscar McConkie Sr. wrote that "the Spirit that emanates from this Presidency [the Godhead] is holy, but it is not the personage named 'Holy Spirit,' and is not a personage at all." The Light of Christ "is like a watchman set in every place. No rendezvous is without it. No weapon can bayonet it away. It is in desert lands and pits, and is upon the mountains, and covers the face of the waters. It encompasses all men and all things."[12]

Thus, in a very real way, many people in the world are more connected to God and to the Light of Christ than they realize. Brother Covey observed: "I believe that what the scientist calls nature is the Spirit of Jesus Christ. I believe that what [many in the Christian world] call God is the Spirit of Jesus Christ. And perhaps this is what all religions call God. . . . I believe that what the humanist would call decency and what a man on the street would call common sense is the Spirit of Jesus Christ."[13]

In the midst of a magnificent sermon to his beloved people, the Nephites, on faith, hope, and charity, Mormon stated: "And now, my brethren, seeing that ye know the light by which ye may judge, which light is the light of Christ, see that ye do not judge wrongfully. . . . Wherefore, I beseech of you, brethren, that ye should *search diligently in*

---

11. *Seventy's Course in Theology*, cited in Lundwall, *Discourses on the Holy Ghost*, 32; emphasis added.
12. *The Holy Ghost*, 5.
13. "Educated Conscience," 128. The Light of Christ seems to be what many in the Christian world would call common grace, as opposed to what they call saving grace, which Latter-day Saints associate with the gift of the Holy Ghost.

the light of Christ that ye may know good from evil" (Moroni 7:18–19; emphasis added). How, exactly, does one "search diligently in the light of Christ"? It seems to me that Mormon is essentially encouraging us as members of the Church of Jesus Christ to, perhaps among other things, (1) rid ourselves of distracting and destructive influences in our lives that might cloud our eternal perspective; (2) spend more time in prayer, meditation, and thoughtful reflection on things of greatest worth; (3) listen carefully to our consciences and hearken to them, being particularly attentive to that inner voice that is the Spirit of Jesus Christ; and (4) act according to what we feel and know to be the right and proper course.

In speaking of the blessings that can come to us as we "search diligently in the light of Christ," President Dieter F. Uchtdorf stated: "If you open your mind and heart to receive the Light of Christ and humbly follow the Savior, you will receive more light. Line upon line, here a little and there a little, you will gather more light and truth into your souls until darkness has been banished from your life. God will open your eyes. God will give you a new heart. God's love, light, and truth will cause dormant things to spring to life, and you will be reborn into a newness of life in Christ Jesus."[14]

Unless we devolve into sin to such an extent that we have defected to perdition, the Light of Christ will be our personal guide, our precious link with God and godliness. That Light "enlightens every man that comes into the world, and . . . strives with the children of men, and will continue to strive with them, until it brings them to a knowledge of the truth and the possession of the greater light and testimony of the Holy Ghost."[15] What a thrill to know that a portion of God's divine light resides within the soul of each of us and is all about us. This supernal truth witnesses to the fact that our Heavenly Father and our Savior desire to do all they can to lift, strengthen, orient, and inspire the human family.

---

14. "Bearers of Heavenly Light," *Ensign*, November 2017, 79.
15. Smith, *Gospel Doctrine*, 67.

Chapter 4

AN ABUNDANT OUTPOURING

*W*e have seen that if individuals will attend to and follow the promptings, the voice of the Light of Christ, they will, either in this life or the next, be led to that higher light that comes through the fulness of the gospel, the new and everlasting covenant (Doctrine and Covenants 84:45–48). We will now consider what we learn from holy scripture and living prophets concerning this higher light, the light of the third member of the Godhead, the Holy Ghost.

THE INFLUENCE OF THE SPIRIT

Think of a family—let's call them the McMasters. They meet with the full-time missionaries from March through June of a given year, learning of the restored gospel, coming to understand its doctrine, practices, requirements, covenants, and ordinances. Each time they meet with the sister missionaries they feel a most unusual spirit in their home—a spirit of peace, of joy, and of love.

The message of the missionaries is not only clearly understood but also enters into the McMasters' hearts and burns like fire. Frequently one of the missionaries will pause in the middle of the discussion, look deeply into the eyes of these choice family members and say something like, "I know, with all my heart, that what we have just taught is true." The family is taught that our Heavenly Father is an exalted "Man of

Holiness" (Moses 6:57); that we have all come from a premortal existence when we were born; that at the time of death we enter the postmortal spirit world; and that through the priesthood keys exercised in temples, we are able to form an eternal family unit. Mother or Father comments, more than once, "Yes, I think I have always believed that."

The family has begun to realize what an unusual and blessed experience they have had for the past four months. The children observe that when the missionaries are in their home there seems to be an added light, an increase in understanding. They also notice that such a rarified atmosphere remains in their home for only a brief time but returns when the sisters come for their next visit. What have they been experiencing? What is the cause of this precious phenomenon? Mr. and Mrs. McMaster and their children have been initiated into the realm of divine experience and have, more particularly, been feeling the *influence* and witnessing the *manifestations* of the Holy Ghost, the third member of the Godhead. They are in the formative stage of gaining a testimony, a conviction that only comes through the influence of the Spirit.

The remarkable change that is taking place within the minds and hearts of family members seems to be less a radical conversion than a sweet remembrance, an inner awareness of another time and place, a distant memory of deep and sacred matters. Eventually they are baptized as a family on a Saturday evening and informed that their confirmations will take place in sacrament meeting the next morning.

A COMPLETE BAPTISM

What if the family members didn't quite understand what was meant by the word *confirmation* and decided on Sunday morning to celebrate their glorious discovery of this pearl of great price and their baptism into The Church of Jesus Christ of Latter-day Saints by visiting grandparents in a distant state for a month?

Simply stated, the McMaster family members have been immersed in the waters of baptism but have not completed the baptismal process.

The Prophet Joseph Smith explained that "the baptism of water, without the baptism of fire and the Holy Ghost attending it, is of no use. They are necessarily and inseparably connected. An individual must be born of water and the spirit in order to get into the kingdom of God."[1] On another occasion he taught: "You might as well baptize a bag of sand as a man, if not done in view of the remission of sins and getting of the Holy Ghost. Baptism by water is but half a baptism, and is good for nothing without the other half—that is, the baptism of the Holy Ghost."[2]

Nephi, son of Lehi, counseled his people and us: "Wherefore, do the things which I have told you I have seen that your Lord and your Redeemer should do [be baptized by immersion by one having proper authority]; for, for this cause have they been shown unto me, that ye might know the gate by which ye should enter." Now note what follows: "For the gate by which ye should enter is repentance and baptism by water; and *then cometh a remission of your sins by fire and by the Holy Ghost*" (2 Nephi 31:17; emphasis added). That is to say, it is only when a person receives the gift of the Holy Ghost that a remission of sins follows. The baptism for the remission of sins comes through the baptism in water, followed by the baptism of the Spirit.

What of the common expression in the Church that "our sins are washed away in the waters of baptism"? Saul of Tarsus was struck down by the Lord on the road to Damascus and brought to Ananias, a local priesthood leader. Ananias explained that he (Saul) would be "[Christ's] witness unto all men of what thou hast seen and heard. And now why tarriest thou? Arise, and be baptized, and wash away thy sins, calling on the name of the Lord" (Acts 22:15–16). In our dispensation, the Lord charged James Covill, a Methodist minister who had expressed interest in the restored gospel, to "arise and be baptized, and wash away your

1. *Joseph Smith* [manual], 90.
2. *Joseph Smith* [manual], 95.

sins, calling on my name, and you shall receive my Spirit, and a blessing so great as you never have known" (Doctrine and Covenants 39:10; see also Alma 7:14). Elder Bruce R. McConkie stated: "Sins are remitted not in the waters of baptism, as we say in speaking figuratively, but when we receive the Holy Ghost. It is the Holy Spirit of God that erases carnality and brings us into a state of righteousness. We become clean when we actually receive the fellowship and companionship of the Holy Ghost. It is then that sin and dross and evil are burned out of our souls as though by fire. The baptism of the Holy Ghost is the baptism of fire."[3]

WHAT IS THE GIFT?

We know from ancient scripture and from the revelations of the Restoration that the Holy Ghost is conferred by the laying on of hands of a worthy holder of the Melchizedek Priesthood (Acts 8:16–20; 19:1–6; 2 Timothy 1:6; 3 Nephi 18:36–37; Moroni 2:2; Doctrine and Covenants 20:41, 43, 68; 25:8; 33:15; 35:6; 39:23; 49:14; 52:10; 53:3; 68:25; 76:52; 138:33). Even after the deaths of the original apostles in the meridian dispensation, the ordinance of the laying on of hands continued for some time. Tertullian (ca. A.D. 198) remarked that "the hand is laid on us, invoking and inviting the Holy Spirit through benediction."[4] Cyprian (ca. A.D. 250), a great defender of the faith following the apostolic period, stated: "It is a small matter to 'lay hands on them that they may receive the Holy Ghost,' unless they receive also the baptism of the Church. For then finally can they be fully sanctified, and be the sons of God if they be born of each sacrament [ordinance]."[5] Cyprian also explained that "prayer being made for [the Samaritans who were taught and baptized by Philip in Acts 8], and hands being imposed, the Holy Spirit should be invoked and

---

3. *New Witness for the Articles of Faith,* 290; see also 239.
4. Tertullian, in *Ante-Nicene Fathers,* 3:672.
5. Cyprian, in *Ante-Nicene Fathers,* 5:378.

poured out upon them, which now too is done among us, so that they who are baptized in the Church are brought to the prelates [high ecclesiastical officers] of the Church, and by our prayers and by the imposition of hands obtain the Holy Spirit, and are perfected with the Lord's seal."[6]

Then what is the difference between receiving the *influence,* or *manifestations,* of the Holy Ghost and receiving the *gift* of the Holy Ghost? One of my colleagues for many years in Religious Education at Brigham Young University was Professor Roger Keller. Roger had completed doctoral studies in theology at Princeton University and been ordained as a Presbyterian minister. While living in Mesa, Arizona, and after becoming acquainted with a number of Latter-day Saints, Roger and his wife, Flo Beth, investigated the doctrine and practices of The Church of Jesus Christ of Latter-day Saints. Eventually the Keller family was baptized, and Roger left the Presbyterian ministry. After working for a couple of years at odd jobs to keep his family fed, Roger was invited to join the Church History and Doctrine department at BYU, where over many years he taught several courses but specialized in world religions. Roger and I had many wonderful conversations on doctrine of The Church of Jesus Christ of Latter-day Saints as well as interfaith relations, an endeavor and passion with which both of us became involved.

One day during one of our many chats, I asked, "You were a Presbyterian minister and are now a high priest and a bishop. Did you feel the Spirit of the Lord while you were a Protestant?"

"Yes, of course," he replied.

I continued, "What is the difference between what you felt and experienced then and what you experience now?"

His answer was simple but very enlightening. It was also not a surprise. He said, "What I feel now is basically what I felt then, with this

---

6. Cyprian, in *Ante-Nicene Fathers,* 5:381.

exception: I now feel the power and guidance of the Holy Spirit in a more powerful way and in a more constant fashion."

In recent years I have read Mosiah 18 with different eyes. You will recall that Alma the Elder escaped from the grasp of wicked King Noah, repented sorely of his previous life, and settled secretly near the Waters of Mormon. There he taught the people and organized a small "church in the wilderness" based on what he had learned from the prophet Abinadi. Having explained to the people the nature of the covenant of baptism, Alma then inquired: "Now I say unto you, if this be the desire of your hearts [to stand as witnesses of God in all places and at all times and thereby obtain eternal life], what have you against being baptized in the name of the Lord, as a witness before him that ye have entered into a covenant with him, that ye will serve him and keep his commandments, *that he may pour out his Spirit more abundantly upon you?*" (Mosiah 18:10; emphasis added).

To be clear, these people had felt the *influence* of the Spirit when they were introduced to the doctrine of Christ, as Alma bore what must have been an amazing testimony. After baptism and confirmation, however, they experienced the Spirit *more abundantly,* or, as my friend Roger put it, more powerfully and more constantly. Let us now state the principle: *The gift of the Holy Ghost is the right to receive the constant companionship of the third member of the Godhead, according to one's faithfulness.* We will speak more in chapter 19 of the constancy of that companionship.

As a modern apostle wrote so beautifully, "The testimony before baptism, speaking by way of analogy, comes as a flash of lightning blazing forth in a dark and stormy night; it comes to light the path on which earth's pilgrims, far from their heavenly home and lost in the deserts and swamps of the world must walk if they are to return to the Divine Presence. The companionship of the Holy Ghost after baptism is as the continuing blaze of the sun at noonday, shedding its rays on the path of life and on all that surrounds it."[7]

CORNELIUS AND THE SPIRIT

After Jesus Christ had prepared and taught his twelve apostles, he sent them out to declare the message of salvation. In doing so, he gave them strict instructions: "Go not into the way of the Gentiles, and into any city of the Samaritans enter ye not: but go rather to the lost sheep of the house of Israel" (Matthew 10:5–6; compare 15:24). God loves all of his children, black and white, bond and free, male and female, Jew and Gentile, and each person will eventually have the opportunity to hear and then either receive or reject the message of salvation. There is, however, a time and a season for individuals and whole nations to be so blessed, and, according to the eternal purposes of God, the gospel truth will be given to them in the Lord's time. He who sees the whole picture will decide when and to whom the blessings of the fulness of the gospel will be delivered. During the three years of our Savior's ministry, the message went first, on a preferential basis, to the Jews, the house of Israel.

Before the resurrected Lord ascended into heaven, however, he charged his apostles in the Old World to preach the gospel to every creature, to baptize them into the Church of Jesus Christ, and then continue to teach and nurture converts to the faith (Matthew 28:19–20

---

7. McConkie, *New Witness for the Articles of Faith,* 262. In response to a question that had been raised by a member of the Church regarding the Holy Ghost, the First Presidency (Joseph F. Smith, Anthon H. Lund, and Charles W. Penrose) wrote in 1916 that the gift of the Holy Ghost "is a special blessing sealed upon baptized repentant believers in Jesus Christ, and is 'an abiding witness.' The spirit of God may be enjoyed as a temporary influence by which divine light and power come to mankind for special purposes and occasions. But the gift of the Holy Ghost, which was received by the apostles on the day of Pentecost, and is bestowed in confirmation, is a permanent witness and higher endowment than the ordinary manifestation of the Holy Spirit" (*Messages of the First Presidency,* 5:3–4).

and note 20a; Mark 16:15–18). Not long after the conversion of Saul of Tarsus (Acts 9), the Almighty determined that it was time to remove the restrictions on those to whom the gospel would be delivered. As is his practice, God worked through his earthly priesthood channels, in this case through the senior apostle, Simon Peter.

Chapter 10 of the Acts of the Apostles opens with a description of a noble Gentile, a Roman centurion named Cornelius, who lived in the coastal area of Caesarea. Cornelius was "a devout man, and one that feared God with all his house, which gave much alms to the people, and prayed to God alway" (Acts 10:2). At about 3:00 P.M. one afternoon, Cornelius was shown a vision in which an angel of God instructed him to send for Peter, who was at the time lodging with a friend in Joppa.

The very next day at noon Peter went atop his dwelling to pray and while doing so was drawn into a heavenly vision. The chief apostle saw "a certain vessel descending unto him, as it had been a great sheet knit at the four corners, and let down to the earth." Within this sheet were displayed all kinds of "wild beasts, and creeping things, and fowls of the air" (Acts 10:11–12).

A voice came to Peter, instructing him to get up, kill the beasts, and eat them. The problem, of course, was that these animals were ritually unclean and therefore strictly forbidden by the kosher statutes of the law of Moses (Leviticus 11).

Peter responded as any observant Jew would have: "Not so, Lord; for I have never eaten any thing that is common or unclean." And then the voice came again, this time with immortal words that would shake the world of Simon Peter and, for that matter, the world of the house of Israel: "What God hath cleansed, that call not thou common" (Acts 10:14–15).

This vision and message were given to Peter two more times, and to be obedient to the voice of heaven, Peter took his journey to Caesarea. By the time Peter reached the home of Cornelius and met that worthy

Gentile, the apostle had come to understand the message of the vision clearly. As Peter was invited into the house, he replied: "Ye know how that it is an unlawful thing for a man that is a Jew to keep company, or come unto one of another nation; but God hath shewed me that I should not call *any man* common or unclean" (Acts 10:28; emphasis added).

Soon thereafter "Peter opened his mouth, and said, Of a truth I perceive that God is no respecter of persons: but in every nation he that feareth him [God], and worketh righteousness, is accepted with him." Peter then taught and testified that Jesus of Nazareth was indeed the Messiah and Lord of salvation: "To him give all the prophets witness" (Acts 10:34–35, 43).

What took place then must have been absolutely unnerving for a Jew such as Simon. "While Peter yet spake these words, the Holy Ghost fell on all them which heard the word." Then Peter witnessed a miracle, for "on the Gentiles also was poured out the gift of the Holy Ghost." Peter's company "heard them speak with tongues, and magnify God. Then answered Peter, Can any man forbid water, that these should not be baptized, which have received the Holy Ghost as well as we? And he commanded them to be baptized in the name of the Lord" (Acts 10:44–48).

Let's take a moment to clarify. Sending the Holy Spirit to the household of Cornelius was indeed *a gift,* a divine blessing that could only have been bestowed by a gracious God. It was not, however, in the strictest sense *the gift of the Holy Ghost,* about which we have been speaking and which comes to an individual or a household only after an authorized baptism by water and the accompanying ordinance of confirmation. "There is a difference between the Holy Ghost and the gift of the Holy Ghost," the Prophet Joseph Smith taught. "Cornelius received the Holy Ghost before he was baptized, which was the convincing power of God unto him of the truth of the Gospel, but *he could not receive the gift of the Holy Ghost until after he was baptized.* Had he not taken this sign or ordinance upon him, the Holy Ghost which convinced him of the truth of God, would have left him."[8]

NO TRUE BAPTISM WITHOUT THE SPIRIT

One of the first principles we learn in the book of Acts relative to the gift of the Holy Ghost is that this saving ordinance must be performed by those authorized administrators who have been properly ordained and that ordination to that power cannot be purchased. Simon (known in Christian history as Simon Magus), who was taught the gospel of Jesus Christ and baptized by Philip, approached Peter and offered money for the power to confer the gift of the Holy Ghost. "Thy money perish with thee," Peter responded boldly, "because thou hast thought that the gift of God may be purchased with money. Thou hast neither part nor lot in this matter: for thy heart is not right in the sight of God. Repent therefore of this thy wickedness" (Acts 8:9, 14–23).

A third episode in the New Testament also teaches about the divine authority needed to confer the gift of the Holy Ghost. Joseph Smith was especially drawn to the story recorded in Acts 19 of the apostle Paul encountering certain disciples at Ephesus who claimed to be Christians but had not so much as heard anything concerning the bestowal of the gift of the Holy Ghost. They indicated that they had been baptized "unto John's baptism. Then said Paul, John verily baptized with the baptism of repentance, saying unto the people, that they should believe on him which should come after him, that is, on Christ Jesus. When they heard this, they were baptized in the name of the Lord Jesus. And when Paul had laid his hands upon them, the Holy Ghost came on them; and they spake with tongues, and prophesied" (Acts 19:2–6).

Joseph Smith explained concerning these disciples at Ephesus that "some sectarian Jew had been baptising like John, but had forgotten to

8. *Joseph Smith* [manual], 97; emphasis added.

inform them that there was one to follow by the name of Jesus Christ, to baptise with fire and the Holy Ghost—*which showed these converts that their first baptism was illegal,* and when they heard this they were gladly baptized."[9]

According to the journal of Wilford Woodruff, under the date of 10 March 1844, Joseph Smith, speaking as if he were Paul, said: "No, John did not baptize you, for he did his work right. And so Paul went and baptized them, for he knew what the true doctrine was and he knew that John had not baptized them."[10] Or, my favorite recitation of this story by the Prophet Joseph: "Unto what were you baptized? And they said, Unto John's baptism. Not so, not so my friends; if you had, you would have heard of the Holy Ghost. But you have been duped by some designing knave who has come in the name of John. . . . John's baptism stood good, but these had been baptized by some imposter."[11]

It is difficult to conceive of the countless ways we are assisted, purified, instructed, and empowered by the Holy Spirit. Nephi taught that the Holy Ghost "is the gift of God unto all those who diligently seek [Christ], as well in times of old as in the time that he should manifest himself unto the children of men. . . . For he that diligently seeketh shall find; and the mysteries of God shall be unfolded unto them, by the power of the Holy Ghost, as well in these times as in times of old, and as well in times of old as in times to come; wherefore, the course of the Lord is one eternal round" (1 Nephi 10:17–19).

Perhaps no one has written more beautifully about the myriad of ways the Spirit transforms fallen humanity than Elder Parley P. Pratt,

---

9. "Baptism," *Times and Seasons* 3, no. 21 (1 September 1842): 904; emphasis added.
10. *Words of Joseph Smith*, 328.
11. *Words of Joseph Smith*, 333.

a member of the Quorum of the Twelve Apostles and one of the most gifted writers and doctrinal thinkers within the restored Church of Jesus Christ. Elder Pratt wrote that the Spirit "quickens all the intellectual faculties, increases, enlarges, expands, and purifies all the natural passions and affections. . . . It inspires virtue, kindness, goodness, tenderness, gentleness, and charity. It develops beauty of person, form, and features. It tends to health, vigor, animation, and social feeling. It develops and invigorates all the faculties of the physical and intellectual man. It strengthens, invigorates, and gives tone to the nerves. In short, it is, as it were, marrow to the bone, joy to the heart, light to the eyes, music to the ears, and life to the whole being."[12]

Surely each of us has thought how glorious it would have been to have lived in the meridian of time, to have heard and seen Jesus of Nazareth speak and teach and lift individuals and congregations of people. But, like Nephi, son of Helaman, we are "consigned that these are [our] days" (Helaman 7:9). Our Lord and Redeemer has not left us alone, however, for in many ways he is still with us. One of those ways is through the gift of the Holy Ghost. Through cherishing and cultivating this sacred endowment of light and power, we are in Christ and he is in us through the Spirit (2 Corinthians 5:17; 1 John 2:24; 4:13; Doctrine and Covenants 50:43). Who could ask for more?

---

12. *Key to the Science of Theology*, 101.

Chapter 5

THE UPWARD REACH
FOR THE SPIRIT

N ow that we know what the gift of the Holy Ghost is, how do we acquire and maintain access to this sacred power and influence? When hands are laid upon the head of an individual who has just been baptized, he or she is first confirmed a member of The Church of Jesus Christ of Latter-day Saints and only then is given the gift of the Holy Ghost. This is no small or inconsequential matter. To be initiated into the Church of Jesus Christ is to enter into a sacred fellowship, the fellowship of believers, the body of Christ, the community of those who have accepted Jesus Christ and his gospel as the only way by which eternal life may come.

WHY WE NEED THE CHURCH

To be initiated into the Church of Jesus Christ is to enter into the kingdom of God. "The kingdom of God is an order of government established by divine authority," wrote Elder Orson Pratt. "God, having made all beings and worlds, has the supreme right to govern them by His own laws, and by officers of His own appointment." Elder Pratt also explained that "the kingdom of God is a theocracy. And as it is the only form of government which will redeem and save mankind, it is

55

necessary that every soul should be rightly and thoroughly instructed in regard to its nature and general characteristics."[1]

We need the Church. Our involvement in the Church is vital in obtaining the gift of the Holy Ghost, critical to our happiness here and our eternal reward hereafter. And yet millions of persons throughout the world have in recent years chosen to disengage from any and all religious organizations. What takes place within the Church, and what takes place within each of us as we become enthusiastically involved in the Church, is essential in keeping ourselves unspotted from the vices of the world (Doctrine and Covenants 59:9) and in coming unto the perfection of the soul for which all followers of the Savior strive. Christianity entails more than prayer, fasting, and searching the scriptures—more than an individual effort to live the principles of the gospel of Jesus Christ. As vital as personal devotion and individual effort are, Christianity is fully lived out only *in community*. God designed that the Church of Jesus Christ should be established "for the perfecting of the saints, for the work of the ministry, for the edifying of the body of Christ: till we all come in the unity of the faith, and of the knowledge of the Son of God, unto a perfect man [or woman], unto the measure of the stature of the fulness of Christ" (Ephesians 4:12–13). In short, the Lord's Church is given to assist and empower us toward that spiritual maturity and perfection of which the scriptures speak.

Without the Church, one cannot receive the requisite ordinances of salvation or exaltation; cannot develop those Christlike qualities and attributes that come only through association and affiliation with other individuals who are striving for the same thing. Nor can one participate in the continuing service and "organized sacrifice" that comes through working closely with others. Without the Church and Church affiliation and involvement, one simply cannot be strengthened by the gospel

---

1. *Orson Pratt's Works*, 32.

light that emanates freely and invitingly from those who are on the covenant path, who are seeking the abundant life and seeking to be perfected in Christ.

President Henry B. Eyring spoke of one person's attempt to go it on his own. "I have heard the boast of a man," President Eyring said, "who walked away from the Church slowly, at first just ceasing to teach his Sunday School class and then staying away from church and then forgetting tithing now and then. Along the way he would say to me: 'I feel just as spiritual as I did before I stopped those things and just as much at peace. Besides, I enjoy Sundays more than I did; it's more a day of rest.' Or, 'I think I've been blessed temporally as much or more as I was when I was paying tithing.' *He could not sense the difference, but I could. The light in his eyes and even the shine in his countenance were dimming.* He could not tell, since one of the effects of disobeying God seems to be the creation of just enough spiritual anesthetic to block any sensation as the ties to God are being cut. Not only did the testimony of truth slowly erode, but even the memories of what it was like to be in the light began to seem to him like a delusion."[2]

The Church of Jesus Christ was and forevermore will be built upon the foundation of apostles and prophets (Ephesians 2:20). These are the chief officers within the household of faith, the presiding authorized administrators, the ones charged to stand as special witnesses of the name of Christ in all the world, the ones commissioned to build up the Church and regulate all the affairs of the same throughout the earth (Doctrine and Covenants 107:23, 34). They are the prophets, seers, and revelators, the ones called to see things "afar off" (Doctrine and Covenants 101:54), to be watchmen on the tower of Israel, the stewards of the household of God. Like Enoch, they see "things which [are] not visible to the natural eye" (Moses 6:36).

As to the other offices and callings that make up the Church

---

2. *Because He First Loved Us*, 7–8; emphasis added.

organization, there will, of course, always be a need for teachers and preachers and pastors (bishops, stake presidents) and patriarchs. But the names and functions of callings and assignments may change as needed, for ours is not only a true Church but also a *living* one (Doctrine and Covenants 1:30). Thus we need not be concerned that in the primitive Church, the Church established by Christ in the first century, we do not find a Presiding Bishopric, regional welfare agents, or single adult representatives. Rather, the Lord's Church will always have some organization in place, but the particular organization may and will differ according to needs, circumstances, and ongoing divine direction. What will not change is that the Church will always be led by properly ordained prophets, seers, and revelators who make known the current mind and will of the Almighty.

President Russell M. Nelson taught that "the purpose of the Church is threefold. It is the means by which the gathering of Israel will occur. It is the means by which the families of gathered Israel will be sealed in holy temples. And the Church is the means by which people of the world will be prepared for the Second Coming of the Lord."[3]

RECEIVING THE HOLY GHOST

After a person is confirmed a member of the Lord's Church, as a part of the same ordinance he or she is instructed to "receive the Holy Ghost." While this ordinance is necessary in order to receive the higher light that comes through the covenant gospel, the pronouncement "receive the Holy Ghost" is not a command to the Spirit to take up his work within the newly baptized Saint. Rather, it is a sacred charge—an obligation, responsibility, assignment, Christian duty—extended to the new member to reach up, to do all within his or her power to obtain and maintain the companionship of the Spirit.

---

3. *Teachings of Russell M. Nelson,* 59.

There are many ways, large and small, by which we invite and cultivate the Spirit. Some of these are the following:

Pray for the Spirit. Nothing could be simpler nor more important than to pray often and intently for the Spirit to be with us. We go before our Heavenly Father in great humility, expressing our keen awareness of our limitations; we plead with him to send his Spirit to be with us. As baptized and confirmed members of the Church, we make it a regular and consistent practice to request the Spirit in everything we say or do. That request for the Spirit to be with us becomes our spiritual lifeline, our direct connection to Deity.

The very act of prayer is in reality a surrender, a submission to a Being greater and holier and more powerful than oneself. In this sense, prayer is a form of worship in which the supplicant is looking to and acknowledging God's divine standing and one's absolute dependence upon the Lord. In the Gospel according to Luke, what many through the centuries have called the Gospel of Prayer, we read that as Jesus himself was finishing his own prayer, "one of his disciples said unto him, Lord, teach us to pray, as John also taught his disciples. And he said unto them, When ye pray, say, Our Father which art in heaven, *Hallowed be thy name.* Thy kingdom come. Thy will be done, as in heaven, so in earth" (Luke 11:1–2; emphasis added). To *hallow* is to honor, consecrate, sanctify, make sacred or holy, venerate. In the realm of things spiritual, to hallow is to worship. And our worship invites the gift of the Holy Ghost. We will discuss in chapter 8 how the Holy Ghost can lead us and even prompt us in prayer.

Search the scriptures. Few endeavors on our part will prove to be more efficacious in our quest to receive and enjoy the Holy Spirit than spending time with holy writ. The standard works are a grand collection of divine revelations and instructions given to holy men in times past. Our immersion in them regularly, however, does more than teach us history, as important as history (especially sacred history) is. The words of God are holy; reading those words, pondering those words, praying about those words, and memorizing and repeating those words will, through the years, make of us holy people. That is, as we encounter earlier revelation and focus our attention on it, we open ourselves to receive current revelation.

The same Spirit that brought light and understanding to Abraham, Moses, Elijah, and Isaiah can and will bring that same light and understanding to you and me. The same Spirit that prompted Jesus and Peter and Paul and John the Beloved can and will prompt and guide us. The same Spirit that engendered faith and courage in Nephi, Jacob, Alma, Mormon, and Moroni can and will make of us bold and courageous disciples. And the same Spirit that worked with and through the choice seer Joseph Smith can and will work with and through us. In short, one of the most powerful and productive catalysts to *individual* revelation is *institutional* revelation. "When we want to speak with God," Elder Robert D. Hales taught, "we pray. And *when we want Him to speak to us, we search the scriptures*; for His words are spoken through His prophets. *He will then teach us as we listen to the promptings of the Holy Spirit.*"[4]

Participate in regular worship. It's not uncommon to hear a Church leader conducting a ward or branch sacrament meeting, after he has welcomed those in attendance, make a comment something like this: "We are met today to worship the Lord." I suppose I have heard some form of that greeting hundreds of times over the years, but it has only been in the past few decades that I have begun to reflect on the meaning of such a comment.

We come together as a body of believers to sing hymns of praise and anthems of adoration; to express genuine thanks and make earnest petitions to our God; to partake of the sacrament of the Lord's Supper and reflect reverently on the life and mission, the sufferings and death and resurrection of our Lord and Savior; to hear the gospel preached

---

4. "Holy Scriptures: The Power of God unto Our Salvation," *Ensign*, November 2006, 26–27; emphasis added.

and testimony borne; and to associate with other individuals who make up our Christian community. Worthy Latter-day Saints enter the house of the Lord to learn, to make covenants, to participate in sacred ordinances, to participate in temple worship. And in all of these acts of worship we are aided immeasurably by the Holy Spirit. Let's ponder a few of those forms of worship and contemplate how the Holy Ghost enhances and magnifies our humble offerings.

We sing the hymns to rejoice in our Redeemer, to offer unending gratitude to our Father in Heaven, to express in song what we may well be unable to express in everyday conversation. One who has no musical talent, one who cannot carry a tune in a bucket, is invited to lift his or her voice in song, knowing full well that it is the feelings of the heart—the yearnings and desires of the inner man or woman—that matter most to the God who "delighteth in the song of the heart" (Doctrine and Covenants 25:12).

In describing the important place of the Holy Spirit in our musical endeavors, Joseph Young, brother of President Brigham Young, explained that Joseph Smith the Prophet "recommended the Saints to cultivate as high a state of perfection in their musical harmonies as the standard of the faith which he had brought was superior to sectarian religion. To obtain this, he gave them to understand that *the refinement of singing would depend upon the attainment of the Holy Spirit.* . . . When these graces and refinements and all the kindred attractions are obtained that characterized the ancient Zion of Enoch, then the Zion of the last days will become beautiful, she will be hailed by the Saints from the four winds, who will gather to Zion with songs of everlasting joy."[5]

Seek to emulate the Savior. A modern revelation states that the Savior "received not of the fulness [of the glory and power of the Father] at the first, but received grace for grace" (Doctrine and Covenants 93:12). To receive *grace for grace* is to receive of the Father as we give to others.

---

5. "Vocal Music," in *History of the Organization of the Seventies,* 14–15.

The revelation continues: "And [Jesus] received not of the fulness at first, but continued from grace to grace, until he received a fulness" (Doctrine and Covenants 93:13). To grow *from grace to grace* implies a developmental process, a progression from one level of spiritual attainment to a higher.

The revelation then sets forth a stunning definition of worship: "I give unto you these sayings"—concerning how and in what manner Christ received grace for grace and grew from grace to grace—*"that you may understand and know how to worship, and know what [Who] you worship, that you may come unto the Father in my name, and in due time receive of his fulness. For if you keep my commandments you shall receive of his fulness, and be glorified in me as I am in the Father; therefore, I say unto you, you shall receive grace for grace"* (Doctrine and Covenants 93:19–20; emphasis added).

We worship God as did our Master, Jesus Christ, by participating in what James called "pure religion"—namely, visiting "the fatherless and widows in their affliction, and [keeping ourselves] unspotted from the vices of the world" (JST, James 1:27). We worship God by following the example of him who went about doing good (Acts 10:38). Thus, perfect worship is *emulation,* or what Thomas à Kempis called the imitation, of Christ. It is to be holy as Jehovah is holy. It is to be pure as Christ is pure. It is to do the things that enable us to become more and more like our blessed Lord.[6]

Deny ourselves of all ungodliness. It is one thing to obtain the Spirit and quite another to maintain it, that is, to remain in a spiritual condition in which the Holy Ghost feels comfortable with us. We live in a day that strongly militates against holiness; a time when time-honored values are ridiculed; a season when those who stand up for morality are marginalized in society. It is, in fact, the day of Satan's power, in which evil is called good and good is called evil, in which darkness is labeled light

---

6. See McConkie, *Promised Messiah,* 568–69.

and light is labeled darkness (Isaiah 5:20; 2 Nephi 15:20). As society tilts and even races toward Gomorrah, it becomes increasingly difficult to ascertain moral truth in the world and dangerous to follow current and future trends. We take our cues from society at our great peril.

Happy is the person whose thoughts are clean and pure. We need to do all in our power to control what goes into our minds. We must use wisdom and discernment in what movies we attend, what videos we watch, what internet sites we watch, what sitcoms we continue to consume. We cannot afford to gauge our viewing according to modern trends and what the box office recommends. Very often, in fact, box office success should serve as a caution. "Enter ye in at the strait gate," the Savior said, "for wide is the gate, and broad is the way, that leadeth to destruction, and many there be which go in thereat: because strait is the gate, and narrow is the way, which leadeth unto life, and few there be that find it" (Matthew 7:13–14).

We must give more careful attention to the music we consume, the pictures that surround us, and what we view on the internet. Thoughts are seedbeds of action. Years ago President Dallin H. Oaks explained to BYU students: "We are surrounded by the promotional literature of illicit sexual relations on the printed page and on the screen. For your own good, avoid it. Pornographic or erotic stories are worse than filthy or polluted food. The body has defenses to rid itself of unwholesome food, but the brain won't vomit back filth. Once recorded it will always remain subject to recall, flashing its perverted images across your mind, and drawing you away from the wholesome things in life."[7]

Another matter prevents many of us from enjoying the Spirit of the Lord in our lives as fully as we might: the tendency to live on the edge, to play percentages with God, to tempt fate, and to place ourselves in circumstances that can contribute to our spiritual undoing and fall. There are those who want to see how far they can go without going

---

7. "Things They're Saying," *New Era*, February 1974, 18.

all the way, those who want to drive as close to the edge of the cliff as possible with no plan whatsoever of falling, those who cunningly creep up on the flame with no intention of ever being burned, those who want to enjoy all the privileges of Babylon but at the same time keep intact their citizenship in Zion. There is no lasting happiness in such approaches to life but rather a type of moral or spiritual schizophrenia. Too many people want to be good—but not too good; others want to be bad—but not too bad. Some want to serve the Lord without offending the devil. James taught that "a double minded man is unstable in all his ways" (James 1:8). We would do well to stay as far away from sin and compromise as we can, to avoid not only evil but also the very appearance of evil (1 Thessalonians 5:22). Prevention is far, far better than redemption. As we will emphasize again and again, the Holy Ghost is extremely sensitive.

President George Albert Smith taught: "There are two influences in the world today, and have been from the beginning. One is an influence that is constructive, that radiates happiness and builds character. The other influence is one that destroys, turns men into demons, tears down and discourages. We are all susceptible to both. The one comes from our Heavenly Father, and the other comes from the source of evil that has been in the world from the beginning, seeking to bring about the destruction of the human family. . . .

"My grandfather used to say to his family, 'There is a line of demarcation, well defined, between the Lord's territory and the devil's. If you will stay on the Lord's side of the line you will be under his influence and will have no desire to do wrong; but if you cross to the devil's side of the line one inch, you are in the tempter's power, and if he is successful, you will not be able to think or even reason properly, because you will have lost the spirit of the Lord.'

"When I have been tempted sometimes to do a certain thing, I have asked myself, 'Which side of the line am I on?' If I determined to be on the safe side, the Lord's side, I would do the right thing every time. So when temptation comes, think prayerfully about your problem, and the influence of the spirit of the Lord will enable you to decide wisely. There is safety for us only on the Lord's side of the line."[8]

Partake of the sacrament each week. When we contemplate for a moment the words of the sacramental prayers, we realize that what we promise God when we partake of the sanctified emblems is that we will take upon us the Savior's name and always remember him—that we will be Christians in word and deed. In addition, we covenant that we will do all in our power to keep our promise to obey God's commandments. And what is the reward for keeping that covenant promise? Simply but powerfully put, "that they may always have his Spirit to be with them" (Moroni 4:3; Doctrine and Covenants 20:77).

To remember Jesus Christ is to rivet our minds upon his life, teachings, tender regard for people, miracles, sufferings, death, and glorious rise from the tomb. A significant measure of personal discipline is needed if we are to focus our attention, our thoughts and feelings, on Jesus. Regular and sober reflection on the Savior brings the Spirit.

It is during those precious moments of pondering that we are able to undertake serious self-analysis, to consider how or in what manner we have kept our covenants and been true to the highest within us. That means, of course, that pondering, meditation, and reflection may and indeed should give rise to recognition of where we may have fallen short and a genuine, earnest desire to repent and improve. The Spirit can and will help us to perceive the truth—things as they really are.

What a sweet privilege it is to partake of the emblems of the Savior's sacrifice. Thinking of Jesus invites the Spirit. Reflecting on the price he paid to win our salvation welcomes the Spirit. And enjoying a remission of sins through the sacrament allows the Spirit to be our dear companion.

Live in a constant state of repentance. While I was serving as a stake

---

8. *Sharing the Gospel with Others,* 43.

president, a lovely young woman came into my office for a temple recommend interview. She was a returned missionary, a serious and dedicated student at BYU, and a gem of a human being. She was happy and enthusiastic about life and optimistic about the future. I knew from chatting with her for only a few moments that she was worthy to attend the temple—her countenance beamed—but I went through the appropriate questions nonetheless. At the end of the formal questions, I did what I had done scores of times before—I asked her, "So how would you describe your spiritual life?"

Almost always members of the Church would reply with "Fine," or "I feel good about how I'm doing," or occasionally, "Well, I'm not perfect, but I'm striving to be." Her already big smile expanded as she answered with enthusiasm, "I'm doing great!"

"Well, how great are you?" I followed up.

Her response was one I had never received before. She said, "President, I haven't had to repent in months!"

I was a little taken aback and said something like, "Wow. You are doing great. I think I've never met anyone who is doing that great."

I knew what the young woman meant. She was explaining that she hadn't done anything so grievous that she would need to confess it to a bishop or so serious that she would feel the need to refrain from partaking of the sacrament.

As I recall, I said: "Think with me for a moment. Improvement is repentance. Refinement is repentance. Correcting personality quirks is repentance. Listening more carefully and attentively to a roommate is repentance. In short, life is repentance."

We then had a wonderful conversation.

Mortality is all about the renovation of the human soul, the re-creation of our nature, and the marvelous quest to become men and women of purpose and power. The restored gospel of Jesus Christ is the gospel of repentance, and we have been charged to "teach nothing but repentance" (Doctrine and Covenants 6:9; 11:9; 19:21, 31). Since we cannot merit anything of ourselves (Alma 22:14), and knowing that we are saved only through the merits, mercy, and grace of the Holy Messiah (2 Nephi 2:8), "all we can do" is repent and seek to live worthy of the sweet influence and direction of the Holy Spirit (Alma 24:10, 11, 15).

Imagine the following scenario. It is Christmas morning. You are gathered with family and close friends in a warm, loving environment. The doorbell rings, and you open the door. There stands a beloved associate of yours, one you have not seen for many years. You are delighted to welcome him into your home and reintroduce him to your family. After smiles, hugs, and pleasant conversation, your friend indicates, in spite of the fact that he would prefer to stay, that he must leave because of other commitments. At that moment he hands you a beautifully wrapped gift and wishes you and yours a merry Christmas.

After a scrumptious breakfast the family gathers around the Christmas tree and begins opening gifts. You have opened all of your gifts but the one given to you by your long-lost friend. The family encourages you to open it, but you refuse. You reply, "I really don't need to open it. It's the thought itself that counts, the very idea that a beloved colleague would take the time and spend the money to bring me a gift. I just want to keep the gift as it is—unwrapped—to remember my friend by."

A rather odd situation, isn't it? The gift has been given, the love of the giver has been expressed, but the recipient refuses to make the effort to enjoy that which is within the attractive wrapping paper. Sometimes we are like the recipient of the gift on Christmas morning. We have been offered a glorious gift, the gift of the Holy Ghost, and we have been counseled by our latter-day prophets that there is no gift greater that we could receive in mortality. But we do not reach up, reach out, yearn and plead for that Spirit to be with us, to guide us, to inspire us, to bring conviction to our hearts and minds, and to sanctify our souls. "For what doth it profit a man if a gift is bestowed upon him, and he receive not the gift? Behold, he rejoices not in that which is given unto him, neither rejoices in him who is the giver of the gift" (Doctrine and Covenants 88:33).

The Holy Spirit bears witness of the grandeur and greatness of the Father and the Son, prompts us to worship them, and assists in making the worship meaningful and transformative. Truly, the Spirit provides a sense of awe and adoration, impresses upon us the sublime truth that through worship we may become like them, and is the means by which we are elevated and empowered to become true sons and daughters of the Almighty. The sobering and sacred trek to becoming partakers of the divine nature (2 Peter 1:4) does not truly begin, however, until we obtain, receive, accept, and then use the gift of the Holy Ghost.

PART II

Knowledge That Protects and Confirms

Chapter 6

DISCERNING TRUE
AND FALSE SPIRITS

⁀

J was called to serve as a bishop in 1978 at the age of thirty-one. To say that I was overwhelmed would be a serious understatement. I had served twice before as a counselor in a bishopric, but that was a different matter entirely. Before, I had been especially effective in saying, "Bishop, whatever you feel is best," knowing that the hard decisions, the sensitive interviews, the difficult disciplinary matters, and the final word rested with the bishop.

I had been a bishop for only a few weeks when I received a phone call fairly early on a Saturday morning. The caller was a man who had recently been baptized into the Church and was making remarkable progress as a new convert in our ward. He asked if I was available to meet with him in an hour, and I indicated that would be fine. Before he hung up the phone, he added, "Bishop, I have had two different dreams in the last week, and I would like you to tell me whether the dreams are from God or not." The next fifty-nine minutes were uncomfortable ones, as I wondered why in the world I had agreed to serve in the capacity of bishop. I made my way into our bedroom and dropped to my knees, pleading with the Lord to make me equal to the task before me.

As we sat down together, the new member began, "Bishop, last week I was reading the Doctrine and Covenants and came across a verse that explained that the bishop is called to discern between what is from God and what is from either the individual or the devil." He opened his Doctrine and Covenants and read, "And unto the bishop of the church, and unto such as God shall appoint and ordain to watch over the church and to be elders unto the church, are to have it given to them to discern all those [spiritual] gifts lest there shall be any among you professing and yet be not of God" (Doctrine and Covenants 46:27). I had probably read that verse a hundred times over the years, but now it affected me dramatically. I gulped and said, "Why don't you relate your dreams to me, and let's see what we come up with."

He told me about both dreams in surprising detail. I sat quietly for a moment, felt a gentle but sure impression, and then replied, "Your first dream seems to me to be very significant and to contain fairly direct guidance for your life; I sense that you ought to pay particular attention to what you saw and heard." The second dream seemed to me unusually strange, even bizarre, and, frankly, no specific guidance or instruction came from it. I expressed those feelings to the member. He stood up immediately, shook my hand, thanked me, and left. A sincere man who was gradually growing into the spirit of revelation had come to his priesthood leader, sought for the gift of discernment to be exercised in his behalf, and the answer had come. Here was an example of a person who was intent on trying the spirits (1 John 4:1).

PROPHETIC DIRECTION

Other than what he had learned from the Doctrine and Covenants, why had this man sought my counsel? Because no one wants to be misled. No one who is earnestly striving to know and carry out the will of the Almighty wants to be led astray, away from the path of light and truth. John the apostle offered vital counsel to the Saints late in the first century: "Beloved, believe not every spirit, but try the spirits whether they are of God: because many false prophets are gone out into the world" (1 John 4:1). When John speaks of "trying" the spirits he means testing, evaluating, judging, discerning. When he speaks of trying "the spirits," he is referring not only to spirit beings or angels who might appear but also pointing toward various "doctrines, tenets, views, theories" that we may encounter in our world.[1] An editorial entitled "Try the Spirits" published in the *Times and Seasons* under date of 1 April 1842, offers prudent and wise counsel. The article emphasizes what the apostle Paul taught so powerfully in his first epistle to the Corinthian Saints—that the things of God can only be understood by and through the Holy Spirit of God (1 Corinthians 2:11–14). "'Try the Spirits,' says John, but who is to do it? The learned, the eloquent, the philosopher, the sage, the divine,[2] all are ignorant. . . . 'Try the Spirits,' but what by? Are we to try them by the creeds of men? . . . Let each man or society make a creed and try evil spirits by it and the devil would shake his sides; it is all that he would ask. . . . We answer that no man can do this without the Priesthood, and having a knowledge of the laws by which spirits are governed. . . . No man knows the spirit of the devil and his power and influence but *by possessing intelligence which is more than human.*" A little later in the article we read the following, which serves as an apt summary of why the followers of the Lord Jesus Christ do indeed need to "try the spirits": "*Nothing is a greater injury to the children of men than to be under the influence of a false spirit, when they think they have the Spirit of God.*"[3]

A few principles to guide the Saints in their discernment of supposed revelations or divine communications were then provided: (1) Was any intelligence communicated through the manifestation? (2) The wicked spirits have their "bounds, limits, and laws by which they are governed or controlled." It is also clear that "they possess a power that none but those who have the priesthood can control." (3) There is nothing "indecorous" about the manner that God communicated with his prophets in

---

1. Bruce R. McConkie, "Foolishness of Teaching," 9.

2. "A minister of the gospel; a priest; a clergyman" (*Webster's 1828 Dictionary of the English Language,* s.v. "divine").

3. "Try the Spirits," *Times and Seasons* 3, no. 11 (1 April 1842): 743–44; emphasis added.

ages past. That is, "there is nothing unnatural in the spirit of God."[4] Paul counseled, "Let all things be done decently and in order" (1 Corinthians 14:40). In short, a divine communication will carry a dignity and sobriety that characterizes matters that are communicated by Deity.

USING DISCERNMENT

The following questions might be asked when seeking to determine whether a doctrine, interpretation, or supposed revelation is from the Lord.

1. *Is the person claiming a divine communication or insight acting within the bounds of his or her respective assignment?* The Lord's house is a house of order, not a house of confusion (Doctrine and Covenants 132:8). Chaos would ensue rather quickly if every person could receive revelations for every other person in the Church, irrespective of stewardship. Joseph Smith taught that it is contrary to the economy of God for any person to receive revelation for those higher in authority than themselves.[5] The Prophet also explained that it is the "privilege of any officer in this Church to obtain revelations, so far as relates to his particular calling and duty in the Church."[6] Through the generations, people have repeatedly insisted that they have received direction for the Church regarding its financial status, its placement of temples, its meetings or schedules, who should be ordained to the priesthood, and its doctrinal positions on this or that topic. No matter the genuineness or sincerity of the supposed recipients, the directives are not of God. The Lord simply does not work that way. His house is a house of order.

2. *Is the recipient of the communication worthy to receive the same?* The revelations indicate that the works of God are brought to pass through those who are clean, who have been purified from the sins of the world (3 Nephi 8:1; Doctrine and Covenants 50:28). If I have

---

4. "Try the Spirits," 745, 747.
5. Letter to John S. Carter, 13 April 1833, 29–30.
6. Discourse, 6 April 1837, 487.

received what I believe to be a revelation from God, then it is perfectly appropriate for me to ask myself sincerely whether I am in a spiritual condition to receive such a communication from God. In addition, if a person claims to be receiving divine guidance for an individual or a group, and it is clearly understood that this person is in violation of the laws of the Church or of the land, we may write it down in stone that the supposed revelation is not of God.

3. *Is the communication in harmony with the teachings in the standard works and those of the living prophets?* When individuals claim to have received word that they should join a polygamous cult or participate in a demonic practice or be disloyal or disobedient to the government of the country in which they live, one wonders how they can justify their position. When others indicate that they have been directed by the Lord to lie or cheat or steal or be immoral, one wonders how such actions can possibly square with the teachings of the Church. Often individuals claim that their case is an exception to the rule. We would do well as a people to stay within the rules and avoid the exceptions and margins, especially when such exceptions violate the law and order of the kingdom of God. Those still convinced that what they are commanded to do is of God would then do well to counsel with their priesthood leaders and then follow the counsel precisely.

4. *Does the communication build our faith and strengthen our commitment?* A vital criterion must be met if a supposed revelation is from God. We might ask such questions as the following: Does this communication build my faith in Joseph Smith and the Restoration? Do I feel more motivated to serve faithfully in the Church and kingdom? Does it buttress my confidence in the Lord's anointed servants today and in the destiny of the Church? God does not and will not work against himself; he will not confuse his people by having them believe or do things that would in any way weaken their hold on the iron rod. Those who suggest that the present Church is not progressive enough, that it

needs to move faster toward this or that social or political or moral end, act outside the bounds of propriety and are walking on slippery paths.

5. *Does this communication bring peace and a state of spiritual well being?* Interpretations or supposed revelations that result in doubt, confusion, inconsistency, and unrest do not come from the Prince of Peace. The Holy Spirit warms, comforts, settles the soul, clarifies, and enlightens. "I will tell you a rule by which you may know the Spirit of God from the spirit of evil," said President George Q. Cannon. "The Spirit of God always produces joy and satisfaction of mind. When you have that Spirit you are happy; when you have another spirit you are not happy. The spirit of doubt is the spirit of the evil one; it produces uneasiness and other feelings that interfere with happiness and peace."[7] "When we enjoy the Holy Spirit," President Wilford Woodruff pointed out, "when we are trying to live our religion here on earth, we are the happiest people on God's footstool, no matter what our circumstances may be."[8]

PATIENCE WITH SPIRITUAL GROWTH

Some members of the Church, presumably dissatisfied with the elementary manner in which a study of the gospel is undertaken, have chosen to turn toward more flashy, more sensational, certainly more dramatic means of gaining great knowledge and participating in unusual experiences. I tend to call this group Mormon Gnostics, who feel that they are possessed of sacred, secret knowledge that has been granted to few others.

These kinds of persons may be characterized by (1) their enthusiasm, almost obsession, for the esoteric, for "deeper" matters of the faith; (2) their claim to be enjoying what might be called extraordinary spiritual experiences—regular visits from the Savior himself or conversations with such notable prophets as Enoch or Melchizedek; (3) their eagerness to discover and broadcast precisely when the Lord Jesus Christ will return

---

7. In *Journal of Discourses*, 15:375.
8. *Wilford Woodruff* [manual], 51.

in glory. When it comes to matters that ought to be left with the prophets and apostles, the Savior is very emphatic that "it shall not be given to any one to go forth to preach my gospel, or to build up my church, except he be ordained by some one who has authority, and *it is known to the church that he has authority and has been regularly ordained by the heads of the church*" (Doctrine and Covenants 42:11; emphasis added).

No one should be in a hurry to qualify for great spiritual experiences. "You cannot force spiritual things," President Boyd K. Packer explained. "Such words as *compel, coerce, constrain, pressure, demand* do not describe our privileges with the Spirit.

"You can no more force the Spirit to respond than you can force a bean to sprout, or an egg to hatch before its time. You can create a climate to foster growth; you can nourish, and protect; but you cannot force or compel. You must await the growth.

"Do not be impatient to gain great spiritual knowledge. Let it grow, help it grow; but do not force it, or you will open the way to be misled."[9]

Or, as Bible scholar N. T. Wright put it, "Despite what you might think from some excitement . . . about new spiritual experiences, God doesn't give people the Holy Spirit in order to let them enjoy the spiritual equivalent of a day at Disneyland."[10]

THE PROPER PLACE OF EMOTION

I have been concerned over the years that too often our youth (and, unfortunately, even some of our more experienced members) are prone to confuse sentimentality with spirituality, tears with testimony. Let me illustrate. One Mutual night as I came out of my bishop's office, I noticed that the members of the Laurel class were huddled in the hall and in the midst of what seemed to be quite a fascinating discussion. They appeared to be talking about one of the young women in their class

9. *That All May Be Edified*, 338.
10. *Simply Christian*, 122.

who had during the last year slipped out of Church activity. I heard one of the young women say, with confidence, "Well, I can tell you this much—she doesn't have much of a testimony." One of the others challenged her. "How can you say that? How do you know?" The first young woman replied, "Well, think about it for a minute. I've seen her bear her testimony many times, and I've never seen her cry once!" There was a pause, a moment of reflection on the part of twelve young women, and then a rather visible concurrence. Most of them nodded in agreement.

Many years ago I taught several classes of high school juniors and seniors in seminary. My fourth period class was a remarkable group. During the first part of the year, however, I noticed that nearly every devotional to start the class and set the spiritual tone involved some kind of death story. Somebody was dying or giving their blood or something of that sort. I took the class president aside after the third week and asked, "Fred, what's the deal with the devotionals?"

He replied, "Yes, aren't they great?"

I said, "I mean, why all the morbid stories in our devotionals? Why are we so hung up with death?"

Fred responded politely, but the look on his face betrayed the fact that my question had totally mystified him. "Brother Millet," he came right back, "How else are we supposed to get the kids to cry?" I said, "Oh, I understand." Then we visited about what a spiritual experience really is.

There's no question that when we have a genuine spiritual experience, we may be touched emotionally. Tears come easily for some of us, and there should never be the slightest embarrassment about such a thing. And yet we do ourselves and our youth a tremendous disservice if we begin to believe that an emotional experience is always a spiritual experience. Tears may come, but they should never be manipulated or elicited or sought for. In the classroom, for example, there is plenty for the gospel teacher to do by way of study, prayer, preparation, organization, and presentation; he or she must not seek to usurp the role of the

Holy Ghost. The Spirit is the Comforter. He is the Revelator. He is the Converter. He is, in reality, the Teacher. We strive to be an instrument in the Lord's hands. We may seek and pray for an outpouring of the Spirit, but we must never attempt to manufacture the same. It is not in our power to do so.

President Howard W. Hunter, in speaking to Church Educational System personnel, said: "I think if we are not careful as . . . teachers . . . , we may begin to try to counterfeit the true influence of the Spirit of the Lord by unworthy and manipulative means. I get concerned when it appears that strong emotion or free-flowing tears are equated with the presence of the Spirit. Certainly the Spirit of the Lord can bring strong emotional feelings, including tears, but that outward manifestation ought not be confused with the presence of the Spirit itself.

"I have watched a great many of my brethren over the years and we have shared some rare and unspeakable spiritual experiences together. Those experiences have all been different, each special in its own way, and such sacred moments may or may not be accompanied by tears. Very often they are, but sometimes they are accompanied by total silence. Always they are accompanied by a great manifestation of the truth, of revelation to the heart.

"Give your students gospel truth powerfully taught; that is the way to give them a spiritual experience. Let it come naturally and as it will, perhaps with the shedding of tears, but perhaps not. If what you say is the truth, and you say it purely and with honest conviction, those students will feel the spirit of the truth being taught them and will recognize that inspiration and revelation have come into their hearts. That is how we build faith. That is how we strengthen testimonies—with the power of the word of God taught in purity and with conviction."[11] If we become confused about what is a genuine spiritual experience and what is not, we open ourselves to deception.

---

11. "Eternal Investments," 3.

From a very young age, the Prophet Joseph Smith seemed to possess an unusual measure of wisdom and discernment when it came to spiritual matters. His mother, Lucy Mack Smith, explained that young Joseph, by the time the angel Moroni appeared in September 1823, "had never read the Bible through in his life: he seemed much less inclined to the perusal of books than any of the rest of our children, but *far more given to meditation and deep study.*"[12] Having studied the life and ministry of Joseph Smith for decades now, I have concluded the following: (1) Joseph was in no way possessive of the gifts and blessings of God; he wanted all of the Saints to come to see and experience and know the things of God, just as he had; and (2) Joseph did not pretend to gifts or manifestations that really did not take place; in short, there is no evidence of which I am aware that Brother Joseph ever tried to fake the workings of the Spirit. In speaking of the time leading up to the First Vision, Alexander Neibaur explained that "Joseph told us [that he had attended] a revival meeting. His mother and brother and sister got religion," and Joseph *"wanted to get religion, too, wanted to feel and shout like the rest, but could feel nothing."*[13]

RELY UPON THE SCRIPTURES

Decades ago those called to serve full-time missions went to Salt Lake City to what was then known as the Mission Home. There for a few days (since language training centers were just coming into being and generally foreign languages were learned in the field) the elders and sisters were instructed in the doctrine of the gospel, in mission rules and procedures, as well as how to maintain good health and hygiene. What is now astonishing to contemplate, however, is that most of the teaching was done by the General Authorities of the Church.

It was early in the week that we were set apart as missionaries. I

---

12. *History of Joseph Smith by His Mother*, 82; emphasis added.
13. Cited in Harper, *Joseph Smith's First Vision*, 66, emphasis added; spelling and punctuation modernized.

remember so very well the beautiful blessing pronounced upon my head by Elder Alma Sonne, an Assistant to the Twelve. In addition, many of the missionaries received their endowment in the Salt Lake Temple that week. I do remember how spiritually overwhelming my first time through the temple was for me; I didn't understand much of what I heard and saw, but I felt an outpouring of the Spirit of God that was greater than anything I had known before. It would take many return visits to the temple before I began to fully appreciate the depth and profundity of the doctrine, covenants, and ordinances.

After we had completed the endowment session, our group of missionaries was led to the large assembly room of the Salt Lake Temple where we were told that solemn assemblies were held. After we were all seated, Elder Harold B. Lee stood behind one of the pulpits and invited the missionaries to ask any questions about the temple they might have. In my case, I was so overwhelmed with what I had undergone that I was not bright enough even to come up with a question! My, would I love to have that invitation today. As I reflect on that day in the temple with Elder Lee, the most impressive thing to me was the way he responded to the questions. In response to almost every question he said, "Well, let's see what the Lord has said about that." He would then open his scriptures and read one or more passages of scripture that proved to be particularly insightful. This happened again and again. I was so impressed with Elder Lee's grasp of the standard works that I found myself making a vow that I would strive with all my might in the years to come to be in a position to assist members of the Church to better understand and appreciate the restored gospel.

The following passages about the preeminent value of the holy scriptures were spoken or written by President Harold B. Lee:

"All that we teach in this church ought to be couched in the scriptures. We ought to choose our texts from the scriptures, and wherever you have an illustration in the scriptures or a revelation in the Book of Mormon, use it, and do not draw from other sources where you can find it here in these books. We call these the standard Church works because they are standard. If you want to measure truth, measure it by the four standard Church works. . . . If it is not in the standard works, you may well assume that it is speculation. It is a man's own personal opinion."[14]

"If there is any teacher who teaches a doctrine that can't be substantiated from the standard Church works—and I make one qualification, and that is unless that one be the President of the Church, who alone has the right to declare new doctrine—then you may know by that same token that such a teacher is but expressing his own opinion."[15]

In speaking of his having had the experience of responding to missionaries' questions in the temple, President Lee remarked: "We always say to them repeatedly as we have finished, 'I want you to notice that all the answers I have given have been given from out of the scriptures. I wouldn't dare attempt to make an answer to your questions anywhere else but from the scriptures or from the statements of a President of the Church.' . . . . Don't dare to go beyond what the Lord has revealed and attempt to use imagination in some cases or to speculate as to these teachings. I wish you would remember that."[16]

It is, of course, to the scriptures that we turn in order to learn doctrine. It is vital that we know the doctrine of the Church; if we do not, we may be unable to properly discern or teach the difference between truth and error. We begin to make sense of the scriptures, begin to grasp their messages and meanings, begin to gain a conviction that the words of scripture were indeed given by "holy men of God [who] spake as they were moved by the Holy Ghost" (2 Peter 1:21)—we do all of this by and through the power of the Holy Spirit, whose mission it is to open our eyes, expand our minds, and settle our hearts.

---

14. *Teachings of Harold B. Lee*, 148–49.
15. *Teachings of Harold B. Lee*, 149.
16. *Teachings of Harold B. Lee*, 153–54.

There is so much beauty and goodness to be found in our world, so many reasons to rejoice in the Lord and in his mighty creations. There is, unfortunately, also much that is not so beautiful and is anything but good. Satan is here on planet Earth, and he and his followers are going about the business of spreading the work of unrighteousness, of lies and deceptions, of doctrinal aberrations and partial truths that result from wresting (twisting or distorting) the holy word, any of which can destroy our souls.

President Brigham Young pointed out that "man can be deceived by the sight of the natural eye, . . . can be deceived by the hearing of the ear, and by the touch of the hand; . . . he can be deceived in all of what are called the natural senses. But *there is one thing in which he cannot be deceived.* What is that? *It is the operations of the Holy Ghost,* the Spirit and power of God upon the creature. It teaches him of heavenly things; it directs him in the way of life; *it affords him the key by which he can test the devices of man, and which recommends the things of God.*"[17]

President Gordon B. Hinckley put the matter simply: "That's the test, when all is said and done. Does it [the prompting] persuade one to do good, to rise, to stand tall, to do the right thing, to be kind, to be generous? Then it is the Spirit of God."[18]

It is my heartfelt prayer that the Lord will empower us with deeper wisdom and greater discernment to "divide asunder all the cunning and the snares and the wiles of the devil," and that he will, by the power of the Holy Ghost, lead the men and women of Christ "in a strait and narrow course across that everlasting gulf of misery . . . and land [our] souls . . . at the right hand of God in the kingdom of heaven" (Helaman 3:29–30).

---

17. In *Journal of Discourses,* 18:230; emphasis added.
18. *Teachings of Gordon B. Hinckley,* 260.

Chapter 7

QUENCHING THE SPIRIT

oward the end of Paul's first epistle to the Thessalonians, the apostle began to provide brief but crucial counsel: "Rejoice evermore. Pray without ceasing. In every thing give thanks. . . . *Quench not the Spirit.* Despise not prophesyings. Prove all things; hold fast that which is good" (1 Thessalonians 5:16–21; emphasis added). Because the Holy Spirit is like an inner fire, a flame that warms the heart and lights the way, Paul pleaded with the Saints not to quench the Spirit, that is, not to put out the flame or extinguish the light.

Jacob, son of Lehi, offered his own commentary on the marvelous allegory of Zenos. Among other things, Jacob counseled his people to "cleave unto God as he cleaveth unto you. And while his arm of mercy is extended towards you in the light of the day, harden not your hearts." Jacob probed further: "Behold, will ye reject these words? *Will ye reject the words of the prophets . . . and deny* the good word of Christ, and the power of God, and *the gift of the Holy Ghost, and quench the Holy Spirit,* and make a mock of the great plan of redemption, which hath been laid for you?" (Jacob 6:5, 8; emphasis added). Similarly, Amulek pleaded with the Zoramites that "ye should no more deny the coming of Christ; that ye *contend no more against the Holy Ghost,* but that ye receive it, and take upon you the name of Christ" (Alma 34:37–38; emphasis added).

THE SENSITIVITY OF THE HOLY GHOST

As the third member of the Godhead, the Holy Ghost cannot dwell in an unclean or impure environment, nor can the Spirit accompany a person who is disobedient or unfaithful or whose behavior is at cross-purposes with the mind and will of God our Father (1 Nephi 10:21; 15:33; Mosiah 2:37; Alma 7:21; 34:36; Helaman 4:24; Mormon 9:3–4). To put it another way, the Holy Ghost is exceedingly sensitive.

We have learned that the Light of Christ, or Spirit of Jesus Christ, both fills the immensity of space and also works upon the heart and mind of individuals, seeking to lead them to the higher light of the Holy Ghost. Of the Light of Christ, President Joseph F. Smith noted: "*It is the Spirit of God which proceeds through Christ to the world, that enlightens every man that comes into the world, and that strives with the children of men, and will continue to strive with them,* until it brings them to a knowledge of the truth and the possession of the greater light and testimony of the Holy Ghost. If, however, he receive that greater light, and then sin against it, the Spirit of God will cease to strive with him, and *the Holy Ghost will wholly depart from him.*"[1]

Please note the word *strive.* It is my impression that we as a people have not fully appreciated the meaning or import of this word. *Strive* is closely related to *strife,* which is "vigorous or bitter conflict, discord, or antagonism." Strife entails "a quarrel, struggle, or clash."[2] To summarize, the Light of Christ will strive—vigorously struggle with, clash—with each one of us until we are led to the higher light. *The Holy Ghost will not strive with us.* Without intending to be in any way irreverent or inappropriate, if I were to resort to language I heard again and again as a boy in Louisiana, I would say, "the Holy Ghost will not mess with us," or "the Holy Ghost will not put up with us," if we remain in sin.

President Boyd K. Packer observed: "If we begin to do things that

1. *Gospel Doctrine,* 67–68; emphasis added.
2. *Random House College Dictionary,* rev. ed., s.v. "strife."

kill the Spirit, . . . then the Spirit will back off. It will leave us alone to find our way. That is a very dangerous place to be in."[3]

That is particularly the case when we are seeking to find answers to our questions. President M. Russell Ballard taught Brigham Young University students that "while searching, studying, and praying for answers, please remember that you have to be living right to get the answers you seek."[4] In that address, President Ballard quoted the following from Latter-day Saint historian Richard L. Bushman: "Guilt clouds the mind. If you are knowingly sinning, you will subconsciously want to separate yourself from God and find reasons for denying his power."[5] Once again, the third member of the Godhead is extremely sensitive.

THE TEMPLE OF GOD

To enjoy the gift of the Holy Ghost in our lives—the Spirit's guidance, warnings, comfort, and sanctifying power—is a consummate privilege. To have the light and knowledge and inspiration of the third member of the Godhead within our hearts and minds is a sacred and priceless opportunity. Thus the apostle Paul inquired of the body of Christ, the Christian community: "Know ye not that ye are the temple of God, and that the Spirit of God dwelleth in you? If any man defile the temple of God, him shall God destroy, for the temple of God is holy, which temple ye are" (1 Corinthians 3:16–17). Shortly thereafter, Paul asked in a similar vein: "What? Know ye not that *your body is the temple of the Holy Ghost which is in you,* which ye have of God, and *ye are not your own?* For *ye are bought with a price:* therefore glorify God in your body, and in your spirit, which are God's" (1 Corinthians 6:19–20; emphasis added).

---

3. *Mine Errand from the Lord,* 95.

4. "Questions and Answers: An Apostle Comes to Campus for a Grandfatherly Chat with the BYU Student Body," 29.

5. Bushman, *On the Road with Joseph Smith,* 110–11, cited in Ballard, "Questions and Answers: An Apostle Comes to Campus for a Grandfatherly Chat with the BYU Student Body," 29.

Paul's words apply to the Church of Jesus Christ itself, as well as to our physical bodies. No sane Latter-day Saint would ever consider dragging into the house of the Lord loud and harsh music, filthy or blasphemous language, or pornographic images. In the same way, no thinking member of Christ's Church would choose to offend the Spirit that was conferred upon us at our confirmation by defiling our bodies with sinful practices or ingesting substances that will defile and destroy our physical body, what Paul here calls the "temple of God." How dare we treat so lightly, so cheaply, and so disrespectfully the physical body for which we yearned and learned and worked for countless ages before we ever came to earth? We knew then, just as we know now, that our body is the instrument of our spirit; that the physical body allows us to gain experience in ways that we could not in the premortal world; and, it is this body—a glorified, exalted, and celestial body—with which we will spend eternity.

I was impressed with something my friend John Bytheway taught. In speaking of the booklet *For the Strength of Youth,* John wrote: "If we were to reduce those forty-six pages to seven words, they might be, 'Don't do things that offend the Spirit.' As a teacher, I love to see the look on the faces of the young people as it dawns on them that *every* standard, rule, and guideline in the pamphlet, *every one,* is about keeping the Holy Ghost with them." Brother Bytheway said further: "Sometimes, someone might counter: 'Well, that movie, that show, that type of depiction doesn't offend me.' However, that's not the standard. It's not about what offends *you*—it's about what offends the Holy Ghost. And since we have each made a covenant to so live that 'we can always have his Spirit to be with [us]' (Moroni 4:3), we have made a covenant not to offend the Holy Ghost by our choice of media."[6]

---

6. *Moroni's Guide to Surviving Turbulent Times,* 52.

ACTIONS OR ATTITUDES THAT OFFEND THE SPIRIT

There are many ways in our busy and distracting world to offend the Spirit and thereby quench the divine influence we might otherwise enjoy. Some of these are the following:

Using our time unwisely. Many years ago it became necessary to convene a disciplinary council for a young man, a Melchizedek Priesthood holder and returned missionary, who had succumbed to serious sexual transgression. Let's call him Tim. The decision of the stake disciplinary council was that he should be disfellowshipped. I worked closely with his bishop and encouraged him to meet with Tim regularly, to guide him through the process of repentance. I also asked that Tim meet with me periodically so that I could check on his progress. As the weeks passed, the bishop and I communicated often. Both of us were quite disappointed that the young man had made very little spiritual progress, although Tim insisted that he had remained free from further sin and that he and the young woman with whom he had been involved had broken off their relationship.

After several months passed, I sat opposite Tim in an interview. I perceived that his countenance had really not changed much since the disciplinary council; there was a darkness about him that was troubling to me. I decided to do some serious probing to determine what in his life was blocking his progress. After about forty-five minutes of inquiring about the state of his soul, I decided to ask him to walk me through a typical day in his life. We were only a few minutes into this phase of the interview when it became very clear where some of the problem lay. Each night, just after dinner, Tim would recline on the sofa and begin to play video games. He explained that he usually continued in the games throughout the night until about nine the next morning. Exhausted and unable to attend his university classes, he would sleep for several hours, eat some dinner, and then repeat the process. He explained that this had been going on since the disciplinary council.

Obviously Tim was failing his classes, simply from nonattendance.

Even more tragic, however, was that he was wasting his time, spending untold hours glued to the screen watching mindless drivel. As I looked into his eyes there came into my mind the words of Amulek in the Book of Mormon. Speaking to the Zoramites, Amulek sounded a sobering warning: "I beseech of you that ye do not procrastinate the day of your repentance until the end." Notice what follows: "For after this day of life, which is given us to prepare for eternity, behold, *if we do not improve our time* while in this life, then cometh the night of darkness wherein there can be no labor performed" (Alma 34:33; emphasis added).

Why is that the case? As Amulek had stated only moments earlier, "*This life is the time for men to prepare to meet God;* yea, behold the day of this life is the day for men to perform their labors" (Alma 34:32; emphasis added). As I see it, to *improve our time* is to *make wise and productive use of the time* that has been allotted to us. If we do not, if we idle away the precious and priceless seconds and minutes and hours that make up this second estate, we will not enjoy the companionship of the Spirit—the comfort, the elevated perspective, the discernment, the sanctifying influence—that could be ours. I am reminded of the poignant words of a beautiful and beloved hymn:

> *Improve the shining moments; don't let them pass you by.*
> *Work while the sun is radiant; work, for the night draws nigh.*
> *We cannot bid the sunbeams to lengthen out their stay,*
> *Nor can we ask the shadow to ever stay away.*

> *Time flies on wings of lightning; we cannot call it back.*
> *It comes, then passes forward along its onward track.*
> *And if we are not mindful, the chance will fade away,*
> *For life is quick and passing. 'Tis as a single day.*

> *As winter-time doth follow the pleasant summer days,*
> *So may our joys all vanish and pass far from our gaze.*
> *Then should we not endeavor each day some point to gain,*
> *That we may here be useful and ev'ry wrong disdain?*

Improve each shining moment. In this you are secure.

For promptness bringeth safety and blessings rich and pure.

Let prudence guide your actions; be honest in your heart;

And God will love and bless you and help to you impart.[7]

Preoccupation and distraction. Many wonderful people throughout the earth, women and men, Latter-day Saints and noble persons of other faiths, people worthy of our Father's direction, do not allow the Spirit to work closely with them because their minds and hearts are obsessed with temporalities, with things of this world (Doctrine and Covenants 121:35). That is tragic. In some cases, such individuals are so focused on succeeding at their employment, of *making a living,* that they allow little time or energy for learning how *to live,* meaning to live by and with the influence of the Holy Spirit.

Others, in an effort to assist their children to lead a full life, race about attending concerts, dance recitals, athletic events, music lessons, civic functions, country clubs, or local service projects—all of which can be, in their own way, good and worthwhile activities. They matter precious little, however, if they monopolize the time and energy of family members to such an extent that family home evening, family prayer, or scripture study (family and personal) are eased off the family's agenda. President Dallin H. Oaks offered wise counsel and cautions when he taught us that there are some matters that are *good,* others that are *better,* and some that are *best.*[8] President Oaks also charged the Latter-day Saints to concern themselves more and more with the "weightier matters."[9]

An equally unfortunate circumstance is a person who earnestly seeks God in prayer for comfort, for instruction, for specific guidance, but who does not carve out a time and place for the Almighty's voice to be heard. "Know that our Father in heaven will always hear your

---

7. "Improve the Shining Moments," *Hymns*, 1985, no. 226.

8. "Good, Better, Best," *Ensign*, November 2007, 104–8.

9. *With Full Purpose of Heart*, 179–90.

prayers," Elder Richard G. Scott explained, "and will invariably answer them. However, His answers will seldom come while you are on your knees praying. Even when you may plead for an immediate response. Rather, He will prompt you in quiet moments when the Spirit can most effectively touch your mind and heart."[10]

Sexual impurity. In a modern revelation embracing "the law of the Church," Jesus Christ gave this warning: "Thou shalt love thy wife [or husband] with all thy heart, and shalt cleave unto her and none else. And he that looketh upon a woman to lust after her *shall deny the faith, and shall not have the Spirit;* and if he repents not he shall be cast out" (Doctrine and Covenants 42:22–23; emphasis added).

What does the Lord mean when he states that one who lusts in his or her heart after another person *will deny the faith?*

Let's turn first to a definition for the word *deny.* One respected dictionary explains that to deny is "to state (that something declared or believed to be true) is not true."[11] This definition seems to imply that if a person continues to harbor the spirit of lust, continues to objectify another child of Almighty God, and does not seek to repent of the same, he or she will lose the Spirit of God and the testimony or conviction of the truthfulness of the gospel of Jesus Christ. Testimony comes by and through the power of the Holy Ghost. Unrepented lust causes us to forfeit the companionship of that sensitive Spirit and to relinquish over time a knowledge of what we once knew most assuredly to be true.

The word *deny* is also defined in that same dictionary as "to withhold the possession, use, or enjoyment of."[12] What this definition brings to mind is the painful realization that lustfulness inevitably results in loss—loss of the Spirit, loss of the promised peace so necessary in times of trouble or trauma, loss of the enjoyment of gospel living, loss of sweet association with those of the household of faith who are

---

10. *21 Principles*, 43.
11. *Random House College Dictionary*, s.v. "deny."
12. *Random House College Dictionary*, s.v. "deny."

laboring tirelessly to cultivate and maintain that sacred gift of the Holy Ghost.

Six months later that same Lord and Savior cautioned that "he that looketh on a woman to lust after her, or if any shall commit adultery in their hearts [see Matthew 5:27–28], they shall not have the Spirit, but shall deny the faith *and shall fear*" (Doctrine and Covenants 63:16; emphasis added). A fascinating addition, is it not? Not only will a lustful person lose the Spirit and deny the faith but he or she will also *fear.*

Remember, fear is the opposite of *faith.* If we are constantly afraid of what will come, forever panicked about some dreaded eventuality, morbidly horrified that the end of the world is imminent, for example, then we are living without faith—faith in God and Christ, trust in the Father's plan of salvation, reliance upon the fact that no matter what may come, what tragedies may unfold, our Lord is at the helm and is in charge. Those who live in unrepented lustfulness may, in quiet and more reflective moments, even fear that one day they will stand face to face with the Keeper of the Gate (2 Nephi 9:41) and be required to give an accounting of how they have used the precious time on earth that has been allotted to them.

Exercising unrighteous dominion. The Savior's gentle invitation to follow him is a kindly summons to "come and see" (John 1:37–39). Even though he knew, more clearly than any other person who dwelt on planet Earth, that his strait path leads to life eternal while the wide path leads to spiritual death (Matthew 7:13–14; 3 Nephi 14:13–14), he would compel no one to accept him and his gospel. Thus from Liberty Jail the Prophet Joseph wrote, "When we undertake to cover our sins, or to gratify our pride, our vain ambition, or to exercise control or dominion or compulsion upon the souls of the children of men, in any degree of unrighteousness, behold, *the heavens withdraw themselves; the Spirit of the Lord is grieved;* and when it is withdrawn, Amen to the priesthood or the authority of that man" (Doctrine and Covenants 121:37; emphasis added).

As an illustration, a man exercises unrighteous dominion in his home when he makes all of the decisions for the family, when he fails to involve his wife and children in family affairs, when he rules the home with an iron hand, when he bullies or pressures family members, when his approach to motivation borders on abuse. A leader exercises unrighteous dominion in a ward or branch when he or she seeks to get the job done at any cost, no matter whose feelings are hurt in the process; when he or she refuses to delegate properly and assumes all the burden of responsibility; when he or she does not allow those within their stewardship to mature in and do their jobs and make the appropriate decisions for their respective quorum or auxiliary. Moral agency is a precious, God-given gift over which the war in heaven was fought. God will not violate it, and a person who does so may soon find himself or herself devoid of power in the priesthood.

President Howard W. Hunter, in speaking to the men of the Church, was most direct: "Presiding in righteousness necessitates a shared responsibility between husband and wife; together you act with knowledge and participation in all family matters. For a man to operate independent of or without regard to the feelings and counsel of his wife in governing the family is to exercise unrighteous dominion."[13]

Ignoring wise counsel. For five years I had the privilege of serving as the director of the Institute of Religion near Florida State University. Those years in Tallahassee are precious to my wife, Shauna, and me. As with any college or university institute, one of the greatest challenges was to search out potential students (especially those who had left home for college and chosen to hide from the Church and certainly from weekday religious education). Consequently, I found that I needed to do whatever was moral to attract them to the building and get them enrolled in one or more classes. That meant I needed to be available to meet their needs and to teach classes when they could make it.

---

13. "Being a Righteous Husband and Father," *Ensign*, November 1994, 51.

A small group of students approached me and requested that I teach an Old Testament class. I really did not know a great deal about the Old Testament, given that I had only taught it once and that was to a rowdy but wonderful group of seminary students four years earlier in the Salt Lake Valley. I agreed to teach the institute class. The young people then asked, "Could we do it at 6:00 A.M., so that we can get to our university classes on time?"

I smiled, gulped, and haltingly replied, "Sure. That would be fine." At least the institute class would not conflict with other classes!

We began the next week, and I found myself actually enjoying my study of the Old Testament. I managed to stay about two class periods ahead of the students. One morning we were moving along fairly well when a young woman raised her hand and posed a question about a potentially sensitive matter. I pondered for a moment to decide how to answer. One option was that I could provide a brief but accurate answer that wouldn't lead us into strange territory. Unfortunately, I had done a great deal of reading on this odd and tangential subject in recent months and realized that I could really impress the students with my extensive knowledge. At that moment, the Spirit of the Lord very clearly prompted me to choose the former option and proceed with the remainder of the lesson. I thought to myself, "But I really do know quite a bit about this matter." The prompting came again, as though the Lord was speaking to me very directly: "Provide an adequate answer for now. That is all you need to do."

Regrettably, I decided to set aside those two very clear warnings. Within ten minutes the room was filled with a spirit of unrest, and confusion began to spread. And, more practically, we wasted a great deal of time that could have been spent on more meaningful matters. The look on the faces of those young adults bespoke both discomfort and disappointment. I did my best to patch things up before the class was over. Finally everyone left the room, and I was left to reflect painfully on what had just taken place. I had ignored the Holy Spirit's effort to keep me from a worthless exercise. I had turned a deaf ear to the voice of that member of the Godhead whose influence and comfort I had, ironically, sought for most earnestly for so many years. My refusal to obey resulted in my quenching the Spirit, driving it out of our midst and leaving each one of us in a stupor of thought. It was an awful experience, one I have never forgotten.

Over the years since then, as I have studied the Book of Mormon, I have read with much interest and an equal amount of regret of an encounter that took place some eighty years before Christ's birth. Alma's missionary companion Amulek was teaching the wicked people of Ammonihah when he was confronted by Zeezrom. "Will ye answer the questions which I shall put unto you?" inquired the crafty lawyer. Then came a timeless and treasured reply, one that I wish I had remembered before my debacle in institute class. "And Amulek said unto him: Yea, if it be according to the Spirit of the Lord, which is in me; for I shall say nothing which is contrary to the Spirit of the Lord" (Alma 11:21–22).

We belong to a church that is a distinctive Christian faith, distinctive in that many facets of our beliefs and lifestyle are little understood or appreciated by men and women of good will all along the religious spectrum. One of our most distinctive doctrines—one that makes us truly one of a kind—is our belief that the channels of divine direction have been cleared, that institutional revelation is coming day by day through living apostles and prophets. This is a singular blessing, a phenomenal comfort in a world that is rapidly spinning out of control. This belief, this assurance that the Almighty is directing his living kingdom through living prophets, seers, and revelators, however, comes with a burden of responsibility.

In a revelation given through the Prophet Joseph Smith in March 1833, the living Christ said: "Verily I say unto you, the keys of this kingdom shall never be taken from you, while thou art in the world, neither in the world to come; nevertheless, through you shall the oracles [revelations, divine direction] be given to another, yea, even unto the church." And now comes the clincher, a sobering directive, a warning: "And all they who receive the oracles of God, *let them beware how they hold them lest they are accounted as a light thing, and are brought under condemnation thereby,* and stumble and fall when the storms descend, and the winds blow, and the rains descend, and beat upon their house" (Doctrine and Covenants 90:3–5; emphasis added). My sober assessment is that mighty storms are now beating upon us, horrific winds and rain are now pounding us with gale force and beating upon our houses of faith.

In what was clearly a prophetic warning, Elder Neal A. Maxwell declared to students at Brigham Young University decades ago: "Make no mistake about it, brothers and sisters; in the months and years ahead, *events will require of each member that he or she decide whether or not he or she will follow the First Presidency.* Members will find it more difficult to halt [hesitate] longer between two opinions [1 Kings 18:21]. . . . In short, brothers and sisters, *not being ashamed of the gospel of Jesus Christ includes not being ashamed of the prophets of Jesus Christ.*"[14]

If we once rejoiced and delighted in being a part of an organization that is led by prophets, seers, and revelators, are we still excited about it today? To liken Alma's words to ourselves (Alma 5:26), we might ask, "If we once felt to sing gratitude and shout praises to the Almighty for sending modern prophets to the earth, do we feel so now?"

Our capacity as members of The Church of Jesus Christ of Latter-day Saints to enjoy the comfort and guidance and inspired direction of the Holy Spirit depends on many things. One crucial factor is whether we are truly loyal to and grateful for those living oracles who have been charged to guide the destiny of this Church in our day and time. "For of him [or her] unto whom much is given much is required; and he [or she] who sins against the greater light shall receive the greater condemnation" (Doctrine and Covenants 82:3).

---

14. "Meeting the Challenges of Today," 149; emphasis added.

President Henry B. Eyring explained that "when a prophet speaks, those with little faith may think that they hear only a wise man giving good advice. Then if his counsel seems comfortable and reasonable, squaring with what they want to do, they take it. If it does not, they consider it either faulty advice or they see their circumstances as justifying their being an exception to the counsel. Those without faith may think that they hear only men seeking to exert influence for some selfish motive." Further, some erroneously suppose that "to take counsel from the servants of God is to surrender God-given rights of independence. But the argument . . . misrepresents reality. When we reject the counsel which comes from God, we do not choose to be independent of outside influence. *We choose another influence*. . . .

"Another fallacy is to believe that the choice to accept or not accept the counsel of prophets is no more than deciding whether to accept good advice and gain its benefits or to stay where we are. But *the choice not to take prophetic counsel changes the very ground upon which we stand. It becomes more dangerous.* The failure to take prophetic counsel lessens our power to take inspired counsel in the future."[15]

Denying what we know to be true. The anti-Christs Sherem and Korihor in the Book of Mormon have a number of characteristics in common. First, they teach that there will be no Christ, that to believe in the coming of the Messiah is foolish (Jacob 7:7, 9; Alma 30:6, 12). Second, they deny prophecy and revelation and insist that no one can know the future, particularly concerning the coming of the Savior (Jacob 7:7; Alma 30:13). Third, they demand a sign, physical evidence of the truthfulness of the gospel of Jesus Christ (Jacob 7:13; Alma 30:43). Fourth, both of them really, truly knew that what the prophets had taught, especially concerning Christ, is true (Jacob 7:19; Alma 30:42).

They chose, however, to speak and act against the truth that lay

---

15. "Finding Safety in Counsel," *Ensign*, May 1997, 25; emphasis added.

deep within them. After bearing his testimony to Korihor, for example, Alma stated: "Behold, I know that thou believest, but *thou art possessed with a lying spirit, and ye have put off the Spirit of God that it may have no place in yo*u; but the devil has power over you, and he doth carry you about, working devices that he may destroy the children of God" (Alma 30:42; emphasis added). It is always a serious offense to sin against knowledge, to act in a manner that is at cross-purposes to what you know to be true.

There is a tendency in our day and time that is deeply troubling. It is a variant of being untrue to the truth within you. In an effort not to appear hyper-righteous, holier-than-thou, or stuffy, and because so often today religious people are either marginalized or ignored, some have sought to give the impression that, Yes, they're members of The Church of Jesus Christ of Latter-day Saints but not like some of those boring types! They want to be considered (often to young people) as cool, with it, rad, bad, or whatever the current word is these days. We all know what hypocrisy is. A hypocrite is not one who holds tightly to high standards and ideals but falls short; if that were the case, all of us would be hypocrites, for we are all less than what we ought to be, ever in need of pardoning mercy. No, hypocrisy is just what its Greek name implies: the hypocrite wears a mask, puts on a show, fakes it, says in public how good he is, but with evil intent lives in private well below the standards of his or her faith.

There is, however, another kind of hypocrisy, one less obvious but just as serious. Elder Neal A. Maxwell spoke of a "second form of hypocrisy, the situation in which *we let ourselves appear worse than we are.* This form of hypocrisy is just as insidious (and may be more wide spread) than the other form of hypocrisy—the situation in which we let ourselves appear better than we are. The second form . . . is apt to be a heightened challenge because of the growing uniqueness and size of the Church; *it will be increasingly tempting for members of the Church to play down their convictions and commitment—to appear less committed than they really are.*"16

THE SIN AGAINST THE HOLY GHOST

In 1 John we read a rather enigmatic passage of scripture: "If any man see his brother sin a sin which is not unto death, he shall ask, and he [God] shall give him life for them that sin not unto death. There is a sin unto death: I do not say that he shall pray for it. All unrighteousness is sin: and there is a sin not unto death" (1 John 5:16–17).

To make sense of these two verses, let's look carefully at the context. It appears that John has been teaching concerning the kinds of prayers that God answers—namely, those that are offered by the power of the Holy Ghost, petitions that are in harmony with the will of God. In other words, John has just taught that we can have confidence in having our prayers answered if they are "according to [God's] will" (1 John 5:14–15).

John then observes that if we should see a fellow Christian, a believer, commit any sin that is "not unto death" then we have every reason to pray for that individual, to ask the Father to grant him or her life, meaning forgiveness, a remission of sins, access to eternal life. In a modern revelation the Lord speaks of those who have "sought occasion against [Joseph Smith] without cause; nevertheless, he has sinned [that is, he is mortal and subject to sin]; but verily I say unto you, I, the Lord, forgive sins unto those who confess their sins before me and ask forgiveness, *who have not sinned unto death*" (Doctrine and Covenants 64:6–7; emphasis added).

There it is again. What is the "sin unto death"?

Elder Bruce R. McConkie wrote: "There are sins which utterly and completely preclude the sinner from gaining eternal life. Hence there are sins for which repentance does not operate, sins that the atoning

---

16. *More Excellent Way*, 62–63; emphasis added.

blood of Christ will not wash away, sins for which the sinner must suffer and pay the full penalty personally."[17]

Elsewhere Elder McConkie explained: "Those who turn from the light and truth of the gospel; who give themselves up to Satan; who enlist in his cause, supporting and sustaining it; and who thereby become his children—by such a course sin unto death. For them there is neither repentance, forgiveness, nor any hope whatever of salvation of any kind. As children of Satan, *they are sons of perdition*."[18] It was of this heinous offense that the Savior himself stated: "All manner of sin and blasphemy shall be forgiven unto men: but the blasphemy against the Holy Ghost shall not be forgiven unto men. And whosoever speaketh a word against the Son of man, it shall be forgiven him: but whosoever speaketh against the Holy Ghost, it shall not be forgiven him, neither in this world, neither in the world to come" (Matthew 12:31–32).[19]

---

17. *New Witness for the Articles of Faith*, 231.

18. *Doctrinal New Testament Commentary*, 3:407; emphasis added. Occasionally the question is raised as to whether there will be "daughters of perdition," that is, whether a woman can commit the unpardonable sin of denying the Holy Ghost. So far as I can determine, there is no authoritative statement one way or the other, although different leaders of the Church through the years have expressed their views. Some have stated that one must hold the priesthood in order to commit this most heinous of sins, but Joseph Smith did not mention any such requirement. Those who chose to follow Lucifer and who stood in support of his amendatory offer in the premortal world are guilty of the unpardonable sin, inasmuch as they denied and defied (Doctrine and Covenants 76:31) significant light and knowledge. It is hard to imagine that all of those we now call devils, the minions of Satan, are men. In addition, one wonders whether the phrase "sons of perdition" is not somewhat like the phrase "sons of God." John teaches that Jesus "came unto his own, and his own received him not. But as many as received him, to them gave he power to become the sons of God, even to them that believe on his name" (John 1:11–12). This passage in John is certainly not to be understood as implying that only men can become the true children of God. Perhaps "sons" of perdition is generic, referring to all human beings.

19. The Prophet Joseph Smith drew a fascinating conclusion from the Savior's remark: "Our Savior says, 'that all manner of sin, and blasphemy shall be forgiven men wherewith they shall blaspheme; but the blasphemy against the

THE UNPARDONABLE SIN

In an effort to assist his errant son Corianton to repent of his sin against the law of chastity, Alma declared: "Know ye not, my son, that these things are an abomination in the sight of the Lord; yea, *most abominable above all sins save it be the shedding of innocent blood or denying the Holy Ghost?* For behold, if ye deny the Holy Ghost when it once has had place in you, and ye know that ye deny it,[20] behold, this is a sin which is unpardonable; yea, and whosoever murdereth against the light and knowledge of God, it is not easy for him to obtain forgiveness; yea, I say unto you, my son, that it is not easy for him to obtain a forgiveness" (Alma 39:5–6; emphasis added).

We have generally understood Alma's explanation here to mean that sexual transgression is so grave[21] that it is surpassed in eternal seriousness only by (1) premeditated murder by members of the Church[22] and (2) the sin against the Holy Ghost. To say that the sin against the Holy Ghost is *unpardonable* is to say that it is not covered by the Atonement of the Lord Jesus Christ and that no amount of personal suffering here or hereafter will compensate for it. That appears to be what the scriptural passage means when it states that "it is impossible for those who *were once enlightened,* and *have tasted of the heavenly gift,* and were made *partakers of the Holy Ghost,* and *have tasted the good*

Holy Ghost shall not be forgiven, neither in *this world,* nor in the *world to come*'; evidently shewing that there are sins which may be forgiven in the *world to come*" (History, 1838–1856, 1322).

20. The expression "and ye know that ye deny it" implies that one cannot commit the unpardonable sin unknowingly or unconsciously, that is, by accident. The son of perdition sins against significant light and knowledge, denies and defies, knowing and understanding just what he is doing.

21. An inspiring and instructive message on the seriousness of sexual immorality is Holland, "Of Souls, Symbols, and Sacraments"; Holland and Holland, *On Earth as It Is in Heaven,* 182–97; see also Holland, "Personal Purity," *Ensign,* November 1998, 75–78.

22. McConkie, *New Witness for the Articles of Faith,* 231.

word of God, and the powers of the world to come, if they shall fall away, to renew them again unto repentance; seeing they crucify to themselves the Son of God afresh, and put him to an open shame" (Hebrews 6:4–6; emphasis added).

Later in that same epistle, we read of those "who [have] trodden under foot the Son of God, and hath counted the blood of the covenant, wherewith he was sanctified, an unholy thing, and hath done despite [insult] unto the Spirit of grace." Then comes this sobering note: "It is a fearful thing to fall into the hands of the living God" (Hebrews 10:29, 31). In the dispensation of the fulness of times, in the revelation setting forth the doctrine of eternal marriage, Christ the Savior stated: "The blasphemy against the Holy Ghost, which shall not be forgiven in the world nor out of the world, is in that ye commit murder wherein *ye shed innocent blood, and assent unto my death,* after ye have received my new and everlasting covenant, saith the Lord God" (Doctrine and Covenants 132:27). Such persons are guilty of essentially shedding the innocent blood of Christ once again; that is, if the Savior were here on earth today, these would seek his blood, as did those of the Lord's enemies in the meridian of time.[23]

FREQUENTLY ASKED QUESTIONS

Perhaps by addressing a few questions we can come to better understand this "sin unto death."

1. What is perdition? You will recall that in the earliest ages of the earth's history, Cain, the son of Adam and Eve, entered into an unholy oath, an alliance, with Satan. Cain became "Mahan, the master of this great secret, that [he could] murder and get gain." Thus arose the first secret combination on earth (Helaman 6:26–27). The Lord warned Cain that if he did not repent he would become the father of

---

23. See McConkie, *New Witness for the Articles of Faith,* 233; see also McConkie, *Doctrinal New Testament Commentary,* 3:346.

Satan's lies—he would help to propagate and spread evil and wickedness and mayhem throughout the planet. Cain would thereby become known as Perdition (Moses 5:18–31). *Perdition* means ruin, destruction, damnation.

2. Can a person of any faith commit the unpardonable sin? No. A person must first have received the gift of the Holy Ghost, which comes only by the laying on of hands by those holding the Melchizedek Priesthood. Persons cannot deny and defy a witness and a conviction they never had. President Joseph F. Smith declared: "No man can sin against light until he has it; nor against the Holy Ghost, until after he has received it by the gift of God through the appointed channel or way."[24]

3. What must a person do to commit the unpardonable sin? In the vision of the glories, Joseph Smith and Sidney Rigdon saw those who, as stated by the Lord, "*know my power, and have been made partakers thereof,* and suffered themselves through the power of the devil to be overcome, and to *deny the truth and defy my power*—they are they who are the sons of perdition, of whom I say that it had been better for them never to have been born; for they are vessels of wrath, doomed to suffer the wrath of God, with the devil and his angels in eternity" (Doctrine and Covenants 76:31–33; emphasis added).

"What must a man do to commit the unpardonable sin?" the Prophet Joseph asked. "He must receive the Holy Ghost, have the heavens opened unto him, and know God, and then sin against Him. . . . He has got to say that the sun does not shine while he sees it; he has got to deny Jesus Christ when the heavens have been opened unto him, and to deny the plan of salvation with his eyes open to the truth of it."[25]

This is clearly much more serious an offense than that committed by someone who gradually slides into the ranks of the less active, or

---

24. *Gospel Doctrine*, 434.
25. Discourse, delivered 7 April 1844.

by someone who previously held a responsible position in the Church deciding that he or she no longer accepts what he or she once believed. Nor is one necessarily guilty of this sin unto death who once had a witness of the Holy Spirit of the truthfulness of the restored gospel and then denies his or her faith and chooses to fight against the Church. Such a person may well be guilty of apostasy and may be severed formally from the faith, but he or she will not necessarily have defected to perdition. President Spencer W. Kimball put this matter into perspective when he wrote: "The sin against the Holy Ghost requires such knowledge that it is manifestly impossible for the rank and file to commit such a sin."[26]

4. Why may those who speak against the Father and the Son be forgiven, whereas those who blaspheme against the Holy Ghost cannot? This question gets at the heart of why the sin against the Holy Ghost is so tragic and eternally consequential. Our five physical senses are absolutely invaluable, enabling us to see and hear and smell and taste and touch. What we may see or hear, however, is not nearly as powerful as the distinctive witness that comes to us through the power of the Holy Ghost.

One of the most informative prophetic statements on this matter was given by President Joseph Fielding Smith, who became the tenth President of the Church. "The reason blasphemy against the Son of God may be forgiven," President Smith explained, "even if the Son be made manifest in a vision or a dream, is that such manifestation does not impress the soul as deeply as does the testimony of the Holy Ghost. The influence of the Holy Ghost is Spirit speaking to spirit, and *the indelible impression is one that brings conversion and conviction to the soul as no other influence can.* The Holy Spirit reveals the truth with a positiveness wherein there is no doubt and therefore is far more impressive than a vision given to the eye."[27]

---

26. *Miracle of Forgiveness*, 123.

27. "The Sin Against the Holy Ghost," *Improvement Era*, July 1955, 495; emphasis added. "Christ is the second person in the Godhead," President Smith

5. How do individuals arrive at the point where they choose to put Christ to an *open shame?* Just as those who are true and faithful come to know the things of God line upon line and precept upon precept, so also do those who deny and defy the truth choose the path of faithlessness gradually, one step after another.

"The change of heart does not come all at once," President Joseph Fielding Smith noted, "but is due to transgression in some form, which continues to lurk in the soul without repentance, until the Holy Ghost withdraws, and then that man is left to spiritual darkness. Sin begets sin; the darkness grows until the love of truth turns to hatred, and the love of God is overcome by the wicked desire to destroy all that is just and true. In this way Christ is put to open shame, and blasphemy exalted."[28]

6. Are we certain we know who are sons of perdition? We clearly know from Joseph Smith's inspired translation of the early chapters of Genesis (the book of Moses) that Cain fell into this category

---

reminded us. "But Christ has himself declared that the manifestations we might have of the Spirit of Christ, or from a visitation of an angel, a tangible resurrected being, would not leave the impression and would not convince us and place within us that something which we cannot get away from which we receive through a manifestation of the Holy Ghost. Personal visitations might become dim as time goes on, but this guidance of the Holy Ghost is renewed and continued, day after day, year after year, if we live to be worthy of it" (*Doctrines of Salvation,* 1:44).

28. *Doctrines of Salvation,* 1:49. "From apostates the faithful have received the severest persecutions," the Prophet Joseph Smith explained. Why? "There is a superior intelligence bestowed upon such as obey the gospel with full purpose of heart, which, if sinned against, the apostate is left naked and destitute of the Spirit of God. . . . When once that light which was in them is taken from them, they become as much darkened as they were previously enlightened. And then, no marvel, if all their power should be enlisted against the truth, and they, Judas like, seek the destruction of those who were their greatest benefactors! What nearer friend on earth, or in heaven, had Judas than the Savior? And his first object was to destroy him!" ("The Elders of the Church in Kirtland, to Their Brethren Abroad," *The Evening and the Morning Star,* vol. 2, no. 19 [April 1834]: 152).

(Moses 5:22–24). What about Judas Iscariot, member of the meridian Quorum of the Twelve Apostles?

Jesus identified Judas as a son of perdition (John 17:12). Let us look deeper into that statement. Elder Bruce R. McConkie suggested: "Jesus' ministry where the Twelve are concerned has succeeded. He has cared for the spiritual well being of the souls entrusted to him. Only Judas has been lost; and even he, though a son or follower of Satan, who is perdition, . . . is probably not a son of perdition in the sense of eternal damnation."[29]

In speaking of Judas's state, President Joseph F. Smith asked: "Did Judas possess this light [the gift of the Holy Ghost], this witness, this Comforter, this baptism of fire and the Holy Ghost, this endowment from on high? . . . And if this be so, you may say, 'he is a son of perdition without hope.' But if he was destitute of this glorious gift and outpouring of the Spirit, . . . then what constituted the unpardonable sin of this poor, erring creature, who rose no higher in the scale of intelligence, honor or ambition, than to betray the Lord of glory for thirty pieces of silver?"[30]

President Joseph F. Smith seems to be asking the all-important question. We know from scripture that the Spirit was given to persons who investigated the message of Jesus and the apostles and gave them conviction of the truthfulness of their message, yet the full endowment and outpouring of the Holy Ghost in the Old World did not take place until the day of Pentecost, some fifty days after Passover and the crucifixion of the Master. "I prefer, until I know better," President Smith added, "to take the merciful view that he may be numbered among those for whom the blessed Master prayed, 'Father, forgive them; for they know not what they do.'"[31]

7. Will those guilty of the unpardonable sin be resurrected?

---

29. *Mortal Messiah*, 4:112–13; see also 198, 202.
30. *Gospel Doctrine*, 434–35.
31. *Gospel Doctrine*, 435.

The apostle Paul was very emphatic that "as in Adam all die, even so *in Christ shall all be made alive*" (1 Corinthians 15:22; emphasis added). This was certainly the testimony of the Nephite prophets (2 Nephi 9:13; Alma 11:41; 33:22; Helaman 14:17; Mormon 9:13). Nonetheless, a verse in the Doctrine and Covenants has caused some to err in supposing that the sons of perdition will not be resurrected. In speaking of what he and Sidney Rigdon beheld in the vision of the glories, Joseph the Prophet wrote that the sons of perdition "are they who shall go away into the lake of fire and brimstone, with the devil and his angels—and the only ones on whom the second death shall have any power." The second death is the second spiritual death that comes to those who are ultimately cast out from the presence of God and Christ forevermore. The Prophet continued: "Yea, verily, *the only ones who shall not be redeemed in the due time of the Lord,* after the sufferings of his wrath. For *all the rest shall be brought forth by the resurrection of the dead,* through the triumph and the glory of the Lamb, who was slain, who was in the bosom of the Father before the worlds were made" (Doctrine and Covenants 76:36–39; emphasis added; see also 88:32).

The doctrine that all who have received a physical body will be resurrected is consistent with what is taught in Doctrine and Covenants 88:28–32. Here the Lord explains that those who are quickened or made alive in this life by a portion of celestial glory will, in the resurrection, "receive of the same, even a fulness." Those who are quickened in this life by a portion of the terrestrial glory will receive a fulness in the resurrection. And the same is true for those quickened or made alive in this life by a portion of the telestial glory. Now note what follows: "*And they who remain* [those guilty of committing the unpardonable sin] *shall also be quickened;* nevertheless, they shall return again to their own place, to enjoy that which they are willing to receive, because they were not willing to enjoy that which they might have received" (Doctrine and Covenants 88:29–32; emphasis added).

The scriptures of the Restoration are consistent in declaring that "they who are filthy"—who have not taken advantage of the cleansing powers of the Atonement of Jesus Christ, who have "done despite" to the spirit of grace—"shall remain filthy still" (2 Nephi 9:16; Mormon 9:14; Doctrine and Covenants 88:35, 102). Salvation in some degree of glory is available for all except the sons of perdition (Doctrine and Covenants 76:43–44).

8. What do we know concerning the ultimate plight of the sons of perdition? We are told in sobering language of their "everlasting punishment, . . . to *reign* with the devil and his angels in eternity [because they have physical bodies and thus power over those spirits who do not[32]]. . . . And the end thereof, neither the place thereof, nor their torment, no man knows; neither was it revealed, neither is, neither will be revealed unto man, except to them who are made partakers thereof. . . . Wherefore, the end, the width, the height, the depth, and the misery thereof, they understand not, neither any man except those who are ordained [decreed, ordered] unto this condemnation" (Doctrine and Covenants 76:45–48; emphasis added).

As early as 1833 members of the Church had begun to speculate about the fate of those guilty of committing the unpardonable sin. In a letter addressed to W. W. Phelps, the Prophet explained: "The Lord never authorized them to say that the devil, his angels, or the sons of perdition, should ever be restored; for their state of destiny was not revealed to man, is not revealed, nor ever shall be revealed, save to those who are made partakers thereof; consequently those who teach this doctrine have not received it of the Spirit of the Lord. Truly Brother Oliver [Cowdery] declared it to be the doctrine of devils."[33]

---

32. Joseph Smith, Account of Meeting and Discourse, 5 January 1841; Smith, Discourse, 16 May 1841 (unknown scribe); see also *Words of Joseph Smith*, 60, 74.

33. Answers to Queries to Brother Phelps's Letter of June 4th; Letter to Church Leaders in Jackson County, Missouri, 25 June 1833.

The Saints of the Most High have been given the power to rise to celestial heights, to go where God and angels are. They also have the capacity—because of who they are, what they know, and what they have felt—to fall farther, to descend to spiritual depths beyond those who have never known the things of the Spirit. Truly, "of him unto whom much is given much is required; and he who sins against the greater light shall receive the greater condemnation" (Doctrine and Covenants 82:3).

Mormon drew a lesson from the experiences of the descendants of Lehi that is both timely and timeless. "And thus we can plainly discern," he taught, "that after a people have been once enlightened by the Spirit of God, and have had great knowledge of things pertaining to righteousness, and then have fallen away into sin and transgression, they become more hardened, and thus their state becomes worse than though they had never known these things" (Alma 24:30; compare 2 Peter 2:20–21).

And so the call to the faithful is to live in a manner befitting a Saint, a sanctified man or woman; to be a true disciple of the Lord Jesus, one who has chosen to separate himself or herself from things wicked, one who endeavors tirelessly to rise well above the average or the ordinary. The call forevermore is to be loyal, to be true to the testimony that has come to us through the power of that sacred endowment we know as the gift of the Holy Ghost. Our safety lies in cultivating, maintaining, rejoicing in, and cherishing the marvelous gift of the companionship of the third member of the Godhead.

Chapter 8

EMPOWERED AND
INSTRUCTED IN PRAYER

⁓

Throughout this book we speak of the various means by which we may receive divine insights—inspiration and revelation—from the Holy Spirit. We will discuss here another significant means by which the Spirit can guide us—in our prayers, including those things for which we should pray. The most important thing we do on the Sabbath is to take the sacrament, or, more formally, partake of the sacrament of the Lord's Supper. This sacred practice was instituted by Jesus as he participated in the Passover meal with his apostles. Christians of various denominations refer to it as Holy Communion, or the Eucharist. We partake of the emblems of the sacrament of the Lord's Supper in remembrance of the broken and torn body and spilt blood of Jesus Christ. That is, this ordinance both commemorates and celebrates the atoning sacrifice of the Savior. As the risen Lord explained to the Nephites, "He that eateth this bread eateth of my body to his soul; and he that drinketh of this wine drinketh of my blood to his soul; and his soul shall never hunger nor thirst, but shall be filled" (3 Nephi 20:8).

The word *ordinance* is often used interchangeably with the word *sacrament* but, as we will see shortly, they are not exactly the same. An ordinance is, first of all, a commandment, a statute, a law (see, for example, Doctrine and Covenants 64:5; 136:4). But an ordinance is also a religious rite, a ceremony. That is the definition with which

Latter-day Saints are more familiar. Saving ordinances, or rites, include baptism, confirmation, ordination to the priesthood, the temple endowment, and temple marriage or sealing.

A *sacrament* is "a very special kind of symbol. . . . A sacrament could be any one of a number of gestures or acts or ordinances that unite us with God and his limitless powers. We are imperfect and mortal; he is perfect and immortal. But from time to time—indeed, as often as is possible and appropriate—we find ways and go to places and create circumstances where we can unite symbolically with him and, in so doing, gain access to his power. Those special moments of union with God are sacramental moments, such as kneeling at a marriage altar, or blessing a newborn baby, or partaking of the emblems of the Lord's Supper. This latter ordinance is the one we in the Church have come to associate most traditionally with the word *sacrament,* though it is technically only one of many such moments when we formally take the hand of God and feel his divine power."[1] Thus all ordinances are sacraments, because they become channels of divine power from God to the individual (Doctrine and Covenants 84:20). Not all sacraments, however, are ordinances. There is a very real sense in which fasting, prayer, scripture study, church attendance, visiting sacred sites, and many other holy practices are sacraments, because they are channels to connect us to the Divine and open us to God's power.

We will now focus our attention on the sacrament of prayer and the divine role the Holy Ghost plays in making prayer more meaningful and efficacious.

THE RESURRECTED SAVIOR TEACHES US TO PRAY

In the Book of Mormon the Lord offers precious counsel on prayer, including what he had taught his disciples on the eastern hemisphere: the need to pray with pure intent and not to be heard of men (3 Nephi 13:5–8); the Lord's Prayer, with alterations that show that he is now

---

1. Holland and Holland, *On Earth as It Is in Heaven*, 193–94.

a resurrected, glorified being, the kingdom of God was now in their midst, and they would soon be initiated into the law of consecration (3 Nephi 13:9–13); and the instruction to pray to the Father in the name of the Son (3 Nephi 18:19–21, 23; 19:6, 8; 27:2, 7, 28). He beckoned to this more righteous remnant of Lehi's descendants, those who had been spared the destructions, to lift their voices heavenward on behalf of the less active, to "meet together oft; and . . . not forbid any man from coming unto you when ye shall meet together, but suffer them that they may come unto you and forbid them not; but *ye shall pray for them,* and shall not cast them out; and if it so be that they come unto you oft *ye shall pray for them unto the Father, in my name*" (3 Nephi 18:22–23; emphasis added).

One of the enlightening ways in which Jesus teaches us to pray is by praying himself. He is our model, our pattern, our prototype. Note in 3 Nephi 17:13–14: "And it came to pass that when they had all been brought, and Jesus stood in the midst, he commanded the multitude [some 2,500 men, women, and children are present; see v. 25] that they should kneel down upon the ground. And it came to pass that when they had knelt upon the ground, Jesus groaned within himself, and said: Father, I am troubled because of the wickedness of the house of Israel." Here we see the sublime sensitivity and omniscient awareness of our Master—he is "merciful and gracious unto those who fear [him], and delight[s] to honor those who serve [him] in righteousness and in truth unto the end" (Doctrine and Covenants 76:5).

On the other hand, Jesus knows perfectly well that "the wicked are like the troubled sea, when it cannot rest, whose waters cast up mire and dirt. There is no peace, saith my God, to the wicked" (Isaiah 57:20–21; compare 48:22). He knows, as Alma taught an errant son, that "wickedness never was happiness" and that those who are "in a state of nature, or . . . in a carnal state, are in the gall of bitterness and in the bonds of iniquity." Not only are they enemies to God—working at cross-purposes to the great plan of happiness—but, tragically, are enemies to themselves, laboring against their best good. In Alma's words, "They are without God in the world, and they have gone contrary to the nature of God; therefore, they are in a state contrary to the nature of happiness" (Alma 41:10–11).

The very earth that Jehovah had created cried out: "Wo, wo is me, the mother of men; I am pained, I am weary, because of the wickedness of my children" (Moses 7:48). Enoch of old, who as a result of his panoramic vision of the destruction of humanity in the days of Noah and the Flood, felt no comfort in the damnation of any part of the Father's children (Moses 7:42–44). Nor does the Good Shepherd take delight in even one lost sheep.

"And when he had said these words"—when Jesus had groaned concerning the wickedness of his covenant people—"he himself also knelt upon the earth; and behold he prayed unto the Father, and *the things which he prayed cannot be written,* and the multitude did bear record who heard him. And after this manner do they bear record: *The eye hath never seen, neither hath the ear heard, before, so great and marvelous things as we saw and heard Jesus speak unto the Father;* and no tongue can speak, neither can there be written by any man, neither can the hearts of men conceive so great and marvelous things as we both saw and heard Jesus speak; and no one can conceive of the joy which filled our souls at the time we heard him pray for us unto the Father" (3 Nephi 17:15–17; emphasis added).

Why could they not be written? Some spiritual experiences are so specific to a particular time and place, so reserved for the ears and eyes and hearts of those who experience them, that it is simply wrong, divinely inappropriate, to speak openly of them, to try to rehearse or record them. In addition, some matters are ineffable, literally unspeakable or unrecordable. Mere words fail us. Telestial and terrestrial expressions cannot do justice to celestial phenomena.

I have reflected reverently on what it would be like to hear my Redeemer importune the Father for me. Listen to the Savior's words to

Peter at the Last Supper: "Simon, Simon, behold, Satan hath desired to have you, that he may sift you as wheat." Now note this most unusual phrase: "But *I have prayed for thee,* that thy faith fail not: and when thou art converted, strengthen thy brethren" (Luke 22:31–32; emphasis added). I have wondered what that senior apostle must have felt to know that Jesus, the Lord of the universe, had been praying for him. Mormon reminds us that the Mediator claims of the Father his "rights of mercy" for us and advocates our cause before the throne of grace (Moroni 7:27–28; compare Doctrine and Covenants 45:3–5).

While sitting in the Conference Center during the concluding general session of the October 2001 semiannual general conference, not many days after the horrors of September 11, 2001, I heard President Gordon B. Hinckley close the conference with a message of hope and encouragement, a reminder that if the people of the covenant would only turn to God, they would be empowered to stand in holy places, poised and unafraid, even in the midst of wars and rumors of wars. "And now as we close this conference," he said, "even though we shall have a benediction, I should like to offer a brief prayer in these circumstances."

The fifteenth President of The Church of Jesus Christ of Latter-day Saints, the prophet, seer, and revelator at that time, the man prepared, foreordained, and called to stand in the shoes of Joseph Smith, then powerfully petitioned the heavens: "O God, our Eternal Father, Thou great Judge of the Nations, Thou who art the governor of the universe, Thou who art our Father and our God, whose children we are, we look to Thee in faith in this dark and solemn time. Please, dear Father, bless us with faith. Bless us with love. Bless us with charity in our hearts. Bless us with a spirit of perseverance to root out the terrible evils that are in this world. Give protection and guidance to those who are engaged actively in carrying forth the things of battle. Bless them; preserve their lives; save them from harm and evil. Hear the prayers of their loved ones for their safety. We pray for the great democracies of the earth which Thou hast overseen in creating their governments, where peace and liberty and democratic processes obtain.

"O Father, look with mercy upon this, our own nation, and its friends in this time of need. Spare us and help us to walk with faith ever in Thee and ever in Thy Beloved Son, on whose mercy we count and to whom we look as our Savior and our Lord. Bless the cause of peace and bring it quickly to us again, we humbly plead with Thee, asking that Thou wilt forgive our arrogance, pass by our sins, be kind and gracious to us, and cause our hearts to turn with love toward Thee. We humbly pray in the name of Him who loves us all, even the Lord Jesus Christ, our Redeemer and our Savior, amen."[2]

The Holy Spirit was there in rich abundance in the Conference Center, and surely the Saints of God felt that sweet and powerful influence in chapels, homes, and other gathering places throughout the world. By the power of the Spirit, I felt a deeper closeness to my Heavenly Father, a stillness and peace within my soul, an assurance that the Almighty was not far away, a love for my family and friends and city and nation and world, even for those who had chosen to carry out those horrid and despicable attacks. About midway through President Hinckley's prayer, it was affirmed to my soul the realization that I too could not fully express the inexpressible, that I was woefully inadequate in forming words into sentences that would convey the meaning of what I was *feeling and seeing*. I felt and I saw. I saw things with new eyes. I saw the power of an effectual, fervent prayer of a very righteous man avail much (James 5:16). I witnessed the simplicity and profundity of mighty prayer, prayer guided by and accompanied with the Holy Ghost. Yes, as Shauna and I left the Conference Center, I felt somewhat like the Nephites and also the two disciples on the road to Emmaus must have felt: "Did not our hearts burn within us as we heard him pray unto the Father for us?" (Luke 24:32).

---

2. "Till We Meet Again," *Ensign*, November 2001, 90.

During his visit to the Nephites, the Savior called the little children unto him, one by one, blessed them, and prayed for them (3 Nephi 17:21–24). Jesus was overcome by the experience and wept. Only one who has looked deeply into the eyes of little children can grasp why. Only one who has sensed how near to the heavens, how close to the angels, how innocent and worthy of our respect, admiration, and awe can know why the Purest of the pure wept as he associated with the purest among the Nephites. Angels came down and ministered personally to the little ones, an event that bespeaks a mighty truth, one that the Lord taught in the Old World: "Take heed that ye despise not one of these little ones; for I say unto you, That in heaven their angels [premortal spirits³] do always behold the face of my Father which is in heaven" (Matthew 18:10). Indeed, how we feel toward little children, how we treat them, how we speak to them—these are fairly accurate measures of how much like the Master we are.

PRAYER FROM ABOVE

On the Lord's second day among his American Saints, Jesus continued to call upon his people, both the disciples and the entire multitude, to pray, to kneel down upon the ground and lift their voices heavenward. "And behold, they began to pray; *and they did pray unto Jesus, calling him their Lord and their God*" (3 Nephi 19:15–18; emphasis added). They prayed to Jesus! How strange. How unusual, especially given that he had specifically instructed them in the proper order of prayer and had commanded them to address their prayers to the Father in the name of the Son. Let us step back, however, and examine what was taking place.

In the midst of the people was the Lord Omnipotent, the great Jehovah, the promised Messiah, the God of Abraham, Isaac, and Jacob. In their midst was "God the second, the Redeemer,"⁴ the God who

---

3. McConkie, *Doctrinal New Testament Commentary*, 1:421.
4. *Joseph Smith* [manual], 42.

ministered to Enoch and Noah and who gave the law to Moses, the God through whom all revelation since the Fall had come.[5] In their midst was the Prototype of salvation, the standard of all saved beings,[6] a resurrected, immortal, glorified Personage. Would we not be driven by our inner sense of love and divine propriety to worship him? Would we not in such circumstances feel enticed, motivated, even impelled to pray to him?

Jesus left their midst for a short time, bowed, and prayed alone. He thanked God the Father for sending the Holy Ghost and explained that "they pray unto me because I am with them" (3 Nephi 19:22). "Jesus was present before them as the symbol of the Father," said Elder Bruce R. McConkie. "Seeing him, it was as though they saw the Father [compare John 14:9]; praying to him, it was as though they prayed to the Father. It was a special and unique situation."[7]

Next comes a marvelous lesson about prayer, not a message spoken directly by Jesus but a sublime message that comes to us because of the disciples' eagerness to pray. Mormon wrote: "And it came to pass that when Jesus had thus prayed unto the Father, he came unto his disciples, and behold, they did still continue, without ceasing, to pray unto him; and *they did not multiply many words, for it was given unto them what they should pray,* and they were filled with desire" (3 Nephi 19:24; emphasis added). When persons determine to purify and perfect their prayer life, to become more than a distant acquaintance with Deity, to capture the peace and power and perspective that come only through communion with the Infinite, then marvelous things begin to happen when they pray, not in every prayer necessarily, but certainly more frequently.

We are to pray to the Father, in the name of the Son, by the power of the Holy Spirit. When we meet that divine standard, especially with the inclusion of the Holy Spirit, then prayer becomes more than a monologue; it becomes a dialogue. Prayer becomes more than

5. See Joseph Fielding Smith, *Doctrines of Salvation,* 1:27.
6. See *Lectures on Faith,* 75–76.
7. *Promised Messiah,* 561.

petitionary; it becomes illuminating and instructive. When we have put away all worldly cares, when we have discarded the sordid, when we have elected to focus our minds and center our hearts, when we have pleaded for forgiveness and come boldly before the throne of grace to receive divine assistance (Hebrews 4:16; compare Moses 7:59), when our private agenda has been set aside and our greatest desire is to communicate—no, to commune—then come those sacred moments of divine light when the Spirit begins not only to settle and soothe but also to teach. Our words begin to reach beyond our thoughts. Our pleas become more heartfelt, and the language of the soul replaces the well-worn words to which we so frequently resort.

Because the Comforter knows all things (Doctrine and Covenants 42:17; Moses 6:61), he knows what lies deep within us, the longings and hopes and desires, the needs that often go unexpressed and thus unmet. That is, as the apostle Paul wrote, the Spirit helps us with our infirmities, for we generally do not know what things we ought to pray for. "But the Spirit itself maketh intercession for us" with strivings that cannot be expressed.[8] "And he that searcheth the hearts knoweth what is the mind of the Spirit, because he maketh intercession with the saints according to the will of God" (Romans 8:26–27). This is known as prayer in the Spirit, and it empowers the Saints of the Most High to pray for those things the Lord would have us pray for. In modern revelation we learn that "he that asketh in the Spirit asketh according to the will of God; wherefore it is done even as he asketh" (Doctrine and Covenants 46:30). Similarly, "and if ye are purified and cleansed from all sin, ye shall ask whatsoever you will in the name of Jesus and it shall be done. But know this, it shall be given you what you shall ask" (Doctrine and Covenants 50:29–30).

Prayer is not, and should not be, merely a product of our own

---

8. The language of the King James Version is as follows: "with groanings which cannot be uttered." In this sermon the Prophet Joseph Smith said that *groanings* should be *strivings* and that *uttered* should be *expressed* (Journal, 2 February 1843).

thoughts and feelings. Prayer is intended to engender communion with Deity. To commune is to "be with." Communion entails more than a monologue, certainly more than reciting a "to-do" list to the Father. Prayer should in fact be a dialogue, a true conversation with speaking, listening, digesting, learning. We know how uncomfortable we are with someone who does not allow real conversation, one who asks questions but never allows an answer. Or we may have encountered a person who delights in finishing our sentences, providing answers to his or her own queries. At best such experiences are frustrating and impolite. I don't think it's inappropriate to desire to speak and be heard. That's what humans do. In prayer we should seek a dialogue, even divine communication, never forgetting who we are addressing.

Have you ever thought how our Heavenly Father must feel about a conversation in which you or I do all the talking and even ask critical and important questions but never allow time or silence for a response? Despite our Father's patience, magnanimity, and all-loving nature, it must at least be disappointing to him. "Be still and know that I am God" is extremely important counsel to us (Psalm 46:10; Doctrine and Covenants 101:16). Maybe it means that before we pray and after we have finished speaking to God, we should spend a little time listening, possibly remaining on our knees but possibly sitting quietly and reverently, anticipating that our Father, through his Spirit, may have something to contribute to the conversation. Will we hear a voice? Perhaps, perhaps not, but we may have an inner awareness, a spirit of peace, acceptance, love. We may find our minds turning toward matters and focusing on people about whom we had not intended to contemplate. We may be sanctified by the solemnity and sublimity of silence. And of course, we may be taught what to pray for.

We need help. We need mediation. And that is where the Comforter, the Revelator, comes in. The Holy Ghost can, if we are open and teachable and patient, make known to us the things of greatest import, the things upon which God would have us ponder and reflect and pray. If we will be still, if we will be quiet, if we will be attentive, if we will be sensitive during and after our prayer, we may find our words reaching beyond our thoughts, just as occurred in the New World during the visit of the risen Lord to the Nephites.

Elder Neal A. Maxwell taught that one reason we should seek for this divine connection "is that only with the help of the Holy Ghost can we be lifted outside the narrow little theater of our own experience, outside our selfish concerns, and outside the confines of our tiny conceptual cells. . . .

"God sees things as they really are and as they will become. We don't! In order to tap that precious perspective during our prayers, we must rely upon the promptings of the Holy Ghost. With access to that kind of knowledge, we would then pray for what we and others should have— *really* have. With the Spirit prompting us, we will not ask 'amiss' [James 4:3]. With access to the Spirit, our circles of concern will expand."[9]

What a thrill it would be to have the Lord inspire us regarding how we should pray and what words we should speak! Prayer thereby would become not only petitionary but marvelously instructive, for we would learn something from what we said.[10] Through this means prayer becomes a significant avenue of revelation and opens us to the mind of God. Can we fathom the joy that settles upon the heart as our Lord and God reveals himself to us and reveals us to ourselves?

In addressing the matter of how to hear the voice of the Spirit, Sheri L. Dew emphasized "how eager the Lord is to unveil the knowledge stored safely inside our spirits concerning who we are and what our mission is, and about the life-changing difference it makes when we know. . . .

"There is nothing more vital to our success and our happiness here than learning to hear the voice of the Spirit. It is the Spirit who reveals to us our identity—which isn't just who we are but who we have always

---

9. "What Should We Pray For?" in *Prayer*, 4.
10. See Marion G. Romney, cited in Packer, *Teach Ye Diligently*, 304.

been. And that when we know, our lives take on a sense of purpose so stunning that we can never be the same again. . . .

"Our spirits long for us to remember the truth about who we are, because the way we see ourselves, our sense of identity, affects everything we do. . . . It affects the very way we live our lives."[11]

"Let us resolve to follow the Savior and work with diligence to become the person we were designed to become," President Dieter F. Uchtdorf charged the Saints. "Let us listen to and *obey the promptings of the Holy Spirit. As we do so, Heavenly Father will reveal to us things we never knew about ourselves.* He will illuminate the path ahead and open our eyes to see our unknown and perhaps unimagined talents."[12]

Do we grasp what sweet privileges can and will come to us as Saints of the Most High when we slow down, pause, reflect, and listen in our prayers? Inspired prayer entails speaking, listening, conversing, communing. Prayer in the Spirit is an entrance, a passageway, into life in the Spirit, which is, in truth, life in Christ.

After the resurrected Savior had ascended to heaven following his first full day of teaching the Nephites, the disciple-apostles separated the multitude into twelve bodies. Then "they did cause that the multitude should kneel down upon the face of the earth, and should pray unto the Father in the name of Jesus. And the disciples did pray unto the Father also in the name of Jesus. And it came to pass that they arose and ministered unto the people." These leaders then taught the

---

11. "Knowing Who You Are—and Who You Have Always Been," *Ensign,* July 2018, 10–11. Truman G. Madsen wrote wisely many years ago: "One begins mortality with the veil drawn, but slowly he is moved to penetrate the veil within himself. He is, in time, led to seek the 'holy of holies' within the temple of his own being" (*Eternal Man,* 20).

12. "Of Regrets and Resolutions," *Ensign,* November 2012, 23; emphasis added.

multitude all that the Lord had taught the day before, "nothing varying from the words which Jesus had spoken." Mormon explained that "they knelt again and prayed to the Father in the name of Jesus." And what was the nature of this prayer? What did they pray for? Note the following magnificent truth: "And they did pray for *that which they most desired; and they desired that the Holy Ghost should be given unto them*" (3 Nephi 19:5–9; emphasis added).

The gift of the Holy Ghost is the greatest gift that God can bestow upon us in this life. There is nothing greater, nothing more important, nothing more crucial to a dynamic Christian life than to spend that life under the guidance and sanctifying power of the Spirit. To live in the Spirit is to live in God's presence, not necessarily in his immediate presence but under the umbrella of the Spirit's sacred influence. That unspeakable influence can then affect every aspect of our lives, particularly the way we approach our Father in Heaven in prayer and learn from him through his Spirit.

> *Oh, bless me when I worship thee*
> *To keep my heart in tune,*
> *That I may hear thy still, small voice,*
> *And, Lord, with thee commune.*
>
> *Lord, grant me thy abiding love*
> *And make my turmoil cease.*
> *Oh, may my soul commune with thee*
> *And find thy holy peace.*[13]

My hope is that we may become a more prayerful people, a more reverent people, a more inspired and divinely guided people. There is so much to be learned, so very much to be experienced, if we will only open ourselves to change, if we will but place ourselves in a position to receive revelation and to be taught from on high.

---

13. "Oh, May My Soul Commune with Thee," *Hymns*, 1985, no. 123.

Chapter 9

KNOWING AND
KNOWING THAT WE KNOW

Our day has been labeled as a post-Christian era, a time when millions of men and women, young and old, have chosen to walk away from organized religion. More than perhaps any time in the history of our nation, a startling number of discontented and frustrated people describe themselves as spiritual but not religious. Estimates of that segment of Americans that have moved into the categories of "nones" (no religious affiliation) and "dones" (finished with religion) range from 20 percent to 25 percent. That is stunning and terribly troubling.

Our day has also been characterized as a time of unbelief. Faith is waning. It would be difficult *not* to hear the strident voices of the militant atheists or the unsettled agnostics who call for the overthrow of all religious entities. Nevertheless, no matter how loudly the faithless decry the simple faith of hundreds of millions, *everyone acts by faith,* whether one realizes it or not.

ARE WE SURE WE KNOW?

Consider the following statements, all of which are quite common:

A social worker declares: "I know there are billions of stars in our Milky Way galaxy."

A seventh grader states: "I know that George Washington, our nation's first president, was a man of courage and integrity."

How would the social worker, or the man on the street or the woman on a bus, *know* there are millions of stars in our galaxy? You answer, "Because that's what astronomers say."

A follow-up question might be, "But how do the scientists know that? Clearly no one has counted all the stars in the heavens, one by one, and so how can anyone draw such a conclusion?"

By using remarkable scientific instruments, astronomers are certainly in a much better position to speak with some authority on this subject than the woman who is an attorney or the man driving a truck. Scientists are able to estimate that there are billions of stars out there. And we take their word for it, because they are privy to knowledge that we of the rank and file do not possess.

Now we ask, how could a twelve-year-old know about President Washington's character or, for that matter, that he ever really lived? After investigation, we learn that the seventh grader was taught about Washington by his history teacher. And what is the source of the teacher's knowledge? The teacher learned about the first president of the United States in elementary school, middle school, high school, and college. He or she read what others had written. The writers of those textbooks did not, however, live in the eighteenth century and hence were not personally acquainted with George Washington or any of our founding fathers. If we were to continue this regression, we might come eventually to the written testimony of someone who knew George Washington personally and left a reliable record about him.

What if a noted atheist, such as Richard Dawkins or Christopher Hitchens or Daniel Dennett, should declare in a public address: "There is no God. I know this for myself." These are brilliant men. Hundreds of thousands of people take their writings very seriously. How would Dawkins *know* there is no God? He might answer that his study of science has led him to conclude that the notion of "God" is not necessary to explain the origin of life or the order of the cosmos. We ask if he or his fellow travelers have searched every inch of the universe to see or locate if God is there? Have they looked behind and under every rock or every tree or every mountain? And I definitely cannot picture Dawkins or Hitchens or Dennett declaring, "I know with all my heart that there is no God, for the Holy Spirit has borne witness to my soul," or "I know without a doubt that there is no God because the laws of physics or biology have so testified."

Now let's pursue a path that is likely much more familiar to us. Picture, if you will, a six-year-old girl standing at the pulpit on the first Sunday of the month and saying, "I know that Jesus lives and that Joseph Smith was a prophet of God." How does she know, especially if Jesus has not come to her in person or if she was not in the Sacred Grove in the spring of 1820? What if a seventy-year-old man, a life-long, faithful member of the Church stands at that same pulpit and states, "I know that God lives, that Jesus is the Christ, and that Joseph Smith was a prophet of God." How does he know? Does he perhaps know in a way that the six-year-old girl does not know?

What does it mean to *know* something in the spiritual realm? A few scriptural passages may be helpful:

The apostle Paul wrote that *"the things of God knoweth no man, except he has the Spirit of God.* Now, we have received, not the spirit of the world, but the Spirit which is of God; *that we might know* the things that are freely given to us of God. . . . For who hath known the mind of the Lord, that he may instruct him? But *we have the mind of Christ"* (JST, 1 Corinthians 2:11–12, 16; emphasis added).

"By the Spirit are *all things made known"* (1 Nephi 22:2; emphasis added).

"Behold, great and marvelous are the works of the Lord. How unsearchable are the depths of the mysteries of him; and it is impossible that man should find out all his ways. And *no man knoweth* of his ways save it be *revealed unto him"* (Jacob 4:8; emphasis added).

"He that believeth these things which I have spoken, him will I visit with the manifestations of my Spirit, and *he shall know and bear record.* For *because of my Spirit he shall know* that these things are true; for it persuadeth men to do good" (Ether 4:11; emphasis added).

"And by the power of the Holy Ghost *ye may know* the truth of all things" (Moroni 10:5; emphasis added).

"Verily, verily, I say unto you, *I will impart unto you of my Spirit,* which shall enlighten your mind, which shall fill your soul with joy; and *then shall ye know, or by this shall you know,* all things whatsoever you desire of me, which are pertaining unto things of righteousness, in faith believing in me that you shall receive" (Doctrine and Covenants 11:13–14; emphasis added).

"To some it is given by the Holy Ghost *to know that Jesus Christ is the Son of God,* and that he was crucified for the sins of the world" (Doctrine and Covenants 46:13; emphasis added).

"Be still and *know that I am God*" (Doctrine and Covenants 101:16; emphasis added).

The scriptures and the prophets proclaim that it is by means of the Holy Spirit that we come to know things in the spiritual realm. I have no question but that the six-year-old girl can know, because the Spirit can touch her young heart. Of course, the seventy-year-old can know by the same means. Faith is built upon evidence, spiritual evidence, and the more experience we have with the Spirit, the more often we are moved upon, prompted, and led by that kindly light, the more evidence we collect in our soul. The more spiritual evidence we have, the stronger will be our faith, and the more powerfully we can testify, "I know!"

What if I were to stand and bear witness that Jesus Christ lives, that he is our Lord and Savior, that he has the power to forgive our sins, purify our hearts, and equip us to live comfortably and everlastingly in a celestial realm hereafter? How can I know? I can know, first of all, because both ancient and modern prophets have so attested; their conviction of these things is shared regularly, consistently, and powerfully. In other words, I can know because the testimony of "special witnesses of the name of Christ in all the world" has gone deep into my heart and taken up lodging there (Doctrine and Covenants 107:23). I could also know by personal experience that Jesus has power to forgive our sins— I know what it feels like to be in sin, and I know, conversely, what it feels like to have my sins remitted by the Savior through the glorious process of repentance. I know that Jesus Christ lives and that he is the Redeemer because he has redeemed me.

A DIFFERENT KIND OF EVIDENCE

More than twenty years ago, a religious leader of another faith and I were driving through a city in the eastern United States to the LDS Institute of Religion in that area. I had agreed, as a part of my time there, to speak to the single adults. During our search for the institute building, we resumed a conversation we had had many times—namely, his impression that Latter-day Saints are prone to rely more on *feelings* than on tangible *evidence* for truth of religious claims.[1] He said to me, as he had said more than once in previous discussions, "All you people care about is how you feel; you care very little about truth or physical evidence." Being just a bit weary of that accusation, I considered carefully what kind of a response I should make to what I felt was a silly and baseless comment.

I asked, "Do you believe in the literal bodily resurrection of Jesus Christ?"

He gave me a look that evidenced the fact that he felt the question was inane. "Of course I believe in the Resurrection, Bob. I'm a Christian."

I pressed him a bit. "Why do you believe in the Resurrection? How do you know it really happened?"

---

1. An excellent article on the proper place of evidence in the life of faith is Welch, "Role of Evidence in Religious Discussion," 259–94.

He answered, "Because the New Testament teaches of the resurrection of Jesus."

I replied, "But how do you know the New Testament accounts are reliable? How do you know the Bible can be trusted? Maybe the story of Jesus rising from the dead is a giant hoax."

"No," he said. "There is strong evidence to support the truthfulness of the Bible."

"Like what?" I asked.

"Well, there are archaeological, historical, and cultural evidences that suggest that what is described in the Gospels actually happened."

I asked, "And so that's how you know the Resurrection is real?"

"I suppose so," he said.

My mind raced. I continued, "You know, when I hear you speak this way, I feel a deep sense of sadness."

"Sadness?" he asked. "Why would you be sad?"

"I was just thinking of a good friend of mine, an older woman in Camden, Alabama," I replied.

"What about her?"

I said, "I was thinking of how sad it is that this wonderful and devoted Christian, a person who has given her life to Jesus, studied and memorized Bible passages like few people I know, whose life manifests her complete commitment to the Savior—in many ways she is the backbone of that little branch of Christians in her area—I grieve that she is not really entitled to know of the truthfulness of the Bible."

"Why is that?" he questioned.

I answered, "Well, she knows precious little about archaeology or languages or culture or history or ancient manuscripts. My guess is that she probably would be unable to spell the word *archaeology*. I suppose she could never really *know* that the Bible is the word of God and that its contents may be relied upon with confidence."

"Of course she can know that the New Testament account is true," he explained. "She has her faith assuring her of the truthfulness of the story of Jesus."

I turned to him, smiled, and asked, "Do you mean she can have faith and can have the power of the Holy Spirit testify to her soul that her Bible is trustworthy?"

"Yes, that's what I mean."

My smile broadened. "Then we've come full circle."

"What do you mean by that?" he asked.

I said, "You're telling me that this good woman, one who has none of the seemingly requisite background or knowledge of external evidence, can have a witness of the Spirit, including deep personal feelings about the Bible, and that those feelings are genuine and heaven-sent."

He tenderly nodded his head.

I called him by name and said, "That's how Latter-day Saints speak of knowing spiritual things."

My friend smiled. "I see where you're going with this," he remarked.

We agreed that both traditional Christians and Latter-day Saint Christians base their faith upon evidence—both seen and unseen. While saving faith is always built upon that which is true, upon an actual historical moment in time, upon something that really took place (whether Jesus's rise from the tomb or Joseph Smith's experience in the Sacred Grove), *true believers will never allow their faith to be held hostage by what science has or has not found at a given time.* I know, for example, that Jesus fed the five thousand, healed the sick, raised the dead, calmed the storm, and rose from the dead—not because I have physical evidence for each of those miraculous events (because I do not), nor even because I can read of these things in the New Testament, which I accept with all my heart. Rather, I know these things actually happened because the Spirit of the Living God bears witness to my spirit that Jesus of Nazareth did all that the scriptures say he did and much more. What additional evidence can possibly be required?

In a very real sense, *believing is seeing.* No member of the Church need feel ill-equipped, inadequate, or embarrassed because he or she cannot produce the gold plates or the complete Egyptian papyri. No Latter-day Saint should ever feel hesitant to bear testimony of those truths that remain in the realm of faith, truth and evidence that are seen only with the "eye of faith" (Alma 5:15; 32:40; Ether 12:19). In speaking specifically of the Book of Mormon, Elder Neal A. Maxwell wrote: "It is the author's opinion that all the scriptures, including the Book of Mormon, will remain in the realm of faith. Science will not be able to prove or disprove holy writ. However, enough plausible evidence will come forth to prevent scoffers from having a field day, but not enough to remove the requirement of faith. Believers must be patient during such unfolding."[2]

In the end, the only way that the things of God can be known is by the power of the Spirit of God. As we have pointed out, these things are what the scriptures call the "mysteries of God" (1 Corinthians 4:1; 1 Nephi 10:9; Doctrine and Covenants 11:7). Another way of stating this is that the only way spiritual truths may be known is by the *quiet whisperings of the Holy Ghost.* How did Alma the Younger know? Was it because he was knocked to the ground by an angel? Was it because he lay immobile and speechless for three days while he underwent a confrontation with himself and his sinful and rebellious past? Being struck down certainly seemed to get his attention! In reality, however, Alma knew as we know. He underwent a dramatic turnaround in his life through the intervention of a heavenly messenger, but the witness that directed his magnificent conversion was the witness of the Spirit.

Here is Alma's own testimony: "Behold, I testify unto you that *I do know that these things whereof I have spoken are true.* And how do ye suppose that I know of their surety? Behold, I say unto you *they are made known unto me by the Holy Spirit of God.* Behold, I have fasted and prayed many days that I might know these things of myself. And

_____

2. *Plain and Precious Things,* 4.

now I do know of myself that they are true; for the Lord God hath made them manifest unto me by his Holy Spirit; and this is the spirit of revelation which is in me" (Alma 5:45–46; emphasis added).

On the other hand, sometimes we sense the significance of a spiritual reality by the loud janglings of the spirited opposition it engenders. In many places, the announcement that a Latter-day Saint temple was to be built there brought opponents and even crazed zealots out of the woodwork. If I did not already know by the quiet whisperings of the Spirit within me that what goes on within temples is true and is of eternal import, I just might sense the significance and blessings of the temple by the kind of opposition that seems almost to flow naturally from those who protest and refuse to see.

Consider another illustration. Why do many people throughout the world write scathing books, deliver biting addresses, and prepare vicious videos denouncing the Book of Mormon? What is it about black words printed on a white page, all of which are uplifting and edifying, inviting individuals to come unto Christ and be perfected in him, that arouses such bitter antagonism? Once again, if I did not already know by the quiet whisperings of the Spirit that the Book of Mormon is truly heaven-sent and, as its subtitle attests, Another Testament of Jesus Christ, I could recognize its significance—its power to settle doctrinal disputes, touch hearts, and transform lives—by the loud and hostile reactions some display toward it.

Hugh Nibley, one of the great defenders of the faith, stated: "*The words of the prophets cannot be held to the tentative and defective tests that men have devised for them.* Science, philosophy, and common sense all have a right to their day in court. But the last word does not lie with them. Every time men in their wisdom have come forth with the last word, other words have promptly followed. *The last word is a testimony of the gospel that comes only by direct revelation.* Our Father in heaven speaks it, and if it were in perfect agreement with the science of today, it would surely be out of line with the science of tomorrow. Let us not, therefore, seek to hold God to the learned opinions of the moment when he speaks the language of eternity."[3]

In an address entitled "Truth and the Plan," President Dallin H. Oaks offered cautions and counsel when it comes to knowing what is true and what is not. "We live in a time of greatly expanded and disseminated information," he pointed out. "But not all of this information is true. We need to be cautious as we seek truth and choose sources for that search. We should not consider secular prominence or authority as qualified sources of truth. We should be cautious about relying on information or advice offered by entertainment stars, prominent athletes, or anonymous internet sources." Later President Oaks reminded us that "when we seek the truth about religion, we should use spiritual methods appropriate for that search: prayer, the witness of the Holy Ghost, and study of the scriptures and the words of modern prophets. I am always sad when I hear of one who reports a loss of religious faith because of secular teachings. Those who once had spiritual vision can suffer from self-inflicted spiritual blindness."[4]

Similarly, Bruce and Marie Hafen wrote that "the presence of a plausible explanation for whatever complex issue we're wrestling with can be reassuring and inform our faith. Yet *our choices to believe can't— and therefore shouldn't—always count on complete rational support.*"[5]

REASON AND REALITY

Up to now we have been emphasizing the importance of the kind of knowledge that comes only by the power of the Spirit to the human heart and mind. We have emphasized that our feelings are very important, particularly since spiritual impressions may well be accompanied by strong emotion. The point is, there must be truth, there must be propositions, to which the Holy Ghost can bear witness.

---

3. *World and the Prophets*, 134; emphasis added.
4. "Truth and the Plan," *Ensign*, November 2018, 25.
5. *Faith Is Not Blind*, 121; emphasis added.

Elder Hafen mentioned that he "noticed a tendency among some Church members, especially younger ones, to see testimony and inspiration as primarily a good feeling. Feelings are especially important when they come as an actual confirmation of other evidence of truth. That confirmation is essential to our spiritual guidance. But in addition to our feelings, a well-grounded testimony also includes other important elements, such as experience and reason. Feeling by itself has a thin root system that is too shallow to support a fully developed testimony, especially when confronting hard questions, adversity, or people who might try to manipulate our feelings. An overemphasis on feeling alone runs the risk of creating a fair-weather faith that is 'all sail and no anchor.'"[6]

In addition, let's be clear that it does matter very much that there was a real Jesus who actually came out of a real tomb as a glorified, resurrected being and who indeed appeared to real people. When it comes to faith (and thus faithfulness and adherence to a cause), it matters very much whether there is an actual event, an objective occurrence, to which we look and upon which we build our faith.

One cannot exercise saving faith or have a genuine, heaven-sent burning in the bosom, a witness of the Holy Spirit, concerning an event that never took place. One cannot exercise faith in something untrue (Alma 32:21) or something that did not happen, no matter how sweet the story, how sincere the originator or author, or how committed the followers. Though it is true that great literature, whether historically true or untrue, may lift and strengthen in its own way and even contain great moral lessons, such works cannot cause a spiritual transformation of the soul, even a mighty change of heart, as only scripture can do (Mosiah 5:2). The scriptures become a divine and heaven-sent channel by which personal revelation comes, a significant means by which we may hear the voice of the Lord (Doctrine and Covenants

---

6. *Spiritually Anchored in Unsettled Times*, 3.

18:34–36). The power of the word, whether spoken or written, is in its source—God our Father and his Son Jesus Christ.

We are able to exercise faith in a principle or doctrine taught and witnessed by real people who were moved upon by the power of the Holy Ghost, actual persons in time and space whose interactions with the Lord and his Spirit were genuine and true and whose spiritual growth we must imitate. Huck Finn may have given the world sage advice, but his words cannot sanctify. Even the sweet testimonies of Demetrius the slave and Marcellus the Roman centurion from Lloyd C. Douglas's *The Robe* cannot enliven the soul in the same way as do the teachings of Alma to Corianton or the letters of Mormon to Moroni. There is a difference, a huge difference.

In regard to the resurrection of Jesus—and the principle surely applies to the First Vision or the translation of gold plates—Christian theologian John W. Montgomery observed: "There is an excellent objective ground to which to tie the religion that Jesus set forth. Final validation of this can only come experientially [as Latter-day Saints would say, by personal revelation]. But it is desperately important not to put ourselves in such a position that the event-nature of the resurrection depends wholly upon 'the faith.' It's the other way around. *The faith has its starting point in the event, the objective event,* and only by the appropriation of this objective event do we discover the final validity of it.

"The Christian faith," Montgomery continued, "is built upon the Gospel that is 'good news,' and there is no news, good or bad, of something that didn't happen. I personally am much disturbed by *certain contemporary movements in theology* which *seem to imply that we can have the faith regardless of whether anything happened or not.* I believe absolutely that the whole Christian faith is premised upon the fact that at a certain point of time under Pontius Pilate a certain man died and was buried and three days later rose from the dead. If in some way you could demonstrate to me that Jesus never lived, died, or rose again, then I would have to say I have no right to my faith."[7]

Our faith is grounded in the work of redemption that was accomplished in a specific garden, and on a designated cross, and in a particular moment in our earth's history. It is not the exact site that matters so much as it is that there was such a site. If Jesus did not in reality suffer and bleed and die and rise from the tomb, then we are spiritually doomed, no matter how committed we may be to the "faith event" celebrated by the first-century Christians. And so it is in regard to the occasion in Palmyra. It matters greatly that the Eternal Father and his Only Begotten Son did appear to a young boy in a grove of trees in New York State. Exactly where the Sacred Grove is, or what specific trees or ground were hallowed by this theophany, is far less significant.

If Joseph Smith did not behold the Father and the Son, if the First Vision was only the sweet dream of a naïve boy, then no amount of goodness and civility on the part of the Latter-day Saints will save us. And so it is in regard to the people and events and teachings of the Book of Mormon. That there was a Nephi and an Alma and a Captain Moroni is vital to the story and, in my view, to the truthfulness and relevance of the Book of Mormon. That the prophetic oracles from Lehi to Samuel preached and prophesied of Christ and taught and administered his gospel is vital in establishing the dispensational concept restored through Joseph Smith. These items reveal far more about the way things are and have been among the people of God in all ages than they do about the way things were in the nineteenth century. Joseph Smith the Seer, in harmony with the principles taught by Ammon to Limhi, may well have restored as much knowledge of things past as of things future (Mosiah 8:17).

There is room in the Church for all types and shapes and sizes of people, and certainly all of us are at differing stages of intellectual

7. *History and Christianity*, 107–8; emphasis added.

development and spiritual maturity. Further, there are many doctrinal issues over which discussion and debate may lead to diverse conclusions, particularly in matters that have not been fully clarified in scripture or by latter-day prophets. At the same time, there are certain well-defined truths—matters pertaining to the divine Sonship of Christ, the reality and power of the Savior's Atonement and literal bodily resurrection, the appearance of the Father and the Son in 1820, and the truthfulness of the Book of Mormon—which, in the uncompromising language of President J. Rueben Clark, "must stand unchanged, unmodified, without dilution, excuse, apology, or avoidance; they may not be explained away or submerged. Without these two great beliefs [the Atonement and resurrection of Christ, and the divine call of Joseph Smith], the Church would cease to be the Church."[8]

In my view, ours is not the task to shift the Church about with its history, practices, and beliefs—as though the living Church were on casters—in order to get it into the path of moving persons who desire a religion that conforms to their own private beliefs or attends to their own misgivings and doubts. I am fully persuaded that no Latter-day Saint needs to surrender cherished values to live in a modern world, that a member of the Church need not fall prey to the "alternate voices" offering alternative explanations for our narrative, foundational events, or institutions.[9] One can have implicit trust in the Church and its leaders without sacrificing or compromising anything.

"The finished mosaic of the history of the Restoration," Elder Neal A. Maxwell taught, "will be larger and more varied as more pieces of tile emerge, adjusting a sequence here or enlarging there a sector of our understanding. . . . There may even be," he added, "a few pieces of tile which, for the moment, do not seem to fit. We can wait, as we must." One day, he promised, "the final mosaic of the Restoration will

---

8. "Charted Course of the Church in Education," 245.
9. See Oaks, "Alternate Voices," *Ensign*, May 1989, 27–30.

be resplendent, reflecting divine design. . . . At the perfect day, we will see that we have been a part of things too wonderful for us. Part of the marvel and the wonder of God's 'marvelous work and a wonder' will be how perfect Divinity mercifully used us—imperfect humanity. Meanwhile, amid the human dissonance, those with ears to hear will follow the beckoning sounds of a certain trumpet."[10]

Because we have been baptized by immersion by the proper priesthood authority for the remission of sins, because we have been confirmed members of The Church of Jesus Christ of Latter-day Saints, because we have received the gift of the Holy Ghost, because we have sought for a testimony of this great latter-day work, a gracious God has given to us knowledge that many in the world may never appreciate, much less understand. While in Liberty Jail, the Prophet Joseph Smith wrote the following: "God shall give unto you *knowledge by his Holy Spirit,* yea, by the unspeakable gift of the Holy Ghost, that has not been revealed since the world was until now; which our forefathers have awaited with anxious expectation to be revealed in the last times, which their minds were pointed to by the angels, as held in reserve for the fulness of their glory; *a time to come in the which nothing shall be withheld*" (Doctrine and Covenants 121:26–28; emphasis added).

Our faith is an active one, a way of life in which each member of the Church—girl or boy, man or woman—is charged to obtain an independent witness of the truth by the power of God's Holy Spirit, to seek after the things of God in the only way those things can be truly known.

As members of The Church of Jesus Christ of Latter-day Saints, it is our privilege to be led by prophets, seers, and revelators. Those who choose to follow their counsel and direction, believe in and teach

10. "Out of Obscurity," *Ensign*, November 1984, 11.

the scriptures, and demonstrate loyalty to the Church—no matter the extent or lack of academic training or intellectual capacity—may well open themselves to ridicule from the cynic and the critic from both inside and outside the Church. Ultimately, doctrinal clarity and an unshakable witness come not through the explorations of scholars alone but through the revelations of God to those we call the living oracles. These things we know through the witness that comes by the power of the Holy Ghost.

PART III

Manifesting His Will

Chapter 10

MATTERS ONLY GOD
CAN MAKE KNOWN

e have spoken of the precious, priceless gift that God our Heavenly Father and his Son Jesus Christ have given to us—the gift of the Holy Ghost. In order for the children of God to learn to walk by faith (2 Corinthians 5:7), the plan of salvation called for a veil of forgetfulness to be placed over our minds, such that we no longer remember what it was like to live and act and learn and grow in the presence of Deity. In the language of the apostle Paul, in this second estate we "see through a glass, darkly" (1 Corinthians 13:12).

Although the great enterprise with which the first two members of the Godhead are intimately involved is to "bring to pass the immortality and eternal life of man" (Moses 1:39), they do not walk and talk with us day by day. They have made provision, however, for each of us to have close contact with the heavens through the third member of that Godhead. That is his mission.

APPRECIATING WHAT WE HAVE

Yes, it is a great and grand *privilege* to be prompted, led, even tutored by God's Holy Spirit. In addition, in a very real way, it is also our *duty* to live in such a manner that the Spirit can abide with and in us. This is the Lord's work in which we are engaged, and it must be done in his way if we are to have ready access to his mind, his purposes, and his power. God is our Principal, and we are his agents. The duty of the agent is to carry out the will of the principal. One must, however, know what that will is before he or she can carry it out. In a modern revelation the Savior spoke of this relationship: "Wherefore, as ye are agents, ye are on the Lord's errand; and whatsoever ye do according to the will of the Lord is the Lord's business" (Doctrine and Covenants 64:29).

My colleague Joseph Fielding McConkie emphasized that "our faith and our doctrine is that every member of the Church has both *the ability and responsibility* to be a prophet. To join the Church is but to enroll in the School of the Prophets. . . . Our doctrine is not simply that if we live righteously we can receive revelation; rather it is that *if we live right there is no power that can prevent our receiving it.*"[1] Or as Joseph Smith put it, "No man can receive the Holy Ghost without receiving revelations." Why? Because "the Holy Ghost is a revelator."[2]

Some years ago my friend Richard J. Mouw, former president of Fuller Theological Seminary, and I were invited to speak to a large group of Evangelical Christian students at a college in the Midwest. Rich spoke first for about twenty minutes, then I spoke for about the same amount of time, and then we talked together about the tenets and teachings of our two faiths. We then opened ourselves to questions from the students. I was particularly nervous about that part of the program, knowing from painful experience that some questions are intended not to acquire information but to confront, challenge, or embarrass. Fortunately, the students were kind and respectful, eager to hear what I had to say about The Church of Jesus Christ of Latter-day Saints and its similarities to and differences from Trinitarian Christians. They asked about our views of the plight of fallen man, the Atonement of the Savior, our belief that we can become like God,

---

1. *Prophets and Prophecy*, 90; emphasis added.
2. *Joseph Smith* [manual], 132.

and the importance of both institutional and individual, or personal, revelation.

When this meeting was over, we were escorted to another room where a reception was held. There we greeted students and members of the larger community, some of whom wanted to seek greater clarity or inquire about other matters. About fifteen minutes into the reception, a young man who appeared to be in his early thirties introduced himself to me, shook my hand, and expressed appreciation for our taking the time and making the effort to come. Let's call him Eric. He paused for a few seconds and said, "My wife and I used to be Latter-day Saints, but a few years ago we left the Church." He explained that they had begun to participate in a Protestant congregation in the city. His next remark caught me by surprise: "After today I wonder whether we made the right decision." He acknowledged that a number of people were waiting to meet us and asked if I would be willing for him to communicate with me. I gave him a business card with my contact information and indicated that I would like that very much.

Eric and I had a number of chats, by e-mail and telephone, as well as a visit I made to his part of the country. In one of our first conversations he said he had sat down one evening and made a list of the things he missed most about being a member of the Church. Some of the teachings and practices he missed and some of the distinctive matters he learned in The Church of Jesus Christ of Latter-day Saints included the following:

- That God loves him
- The importance of the family
- Why it is important to honor the Sabbath day
- A deeper love for the Bible
- That it is not a sin to be happy
- How to keep the body and the mind healthy
- The importance of tithes and offerings

- The beauty of eternal relationships
- A love for family history
- That sins can be forgiven, that there is hope
- How to love Jesus Christ
- That Jesus Christ loves us

Sometimes it might take someone like Eric, who has left the Church but now reflects soberly on what life within the Church meant to him, to help us appreciate—no, cherish—the sweet blessings and privileges that are, for you and me, within easy reach. To repeat what Stephen R. Covey said, "Sometimes we [members of the restored Church of Jesus Christ] are like fish that discover water last."

Perhaps these two items I learned from Eric are the most important:

- The possibility that God still speaks today
- The feeling of God speaking to and through us (sadly, Eric had not experienced that feeling since leaving the Church)

Elder Neal A. Maxwell, in his inimitable style, observed that "we are so blessed to know there is a tutoring and loving Father-God, not some impersonal life-force, nor a distracted, absentee monarch presiding somewhere in space. . . . Meanwhile, for those who have eyes to see and ears to hear, *the Father and the Son, astonishingly, are giving away the secrets of the universe.* If only we can avoid being offended by their generosity!"[3]

SHOW AND TELL

In 2 Nephi 31 is set forth one of the most beautiful and impressive presentations of the gospel, "the doctrine of Christ," in all of scripture

---

3. *Meek and Lowly*, 44, 102; emphasis added; see also Maxwell, *Moving in His Majesty and Power*, 20. President Russell M. Nelson quoted part of Elder Maxwell's statement in "Revelation for the Church, Revelation for Our Lives," *Ensign*, May 2018, 95.

(vv. 2, 21). Nephi speaks first of the baptism of Jesus at the hands of John the Baptist and emphasizes that our Lord, though pure, holy, and without sin, submitted to this saving ordinance. He did so to "fulfil all righteousness" (2 Nephi 31:5–6; compare Matthew 3:15). That is, Christ showed "unto the children of men that, according to the flesh he humbleth himself before the Father, and witnesseth unto the Father that he would be obedient unto him in keeping his commandments" and, particularly, the commandment to be baptized. The Master showed "unto the children of men the straitness of the path, and the narrowness of the gate, by which they should enter" into the kingdom of God (2 Nephi 31:7–9; see also John 3:3–5).

Later in that same chapter Nephi charges his people (and us) to "follow the Son, with full purpose of heart" and submit to baptism. Nephi explains that after we have obeyed the command to be baptized, "then shall ye receive the Holy Ghost; yea, then cometh the baptism of fire and of the Holy Ghost; and then can ye speak with the tongue of angels, and shout praises unto the Holy One of Israel" (2 Nephi 31:13).

We will address in more detail later what it means to speak with the tongue of angels. For now, we turn to 2 Nephi 32. There Nephi begins to explain that to speak with the tongue of angels is to speak by the power of the Holy Ghost, to speak "the words of Christ." Nephi continues: "Wherefore, I said unto you, feast upon the words of Christ; for behold, the words of Christ will *tell you all things what ye should do.*" He adds that "if ye will enter in by the way, and receive the Holy Ghost, [He] will *show unto you all things what ye should do*" (2 Nephi 32:2–3, 5; emphasis added).

What about those painful and difficult situations in which we are diligently and most earnestly seeking divine guidance on a matter of great significance for ourselves and our family and no clear answer comes? What do we do if after weeks or months of searching, pondering, fasting, and praying we still are unsure about the course we should pursue? President Brigham Young said that men and women "must be able to demonstrate that [they are] for God and to develop [their] own resources so that [they] can act independently and yet humble." Then follows this profound truth: "It is the way it is because *we must learn to be righteous in the dark.*"[4]

On another occasion President Young declared: "If I do not know the will of my Father, and what He requires of me in a certain transaction, *if I ask Him to give me wisdom* concerning any requirement in life, or in regard to my own course, or that of my friends, my family, my children, or those that I preside over, and get no answer from Him, and then *do the very best that my judgment will teach me, He is bound to own and honor that transaction,* and He will do so to all intents and purposes."[5]

I believe there is more to President Young's second comment than meets the eye. It is certainly true that we should pray with all our hearts for direction and then make the wisest decisions we can. It is my conviction, however, that even on those occasions when we feel very alone—when we wonder if God is even listening—if we are striving to be worthy, seeking earnestly to maintain the influence of the Spirit in our lives, God is in fact directing our paths, for he has so promised us. No doubt there are certain seasons of our life in which we are called upon to proceed without the clear direction of the Spirit. That does not mean we are all alone. Nor does it necessarily mean that we are unworthy. I believe that one day, when we are allowed to review the scenes of mortality from a grander perspective, we will be astounded at how closely our Heavenly Father directed our paths, orchestrated the events of our life, and in general led us by that kindly light we know as the Holy Spirit.

I believe that over the years the Spirit of the Lord works in a quiet

---

4. Office Journal, 28 January 1857; emphasis added.

5. In *Journal of Discourses,* 3:205; emphasis added.

but consistent manner to educate our conscience, enhance our perspective, and polish our wisdom and judgment. After all, the Prophet Joseph explained, one of the assignments of the Holy Ghost is to convey pure intelligence through expanding the mind, enlightening the understanding, and storing the intellect with knowledge.[6] It may be that one day we will look back on those seasons in which we felt required to make decisions on our own and discover that the Lord had been, through the honing and refining processes in our souls, leading us along in paths of his choosing. That is, maybe one day we will learn that our own wisdom and judgment were not just our own.

THE TRUTH OF ALL THINGS

One of the first scriptural passages I memorized as a green and overwhelmed full-time missionary was Moroni 10:4–5, two verses that have probably been quoted or read to persons investigating the Church more often than any other passage. I have a conviction, borne of the Spirit, that what Moroni teaches in those verses is true—that one can come to know that the Book of Mormon is an actual, historical, scriptural record consisting of God's revelations and manifestations to the ancient inhabitants of America.

Let's turn our attention to verse 5: "And by the power of the Holy Ghost ye may know the truth of all things." On more than one occasion I have heard members of the Church quote this verse to emphasize that by the power of God's Holy Spirit we can come to know every truth, every fact, every proposition in the sciences, the arts, literature, etc. That is certainly possible, I suppose, but obviously not very probable in this life. We simply do not have that much time. Rather, Moroni is teaching that it is by the power of the Spirit that *we may know when something is true and when it is not*. That is, the Holy Ghost

---

6. See Discourse, between ca. 26 June and ca. 2 July 1839; see also *Words of Joseph Smith*, 4.

will enable us to discern truth from error. "Ask the Father in my name," a modern revelation counsels the Saints, "in faith, believing that you shall receive, and you shall have the Holy Ghost, which manifesteth all things which are expedient unto the children of men" (Doctrine and Covenants 18:18).

I have been fascinated and inspired by plain and precious truths restored through the Prophet Joseph Smith's translation of the Bible. Between the time when the twelve-year-old Jesus was teaching the doctors of the law at the temple and when he began his formal ministry, we learn: "Jesus grew up with his brethren, and waxed strong, and waited upon the Lord for the time of his ministry to come." What follows is absolutely remarkable: "And he served under his father [presumably Joseph], and *he spake not as other men, neither could he be taught; for he needed not that any man should teach him.* And after many years, the hour of his ministry drew nigh" (JST, Matthew 3:24–26; emphasis added).

It was not that Jesus could not or would not learn from his mother, Mary, and stepfather, Joseph, or even from the Jewish teachers in the local synagogue, for he certainly must have learned a great deal. There are some things, however, that no mortal can teach, some elements of divine wisdom that can come only from on high, some insights into heavenly things that can be acquired only from God the Eternal Father through the power of his Holy Spirit.

John the Beloved expressed a profound truth when he wrote to the Saints at the end of the first century that "the anointing [of the Holy Spirit] which ye have received of him [God] abideth in you, and *ye need not that any man teach you:* but as the same anointing *teacheth you of all things,* and is truth, and is no lie, and even as it hath taught you, ye shall abide in him" (1 John 2:27; emphasis added).

Once again, what the Holy Spirit does is emphasize what is true, what is right, what is good. In short, the Spirit leads us to do good, to do justly, to walk humbly, and to judge righteously (Doctrine and

Covenants 11:12). "You don't have to wonder about what is true," President Russell M. Nelson testified. "You don't have to wonder whom you can safely trust. . . . Regardless of what others may say or do, no one can ever take away a witness borne to your heart and mind about what is true."[7]

One of the truly important ways in which the Spirit shows us the path to pursue is by quickening our memory, or, to borrow a phrase from Alma, the Spirit "enlarges the memory" of persons who are striving to do or say what they should (Alma 37:8). We remember that it was at the Last Supper when the Savior taught his apostles: "The Comforter, which is the Holy Ghost, whom the Father will send in my name, he shall teach you *all things,* and *bring all things to your remembrance,* whatsoever I have said unto you" (John 14:26; emphasis added).

Elder Maxwell spoke of how the Spirit will often teach us "by the medium of memory." This process of our memory being enlarged is actually the means of "accessing the divine database instead of relying solely on our small set of experiences."[8] We can be certain that much, if not most, of the time when we remember lessons from the past that have vital, perhaps even eternal significance, such lessons were brought home to us, returned to our consciousness, by the Lord through his Holy Spirit.

President Henry B. Eyring explained: "More precious than a memory of events is the memory of the Holy Ghost touching our hearts and His continuing affirmation of truth. More precious than seeing with our eyes or remembering words spoken and read is recalling the feelings that accompanied the quiet voice of the Spirit. Rarely I have felt it exactly as the travelers on the road to Emmaus did [Luke 24:13–32]—as

---

7. "Revelation for the Church, Revelation for Our Lives," *Ensign,* May 2018, 95.
8. *Men and Women of Christ,* 106.

a soft but unmistakable burning in the heart. More often it is a feeling of light and quiet assurance."[9]

In 1967 when I entered the Mission Home in Salt Lake City (it preceded the Missionary Training Centers), missionaries were set apart for their missions by General Authorities. Elder Alma Sonne, an Assistant to the Twelve, was assigned to set me apart. In the blessing, he said much about difficulties and challenges I would face in the months ahead, and he blessed me with the wisdom and strength to face them. There were several other matters he mentioned that I am now unable to recall. One thing, however, I do recall very well. He said to me, "Elder Millet, I bless you that from this time forth you will have no difficulty remembering the scriptures, using them and drawing upon them." I was delighted to hear such language at the time, but in the years since, I have treasured that message and promise. Of all with which I have been blessed in scores of priesthood blessings, ordinations, and settings apart, nothing has meant more to me.

On many, many occasions the words of holy scripture or the teachings of latter-day prophets have come into my mind while I was teaching a class or delivering a sermon. In addition, my own life experiences have come to mind to serve as applications for scriptural passages that were being studied at the time. Thank heaven for memory! Thank heaven for the gift of the Holy Ghost, the third member of the Godhead, whose role it is to quicken our memory and bring all things to our remembrance (John 14:26).

THE ENTICINGS OF THE HOLY SPIRIT

In teaching his son Jacob the plan of salvation, Lehi made reference to Adam, Eve, the tree of knowledge of good and evil, and the tree of life in the Garden of Eden before the Fall. "Wherefore, the Lord God gave unto man that he should act for himself. Wherefore, man could

---

9. "His Spirit to Be with You," *Ensign*, May 2018, 87.

not act for himself save it should be that he was enticed by one or the other" (2 Nephi 2:10–16; compare 2 Nephi 9:39).

Each one of us is an expert witness on what it means to be enticed by evil, by Satan or his followers. It is an everyday experience, one we comprehend only too well, one we have experienced many, many times. What does it mean, however, to be *enticed by good,* by the Lord, through his Spirit? An angel taught King Benjamin that "the natural man is an enemy to God, and has been from the fall of Adam, and will be, forever and ever, *unless he yields to the enticings of the Holy Spirit,* and putteth off the natural man and becometh a saint through the atonement of Christ the Lord" (Mosiah 3:19; emphasis added).

To entice is "to lead on by exciting desire; to allure."[10] As we have noted, the Light of Christ, or the Spirit of Jesus Christ, is given to every person who receives a physical body. That divine light, that sacred essence, not only fills the universe and is in and through all things but it is also a personal guide, an individual moral monitor, the foundation of our reason and our conscience. It strives with us, struggling against the natural man or woman, the unredeemed person, to point out the right and proper way to go. It leads those who have not yet received the fulness of the gospel and the saving ordinances to that higher light we know as the influence and then the gift of the Holy Ghost, the latter of which comes only following an authorized baptism and confirmation. Thus in a very real way, the Light of Christ is enticing us all the time, ever pointing us to the good, the wise, alluring us onto the path that eventually leads to greater light. So it is with the Holy Ghost. That Spirit is forevermore enticing us to stay on what President Nelson called the "covenant path."[11]

A most beloved scriptural passage is the Twenty-Third Psalm. Let's look at that marvelous expression of praise and gratitude. Please note

---

10. *Random House College Dictionary*, s.v. "entice."
11. "Drawing the Power of Jesus Christ into Our Lives," *Ensign*, May 2017, 41.

how often the Psalmist (presumably King David) speaks of the enticings of God, the tender and loving manner in which the Almighty directs, empowers, protects, prepares, and draws us to him:

"The Lord is my shepherd; I shall not want. He *maketh me to lie down* in green pastures: he *leadeth me* beside the still waters. He *restoreth my soul:* he *leadeth me* in the paths of righteousness for his name's sake. Yea, though I walk through the valley of the shadow of death, I will fear no evil: for *thou art with me; thy rod and thy staff *they comfort me.* Thou *preparest a table before me* in the presence of mine enemies: thou anointest my head with oil; my cup runneth over." We come now to the touching climax to this psalm: "Surely *goodness and mercy shall follow me* all the days of my life: and I will dwell in the house of the Lord for ever" (Psalm 23:1–6; emphasis added).

There are at least two ways to understand the final verse. The most obvious is that "because Jehovah is ever with me, goodness and mercy will come to me all my days." There is, however, a more subtle meaning implied, one directly associated with the "enticings of the Holy Spirit." Some scholars have suggested that the words *follow me* may imply "stay after me," "track me," "dog my steps," not in a pejorative sense but rather in an all-loving, ever-solicitous manner. As one paraphrase of this passage has it, "Your beauty and love *chase after me* every day of my life."[12] Truly God is the omniscient and omniloving One who follows, prompts, even impels us all the days of our lives.

It is not uncommon during a lesson or a sermon for an idea or several ideas to crowd into my mind. These have often been scriptural references, prophetic teachings, or personal experiences linked or associated with the principle or doctrine I am teaching. Many years ago I made a decision, one that I now realize was very important: unless the idea that has just entered my conscious awareness is bizarre or

---

12. Peterson, *The Message*, 937; emphasis added.

unbelievably strange, I will insert that thought or perspective into my message. To date, I have never been disappointed with the result.

Sister Michelle D. Craig of the General Presidency of the Relief Society spoke of promptings to serve others that have come to her. "Sometimes when I have an impression to do something for someone," she explained, "I wonder if it was a prompting or just my own thoughts. But I am reminded that 'that which is of God inviteth and enticeth to do good continually; wherefore, every thing which inviteth and enticeth to do good, and to love God, and to serve him, is inspired of God' (Moroni 7:13). Whether they are direct promptings or just impulses to help, a good deed is never wasted . . . and is never the wrong response."[13]

Similarly, Elder Ronald A. Rasband wrote: "We must be confident in our first promptings. Sometimes we rationalize; we wonder if we are feeling a spiritual impression or if it is just our own thoughts. When we begin to second-guess, even third-guess, our feelings—and we all have—we are dismissing the Spirit; we are questioning divine counsel."[14]

Nephi spoke a timeless and comforting truth when he sought to encourage his faithless brothers: "I will go and do the things which the Lord hath commanded, for I know that the Lord giveth no commandments unto the children of men, save he shall prepare a way for them that they may accomplish the thing which he commandeth them" (1 Nephi 3:7; compare 17:3; Doctrine and Covenants 5:34).

That passage, one that every Primary child has heard numerous times, has deep and significant meaning. "Spirituality yields two fruits," Elder Richard G. Scott wrote. "The first is inspiration to know what to do. The second is power, or the capacity to do it. These two capacities come together."[15] Elder Scott also said: "The scriptures teach, and I

---

13. "Divine Discontent," *Ensign*, November 2018, 53–54.
14. *Led by Divine Design*, 17.
15. *21 Principles*, 24.

have been led to confirm, that *we will never be prompted by the Holy Ghost to do something we cannot do.* It may require extraordinary effort and much time, patience, prayer and obedience, but we can do it."[16]

THE MYSTERIES AND PEACEABLE THINGS

It is not uncommon for someone to ask a question in one of the classes or quorums in the Church only for another class member or the discussion leader to reply with something like, "I think we had better leave the mysteries alone."

Let's think about that. Clearly there are matters that have not been revealed or clarified by those holding prophetic or apostolic keys. Examples of such matters might be the size and location of Kolob, exactly what the premortal intelligence is, what God was like before he was God, how many Saviors there are, what life will be like if we should eventually attain godhood, and so forth. Discussing such things would no doubt result, in many respects, in the pooling of ignorance, for God has revealed little or nothing about these things at this point in time. Truly, "there are many mysteries which are kept, that no one knoweth them save God himself" (Alma 40:3).

And yet there is a definition of *mystery* that has a much more positive connotation. President Harold B. Lee explained that a mystery "may be defined as a truth which cannot be known except by revelation."[17] On the very first page of the Book of Mormon, in the first verse, Nephi informs readers that in the course of his days he had been "highly favored [blessed] of the Lord in all my days; yea, having had a great knowledge of the goodness and the mysteries of God, therefore I make a record of my proceedings in my days" (1 Nephi 1:1). Nephi's younger brother Jacob exulted: "Behold, great and marvelous are the works of the Lord. How unsearchable are the depths of

---

16. *21 Principles*, 12; emphasis added.
17. *Ye Are the Light of the World*, 211.

the mysteries of him; and it is impossible that man should find out all his ways. And *no man knoweth of his ways save it be revealed unto him;* wherefore, brethren, despise not the revelations of God" (Jacob 4:8; emphasis added; see also Alma 12:9).

To give greater emphasis to this positive view of the mysteries of God, note the phenomenal promise of the Lord in a modern revelation: "If thou shalt ask, thou shalt receive revelation upon revelation, knowledge upon knowledge, that thou mayest know *the mysteries and peaceable things*—that which bringeth joy, that which bringeth life eternal" (Doctrine and Covenants 42:61; emphasis added; compare 36:2; 39:6; Moses 6:61). We have been taught that "whatever principle of intelligence we attain unto in this life, it will rise with us in the resurrection. And if a person gains more knowledge and intelligence in this life through his diligence and obedience than another, he will have so much the advantage in the world to come" (Doctrine and Covenants 130:18–19). Truly the more we come to know by revelation the things of God, the greater the joy we feel within our souls and the nearer we are to the place where God dwells.

THE WORK OF THE CHURCH

The Church of Jesus Christ must, if it is to carry out its divine mandate, be led and directed by its Head, the Lord Jesus Christ himself. In his first general conference as President of the Church, President Joseph Fielding Smith bore this powerful testimony: "I desire to say that no man of himself can lead this church. It is the Church of the Lord Jesus Christ; he is at the head. The Church bears his name, has his priesthood, administers his gospel, preaches his doctrine, and does his work. . . .

"If this were the work of man, it would fail, but it is the work of the Lord, and he does not fail. And we have the assurance that if we keep the commandments and are valiant in the testimony of Jesus and are true to every trust, the Lord will guide and direct us and his church in the paths of righteousness, for the accomplishment of all his purposes."[18]

The resurrected Christ himself proclaimed to the assembled Nephites that in order for the Church to truly be his Church, it needed to be called after him and have his name. That is, "whatsoever ye shall do, ye shall do it in my name; therefore ye shall call the church in my name." But of course, any group of people could call their denomination the Church of Jesus Christ. Would they then truly be his church? No, for the Lord set forth another requirement, a vital one: "If it be called in my name then it is my church, *if it so be that they are built upon my gospel*. . . . And if it so be that the church is built upon my gospel *then will the Father show forth his own works in it*" (3 Nephi 27:7–10; emphasis added).

The Father shows forth his own works in the true Church through the workings of the Holy Spirit. Girls and boys, women and men are called to serve in the Church by divine direction. Sermons are delivered and lessons are taught by the power of the Spirit. Solutions to pressing issues or sobering problems are made known as God brings to pass his purposes through the whisperings of the Holy Ghost. The revelations declare that "the elders are to conduct the meetings as they are led by the Holy Ghost, according to the commandments and revelations of God" (Doctrine and Covenants 20:45). In speaking of the spiritual spontaneity that ought to characterize the Lord's living Church, Moroni informs us that the meetings of the ancient American Church of Jesus Christ "were conducted by the church after the manner of the workings of the Spirit, and by the power of the Holy Ghost; for as the power of the Holy Ghost led them whether to preach, or to exhort, or to pray, or to supplicate, or to sing, even so it was done" (Moroni 6:9). Similarly, in our dispensation the Savior taught the early Saints that while handbooks, guidelines, and established policies and procedures do serve an important function, "it

---

18. In Conference Report, April 1970, 113.

always has been given to the elders of my church from the beginning, and ever shall be, to conduct all meetings as they are directed and guided by the Holy Spirit" (Doctrine and Covenants 46:2).

A tender scene in the Book of Mormon takes place as Alma the Elder is preparing to baptize new believers in the Waters of Mormon: "And now it came to pass that Alma took Helam, he being one of the first, and went and stood forth in the water, and cried, saying: O Lord, pour out thy Spirit upon thy servant, that he may do this work with holiness of heart" (Mosiah 18:12). Alma then states his authority and immerses Helam. Truly, no holder of the priesthood wants to perform any sacred, saving ordinance without being led and inspired and accompanied by the Spirit. Perhaps that is what Moroni had in mind when he explained, near the end of the Book of Mormon, how persons were ordained to the priesthood in his day by the laying on of hands: "And after this manner did they ordain priests and teachers, according to the gifts and callings of God unto men; and they ordained them by the power of the Holy Ghost, which was in them" (Moroni 3:4; compare Doctrine and Covenants 18:32; 20:60). In the words of the Prophet Joseph Smith, "The Holy Ghost is God's messenger to administer in all those priesthoods."[19]

In short, the great "Apostle and High Priest of our profession, Christ Jesus" (Hebrews 3:1), empowers, illuminates, inspires, and qualifies those called to work in the Church of Jesus Christ. As one Christian scholar noted wisely: "I have sometimes heard Christian people talk as though God, having done what he's done in Jesus, now wants us to do our part by getting on with things under our own steam. But that is a tragic misunderstanding. It leads to arrogance, burnout, or both. Without God's Spirit, there is nothing we can do that will count for God's kingdom. *Without God's Spirit, the church simply can't be the church.*"[20]

---

19. Journal, 27 August 1843; "Remarks by President Joseph Smith on Sunday Morning August 27th 1843."
20. Wright, *Simply Christian*, 122–23; emphasis added.

There are simply not enough pages in a book of this sort—or enough books that could be written—to discuss all that we might want to consider when it comes to the receipt of personal revelation, the promptings and enticings of God's Holy Spirit, the myriad ways by which an omniscient Father in heaven makes known his mind and will to his earthly children.

The Book of Mormon writer Jarom spoke a profound truth when he stated that "as many as are not stiffnecked and have faith, have communion with the Holy Spirit" (Jarom 1:4). To *commune* is literally to "be with." Jesus communed with his Father; his Father was "with him." That is the basis of spirituality. President David O. McKay defined spirituality as "the consciousness of victory over self, and of communion with the Infinite."[21] The invitation to come to know God and to know and carry out his will is extended to all those who have received and who cultivate and strive to maintain the Holy Spirit in their daily walk and talk. In that way, we can do our part to build up the kingdom of God and establish his righteousness in the earth (JST, Matthew 6:38).

---

21. *Gospel Ideals*, 390.

Chapter 11

AVENUES OF DIVINE GUIDANCE

*I*n the Lord's Preface to the Doctrine and Covenants, he points out that the revelations "are of me, and were given unto my servants in their weakness, *after the manner of their language, that they might come to understanding*" (Doctrine and Covenants 1:24; emphasis added). Our Lord is a perfect communicator who yearns for his children to seek after him, to strive to know his mind and will, and, most importantly, to understand the messages he delivers. Thus, Nephi explained, God gives "light unto the understanding; for *he speaketh unto men according to their language, unto their understanding*" (2 Nephi 31:3; emphasis added).[1] Let's now reflect briefly on several means by which we are taught and directed by the Holy Spirit.

A PERSONAL APPEARANCE OF GOD

Surely there is nothing that God the Eternal Father and his Only Begotten Son Jesus Christ desire more than for God's children to live in such a manner that they are able to enjoy the enlightening and

---

1. Elder George A. Smith put it this way: "When the Lord reveals anything to men, He reveals it in language that accords with their own. If any of you were to converse with an angel, and you used strictly grammatical language, he would do the same. But if you used two negatives in a sentence the heavenly messenger would use language to correspond with your understanding" (in *Journal of Discourses*, 12:335).

enlivening powers of the Holy Spirit on a consistent and regular basis. Not only does such living equip us to "always have his Spirit to be with [us]" (Moroni 4:3; Doctrine and Covenants 20:77), but it also prepares us for the ultimate manifestation of one day being qualified and spiritually ready to enter into the personal presence of Deity. In the language of Amulek, "this life is the time for men to prepare to meet God" (Alma 34:32). We will speak in chapter 18 at greater length of the blessings of seeing the face of the Father and the Son: We need only remind ourselves now of the precious promise that "inasmuch as you strip yourselves from jealousies and fears, and humble yourselves before me, for ye are not sufficiently humble, the veil shall be rent and you shall see me and know that I am" (Doctrine and Covenants 67:10). We must balance this exciting and unspeakable possibility with the appreciation for and understanding that "it shall be in his own time, and in his own way, and according to his own will" (Doctrine and Covenants 88:68).

VISIONS OR DREAMS

While visions and revelations are listed among the spiritual gifts that Latter-day Saints certainly believe in and enjoy (Articles of Faith 1:6), they may not be everyday experiences. As we noted in chapter 3, the Old Testament prophet Joel prophesied that in the last days the Lord would "pour out [his] spirit upon all flesh; and your sons and your daughters shall prophesy, your old men shall dream dreams, your young men shall see visions" (Joel 2:28).

When persons are granted a vision, they are allowed to see "things which [are] not visible to the natural eye" (Moses 6:36). We often speak of a vision allowing one to see "within the veil," meaning the thin veil that separates this world from the eternal world. Of course, Latter-day Saints are particularly prone to think of Joseph Smith's First

Vision,[2] inasmuch as it was the initial divine manifestation of this final dispensation. This vision represented a parting of the veil that allowed young Joseph to see and converse with the Father and the Son, the first two members of the Godhead, and to do so by the power of the Holy Ghost. Like Moses, this young latter-day prophet was, through the lifting powers of the Spirit, *transfigured,* elevated to a higher spiritual plane (Moses 1:9–11, 14; compare Joseph Smith–History 1:16–17, 20). The theophany in Palmyra was the glorious beginning of the revelations of God to the human family in these last days.

On 16 February 1832 the Prophet Joseph received the vision of the degrees of glory. In introducing the vision, Joseph and Sidney Rigdon bore witness: "We, Joseph Smith, Jun., and Sidney Rigdon, *being in the Spirit* on the sixteenth day of February, in the year of our Lord one thousand eight hundred and thirty-two—*by the power of the Spirit our eyes were opened and our understandings were enlightened,* so as to see and understand the things of God" (Doctrine and Covenants 76:11–12; emphasis added).

In introducing the vision of the celestial kingdom, received in January of 1836 in the Kirtland Temple, the Prophet recorded that "the heavens were opened upon us, and I beheld the celestial kingdom of God, and the glory thereof, whether in the body or out I cannot tell" (Doctrine and Covenants 137:1). That is reminiscent of an experience described by the apostle Paul. Speaking somewhat modestly of himself, he wrote: "I knew a man in Christ above [more than] fourteen years ago, (whether in the body, I cannot tell; or whether out of the body, I cannot tell: God knoweth;) such an one caught up to the third

---

2. While we as members of the restored Church of Jesus Christ speak of Joseph Smith's First *Vision,* we might with equal propriety speak of the young Prophet's First *Visitation,* since we believe that the Father and Son appeared to Joseph— were in his immediate presence—in the grove in upstate New York on that spring day of 1820.

heaven." He then went on to speak of being "caught up into paradise" and hearing unspeakable words (2 Corinthians 12:2, 4).

On 3 April 1836, one week after the dedication of the Kirtland Temple, the Savior appeared to Joseph Smith and Oliver Cowdery and accepted the temple. Then Moses, Elias, and Elijah appeared and restored significant keys of the priesthood. In introducing this vision, Joseph stated: "*The veil was taken from our minds, and the eyes of our understanding were opened.* We saw the Lord standing upon the breastwork of the pulpit, before us; and under his feet was a paved work of pure gold" (Doctrine and Covenants 110:1–2; emphasis added).

Eighty-two years later, the Prophet's nephew Joseph F. Smith was blessed to receive what we now know and treasure as the vision of the redemption of the dead (Doctrine and Covenants 138), a precious glimpse into the postmortal spirit world. President Smith beheld as the crucified Lord entered paradise and opened the door for the gospel to be taught and redemption to be made available for those who had never been blessed to have the fulness of the gospel in their lives. After speaking of how he had pondered upon the scriptures—and specifically the apostle Peter's declaration that Jesus had gone into the spirit world following his death (1 Peter 3:18–20; 4:6)—President Smith declared: "As I pondered over these things which are written, *the eyes of my understanding were opened, and the Spirit of the Lord rested upon me,* and I saw the hosts of the dead, both small and great" (Doctrine and Covenants 138:1–11; emphasis added).

Do we see the pattern? Do we grasp the fact that a supernal work of the Holy Ghost is to open our eyes, take the veil therefrom, and enlighten our understandings, all that we may "see and understand the things of God" (Doctrine and Covenants 76:12)? We hasten to add, however, that visions are not reserved for prophets only. God does not just bless and endow office holders. In the words of Nephi, our Heavenly Father "is the same yesterday, today, and forever; and the way is prepared for all men [and women] from the foundation of the world, if it so be that they repent and come unto him. For he that diligently seeketh shall find; and the mysteries of God shall be unfolded unto them, by the power of the Holy Ghost" (1 Nephi 10:18–19). The rank and file members of the Church of Jesus Christ—those who have come out of the world of darkness into the Lord's marvelous gospel light (1 Peter 2:9)—these are they who, according to the will and wisdom of God, are granted visions. The Prophet Joseph Smith taught that "it is the privilege of the children of God to come to God and get revelation. . . . God is not a respecter of persons; we all have the same privilege."[3] A more emphatic statement is that "God hath not revealed anything to Joseph, but what He will make known unto the Twelve, and even the least Saint may know all things as fast as he is able to bear them."[4]

In addition, on sacred occasions, those loved ones who have passed through death into the postmortal spirit world are permitted to minister or appear to family members who are in need of comfort, divine guidance, or warnings. At the April 1916 general conference, President Joseph F. Smith delivered a powerful address entitled "In the Presence of the Divine," in which he spoke of the nearness of deceased family members. President Smith explained that "surely those who have passed beyond, can see more clearly through the veil back here to us than it is possible for us to see to them from our sphere of action. I believe we move and have our being in the presence of heavenly messengers and of heavenly beings. We are not separate from them.

"We begin to realize . . . that we are closely related to our kindred, to our ancestors, to our friends and associates and co-laborers who have preceded us into the spirit world. We cannot forget them; we do not cease to love them; . . . they see the dangers that beset us; they . . . see the temptations and the evils that beset us in life and . . . hence their

3. *Joseph Smith* [manual], 132.
4. Discourse, between ca. 26 June and ca. 2 July 1839; see also *Words of Joseph Smith*, 4.

solicitude for us, and their love for us, and their desire for our well be-ing, must be greater than that which we feel for ourselves."[5]

President George Albert Smith likewise emphasized that "those who are on the other side [of the veil] are . . . anxious about us. They are praying for us and for our success. They are pleading, in their own way, for their descendants, for their posterity who live upon the earth."[6]

Visions are given to persons in a waking state, whereas inspired *dreams* come while the recipients sleep. Though not all dreams are vi-sions, some are. "One of the most memorable and powerful patterns of communication by the Spirit," Elder Richard G. Scott pointed out, "is through dreams. I have learned that when the transition from being fully asleep to being fully awake is almost imperceptible, it is a signal that the Lord has taught something very important through a dream."[7]

Joseph of old who was sold into Egypt had inspired dreams and interpreted others' dreams (Genesis 37:5–11; 40:1–19; 41:1–8, 14–38). Lehi's dream, also viewed by his son Nephi, was a dream-vision (1 Nephi 8, 11–14). King Nebuchadnezzar's dream concerning the nations and kingdoms of the earth and the latter-day establishment of the kingdom of God, was clearly a vision (Daniel 2).

While I served as a full-time missionary in the Eastern States, then-Elder Harold B. Lee, who visited New York City often to attend busi-ness meetings, spoke periodically to the elders and sisters. So many of the things he taught us changed my life with respect to how I viewed

---

5. *Messages of the First Presidency*, 5:6–7.

6. *Teachings of George Albert Smith*, 27. Elder Parley P. Pratt wrote poetically: "With what tenderness of love, with what solicitude of affection will they [loved ones on the other side of the veil] watch over our slumbers . . . and seek to com-municate with our spirits, to warn us of dangers or temptation, to comfort and soothe our sorrow, or to ward off the ills that might befall us, or perchance to give us some kind of token of remembrance or undying love!" (*Key to the Science of Theology*, 121–22).

7. *21 Principles*, 76.

the scriptures, how I came to love, admire, and sustain Church leaders, and how I tried to prepare myself to receive divine guidance. On one occasion, he said to the missionaries: "Never disregard any dream, especially one that tends to stay with you, one that you cannot seem to shake."

In an address delivered to students at Brigham Young University on the many ways by which God can reveal himself to us, Elder Lee later commented: "Now there's one more way by which revelations may come, and that is by dreams. Oh, I'm not going to tell you that every dream you have is a direct revelation from the Lord—it may be fried liver and onions that have been responsible for an upset or a disorder. But *I fear that in this age of sophistication there are those of us who are prone to rule out all dreams as of no purpose, and of no moment.* And yet all through the scriptures there were recorded incidents where the Lord, by dreams, has directed His people."[8]

Allow me to be a bit personal here. My father was a man whose inspired dreams significantly affected his life and the life of our family. He was encouraged by them, warned by them, and taught valuable lessons through them. In light of what I observed in my dad's life, Elder Lee's counsel has been of enormous importance to me and my family. While I would not say that such dreams have been a frequent occurrence, they have been given to me often enough to teach me to discern very carefully between a dream that is divinely sent and has a meaningful message and a dream that may have resulted from something unusual I ate for dinner that evening.

My dad passed away in March 1988. Because my wife and children and I had lived in either Florida, Georgia, or Utah for so many years, we were able to see Mom and Dad in Louisiana only once or twice each year. Dad did everything he could to be a positive and inspiring influence in our lives during the short week or two that we were able

8. *Stand Ye in Holy Places*, 142; emphasis added.

to spend with them. I do not hesitate to say, however, that his presence and influence have been felt far more often and far more profoundly since his death than they ever were before. That special care and concern have been felt and experienced often through dreams. It has always been the case that when I awoke following such a dream, I have felt an unusual spiritual presence, such that I knew very well to attend carefully and quickly to what I had just been taught.

A STILL, SMALL VOICE

After Elijah the prophet had finished his contest with the wicked priests of Baal, after it had become clear to the Israelites in attendance that Jehovah was God, it seems that Elijah had supposed that such a miracle would result in a more dedicated and committed people, and certainly not that they would conspire to take his life. Unfortunately, there did not seem to be a dramatic or even noticeable change in the hearts of the people. Elijah "went a day's journey into the wilderness" and even considered in his most deflated moment that he was ready to die. He fell asleep under a juniper tree. An angel touched and awoke him and invited him to have something to eat, after which he "went in the strength of that meat [food] forty days and forty nights unto Horeb the mount of God. And he came thither unto a cave, and lodged there; and, behold, the word of the Lord came to him, and [the angel] said unto him, What doest thou here, Elijah?" Elijah explained to the angel his frustration and pain: "the children of Israel have forsaken thy covenant, . . . and I, even I only, am left; and they seek my life, to take it away."

The angel directed Elijah, "Go forth, and stand upon the mount before the Lord. And, behold, the Lord passed by, and a great and strong wind rent the mountains, and brake in pieces the rocks before the Lord; but *the Lord was not in the wind:* and after the wind an earthquake; but *the Lord was not in the earthquake:* and after the earthquake a fire; but *the Lord was not in the fire:* and after the fire *a still small voice*"

(1 Kings 19:4–12; emphasis added). The expression "still small voice" is very familiar to Latter-day Saints, for we hear frequently from our leaders of our need to purify our lives so that we will be in a position to hear that voice. It is fascinating to learn how this expression is rendered in other translations of the Bible. In the New American Standard Bible it is "a gentle blowing"; in the Revised English Bible it is "a faint murmuring sound"; in the English Standard Bible it is "a low whisper"; in the New International Version it is "a gentle whisper"; and in the New Revised Standard Version it is "sheer silence." The language in the Doctrine and Covenants follows that of the King James Version—"still small voice" (Doctrine and Covenants 85:6).

The voice of God came to a group of Lamanites who had been taught the gospel by Nephi and Lehi, sons of Helaman. Of that voice, Mormon writes that "it was not a voice of thunder, neither was it a voice of a great tumultuous noise, but behold, it was *a still voice of perfect mildness, as if it had been a whisper,* and it did pierce even to the very soul" (Helaman 5:30; emphasis added). Mormon offered a very similar description of the voice of God the Father introducing his Beloved Son to the Nephites. It was "not a harsh voice, neither was it a loud voice; nevertheless, and notwithstanding it being a small voice it did pierce them that did hear to the center, insomuch that there was no part of their frame that it did not cause to quake; yea, it did pierce them to the very soul, and did cause their hearts to burn" (3 Nephi 11:3).

What is the message of these sacred episodes for us? So very often men and women expect God's answers and his actions to be powerful, dramatic, sensational, but most of the time our Heavenly Father, his Son Jesus Christ, and the Holy Ghost work quietly, peacefully, and, if we are not carefully attentive, almost imperceptibly. As one study Bible put it, "The emphasis on Mount Carmel [where Elijah challenged the priests of Baal] had been on *God's spectacular ways,* particularly his use of fire. The emphasis here is on *God's quiet ways.* He is not to be found in the spectacular elements of the storm outside the cave but instead in a low whisper."[9]

When President Gordon B. Hinckley was interviewed by CBS commentator Mike Wallace, one of the questions Mr. Wallace addressed to the prophet was, "The Mormons, Mr. President, call you a 'living Moses,' a prophet who literally communicates with Jesus. How do you do that?" President Hinckley's answer was most interesting: "Let me say first that there is a tremendous history behind this church, a history of prophecy, a history of revelation, and a backlog of decisions which set the pattern of the Church so that there aren't constantly recurring problems that require any special dispensation. But there are occasionally things that arise where the will of the Lord is sought, and in those circumstances I think the best way I could describe the process is to liken it to the experience of Elijah as set forth in First Kings. Elijah spoke to the Lord and there was a wind, a great wind, and the Lord was not in the wind. And there was a tempest, or an earthquake, and the Lord was not in the earthquake. And there was a fire, and the Lord was not in the fire. And after the fire *a still, small voice, which I describe as the whisperings of the Spirit.* Now, let me say, categorically, that *the things of God are understood by the Spirit of God, and one must have and seek and cultivate that Spirit, and there comes understanding and it is real.* I can give testimony of that."[10]

"I learned," Elder Ronald A. Rasband taught, "that the Holy Ghost speaks to us through thoughts in our mind and peaceful feelings in our heart. . . . Sometimes the voice was very soft. I had to be quiet on the inside and on the outside to recognize it. And if I didn't listen the first

---

9. *English Standard Version Study Bible*, 636; emphasis added.

10. In Dew, *Go Forward with Faith*, 585–86; emphasis added. President Wilford Woodruff observed that "man is apt to look too high or expect too great things so that they often times mistake the Spirit of God and the inspiration of the Almighty. It is not in the thunder or whirlwind that we should look for the Spirit of God but in the still small voice" (*Wilford Woodruff* [manual], 50).

time or the second time, it became softer and softer until I couldn't feel it any more."[11]

PEACE

Another means by which Deity communicates with humanity, one that is linked closely to the still, small voice, is *peace.* Indeed, one of the precious but often overlooked aspects of revelation through our feelings is peace. In one sense, to be at peace is to have received a meaningful revelation, to have the inner awareness that God is pleased with one's life and that the course charted by the individual is in harmony with the divine will (Doctrine and Covenants 59:23). In another sense, peace is a means by which the Lord responds to petitions and answers prayers. "Blessed art thou," the Savior said to Oliver Cowdery, "for what thou hast done; for thou hast inquired of me [concerning the truthfulness of the Restoration], and behold, as often as thou hast inquired thou hast received instruction of my Spirit. . . . Behold, thou knowest that thou hast inquired of me and I did enlighten thy mind; and now I tell thee these things that thou mayest know that thou has been enlightened by the Spirit of truth." The Lord then continued with his instructions and an invitation: "Verily, verily, I say unto you, if you desire a further witness, cast your mind upon the night that you cried unto me in your heart, that you might know concerning the truth of these things" (Doctrine and Covenants 6:14–15, 22).

As a schoolteacher in the area, and while residing in the Joseph Smith Sr. home, Oliver had inquired of the Lord concerning the truthfulness of the Smith family's claims concerning Joseph Jr. and the coming forth of the Book of Mormon. This information is found in the earliest (1832) history prepared by the Prophet Joseph. The account speaks of the Prophet receiving once again the plates after being chastened by God for allowing the 116 manuscript pages to be lost: "After much humility

11. *Led by Divine Design,* 24–25.

and affliction of soul, I obtained them again when *the Lord appeared unto a young man by the name of Oliver Cowdery and shewed unto him the plates in a vision and also the truth of the work* and what the Lord was about to do through me, his unworthy servant."[12] "Did I not speak peace to your mind concerning the matter?" the Lord asked. "What greater witness can you have than from God?" (Doctrine and Covenants 6:23).

It is a remarkable thought that even more powerful than the vision Oliver saw in his initial investigation of the restored gospel, was the peace that came to him in the Smith home in answer to his prayer. It was a peace that was conveyed through the power of the Holy Spirit, a peace that assured and reassured him that the course he was then pursuing was approved of God. Through the Psalmist, Jehovah spoke: "Be still, and know that I am God" (Psalm 46:10; compare Doctrine and Covenants 101:16).

"The world grows increasingly noisy," President Boyd K. Packer observed. "Raucous music, with obscene lyrics blasted through amplifiers while lights flash psychedelic colors, characterizes the drug culture. Variations of these things are gaining wide acceptance and influence over our youth. . . . This trend to more noise, more excitement, more contention, less restraint, less dignity, less formality is not coincidental nor innocent nor harmless. The first order issued by a commander mounting a military invasion is the jamming of the channels of communication of those he intends to conquer. . . . No one of us can survive in the world of today, much less in what it soon will become, without personal inspiration."[13]

THOUGHTS AND FEELINGS

In early June 1829, Oliver Cowdery went to Harmony, Pennsylvania, to work with the Prophet Joseph Smith in translating the gold plates.

---

12. *Personal Writings of Joseph Smith*, 12; emphasis added.
13. "Reverence Invites Revelation," *Ensign*, November 1991, 22–23.

During that time several revelations were given to Joseph and Oliver. One of them stated: "Oliver Cowdery, verily, verily, I say unto you, that assuredly as the Lord liveth, who is your God and your Redeemer, even so surely shall you receive a knowledge of whatsoever things you shall ask in faith, with an honest heart. . . . Yea, behold, *I will tell you in your mind and in your heart, by the Holy Ghost,* which shall come upon you and which shall dwell in your heart. *Now, behold, this is the spirit of revelation; behold, this is the spirit by which Moses brought the children of Israel through the Red Sea on dry ground"* (Doctrine and Covenants 8:1–3; emphasis added).

Let's reflect for a moment. Moses was the head of a dispensation, the Lawgiver, the deliverer of the Israelites from Egyptian bondage, the most meek man on earth during his time (Numbers 12:3). Moses was eventually translated, taken from the earth without tasting death (Alma 45:17–19).[14] Jehovah explained to Aaron and Miriam, Moses's brother and sister, that while He usually communicated with his prophets through visions and dreams, with Moses he spoke face to face (Numbers 12:6–8; Exodus 33:11). Yet Doctrine and Covenants 8:3 indicates that Moses—like all prophets, and, for that matter, all men and women—walked and was led most often and most surely by the kindly light and whisperings of the Holy Spirit. It was by means of these thoughts (in his mind) and feelings (in his heart) that Moses knew to part the Red Sea and enable the children of Israel to cross over on dry ground.

Regarding thoughts coming into our minds, the Prophet Joseph Smith stated that "a person may profit by noticing the first intimation of the spirit of revelation; for instance, when you feel pure intelligence flowing into you, it may give you sudden strokes of ideas, so that by noticing it, you may find it fulfilled the same day or soon; (i.e.) those things that were presented unto your minds by the Spirit of God, will come to pass; and thus by learning the Spirit of God and

---

14. Joseph Fielding Smith, *Doctrines of Salvation*, 3:107–12.

understanding it, you may grow into the principle of revelation, until you become perfect in Christ Jesus."[15]

We add here that almost always a revelation from God will be rational, will make sense, will be in harmony with the commonly accepted standards and ideals set down by God and prophets and the laws of the land. "In the Church," President Boyd K. Packer pointed out, "we are not exempt from common sense. You can know to begin with that you won't be prompted from any righteous source to steal, to lie, to cheat, to join anyone in any kind of moral transgression."[16] Yes, God did command Abraham to sacrifice Isaac and Nephi to slay Laban, but these were rare exceptions, and both Abraham and Nephi were prophets and seers; they knew the voice of the Lord implicitly and thus could be guided by the Spirit, which became a constant companion. We would be well advised to abide by the rule and leave the exceptions to God and his prophets. The Lord will not reveal to an individual member of the Church anything that is out of harmony with law and order and good judgment or in conflict with the order of the Church. Further, God will never call upon his people to perform an action that is unnatural or indecorous in the eyes of God and man.[17]

This is not to say that a revelation from God might not strike us as unusual, perhaps even at variance with the way we feel about things. President John Taylor spoke of an occasion when he was instructed by the Prophet Joseph Smith relative to personal revelation. "I well remember," he said, "a remark that Joseph Smith made to me upwards of forty years ago. Said he, 'Elder Taylor, you have been baptized, you have had hands laid upon your head for the reception of the Holy Ghost, and you have been ordained to the holy priesthood. Now, if you will continue to follow the leadings of that spirit, it will always lead you

---

15. *Joseph Smith* [manual], 132.
16. "Prayers and Answers," *Ensign*, November 1979, 21.
17. "Try the Spirits," *Times and Seasons* 3, no. 11 (1 April 1842): 745.

right. Sometimes it might be contrary to your judgment; never mind that, follow its dictates; and if you be true to its whisperings it will in time become in you a principle of revelation so that you will know all things.'"[18]

When the Prophet Joseph received what we know as the vision of the glories (Doctrine and Covenants 76), this magnificent revelation was difficult for some of those early converts to the restored Church to accept. Most had come from Protestant churches, which of course teach only of a heaven and a hell hereafter. Even our beloved Brigham Young, who had Methodist roots, struggled for a time with this wholly new concept to which Jesus had referred when he spoke of his Father having many mansions (John 14:2).

President Young stated that when the concept of varying degrees of glory "first came to me, it was so directly contrary and opposed to my education and traditions. I didn't reject it, but I could not understand it. *I would think and pray, read and think, pray and reflect,* until I knew and fully understood it myself, by the visions of the Holy Spirit."[19]

The Spirit can also make things known to us through our *feelings.* "We hear the words of the Lord most often by a feeling," President Ezra Taft Benson taught. "If we are humble and sensitive, the Lord will prompt us through our feelings. That is why spiritual promptings move us on occasion to great joy, sometimes to tears. . . . *The Holy Ghost causes our feelings to be more tender. We feel more charitable and compassionate. We are calmer. We have a greater capacity to love.* People want to be around us because our very countenances radiate the influence of the Spirit."[20]

President Packer offered valuable instruction when he taught that

18. *Joseph Smith* [manual], 132–33.

19. Discourse, 29 August 1852; Minutes, *Deseret News Extra,* 14 September 1852, 22–25.

20. *Come unto Christ,* 20; emphasis added.

"these delicate, refined spiritual communications are not seen with our eyes nor heard with our ears. And even though it is described as a voice, it is a voice that one feels more than one hears [see 1 Nephi 17:45]. . . . The Spirit does not get our attention by shouting or shaking us with a heavy hand. Rather it whispers. It caresses so gently that if we are preoccupied we may not feel it at all. . . . . Occasionally it will press just firmly enough for us to pay heed. But most of the time, if we do not heed the gentle feeling, the Spirit will withdraw and wait until we come seeking and listening and say in our manner and expression, like Samuel of ancient times, 'Speak, for thy servant heareth.'"[21]

There may well be as many means of divine communication as there are individuals to receive them. The Lord through his Spirit communicates to us through patriarchal blessings, father's blessings, confirmations, ordinations, and settings apart. He speaks to us as our teachers or leaders speak or counsel us by the power of the Spirit. The head of this dispensation declared that "We believe that we have a right to revelations, visions, and dreams from God, our heavenly Father; and light and intelligence, through the gift of the Holy Ghost, in the name of Jesus Christ, on all subjects pertaining to our spiritual welfare; if it so be that we keep his commandments, so as to render ourselves worthy in his sight."[22]

"If we will live worthy," President Harold B. Lee declared, "then the Lord will guide us—by a personal appearance, or by His actual voice, or by His voice coming into our mind, or by impressions upon our heart and our soul. And oh, how grateful we ought to be if the Lord sends us a dream in which are revealed to us the beauties of the

21. *That All May Be Edified*, 335–37; President Packer was referring to the incident in 1 Samuel 3:10.
22. *Joseph Smith* [manual], 132.

eternity or a warning and direction for our special comfort. Yes, if we so live, the Lord will guide us for our salvation and our benefit."[23]

Sister Julie B. Beck, former General President of the Relief Society, testified that "the ability to qualify for, receive, and act on personal revelation is the single most important skill that can be acquired in this life."[24] "As we pursue the journey of life," President Thomas S. Monson counseled simply, "let us learn the language of the Spirit."[25] I know from all that I have read and heard—but more important, I know from all I have experienced—that God is merciful and gracious to those who honor and serve him. "Yea, even the wonders of eternity shall they know, and things to come will I show them, even the things of many generations. And their wisdom shall be great, and their understanding reach to heaven" (Doctrine and Covenants 76:8–9). The gift of the Holy Ghost places such consummate blessings within our reach, all in the Lord's "own time, and in his own way, and according to his own will" (Doctrine and Covenants 88:68). May we be prepared and in readiness for when the Almighty chooses to part the veil and impart sacred matters to us.

23. *Stand Ye in Holy Places*, 144.
24. "And upon the Handmaids in Those Days Will I Pour Out My Spirit," *Ensign*, May 2010, 11.
25. "The Spirit Giveth Life," *Ensign*, May 1985, 70.

Chapter 12

THE SPIRIT WORKS
THROUGH MORTALS

God spoke through the prophets anciently, and their teachings were absolutely essential to persons living in that day. One of the fascinating features of the economy of God is the fact that those same messages find lodgment in the hearts of persons living hundreds, even thousands of years later. It is not just that the principles set forth in ancient scripture are very often applicable to our lives, as significant as that is. It is also astonishing how frequently women and men read a passage of scripture and then God, in an act of pure grace and through the work of the Holy Spirit, causes those few verses to leap off the page, as though that scriptural message had been given to the reader in the first instance. Holy scripture is thereby eternally relevant.

In addition, far more often than we realize, our Father in heaven communicates important matters to us through the instrumentality of sensitive, caring persons who come into our life at just the right time, sometimes just the right moment. We would be wise to follow the scriptural injunction: "Be not forgetful to entertain strangers: for thereby some have entertained angels unawares" (Hebrews 13:2).

THROUGH THE WORDS OF PROPHETS

Through the years I have on many occasions felt the Spirit whispering to me through the holy scriptures. While most of the time the scriptures tend to settle my soul, quiet my inner noise, or solidify my doctrinal understanding, on other occasions they have provided specific counsel or particular direction. As an example, during the early part of my full-time mission, my companion and I spent a great deal of time and energy tracting or doing door-to-door contacting. In looking back, tracting did tend to build one's discipline, form one's character, and assist young elders and sisters to feel more confident in greeting and testifying to total strangers. And yes, there have been many, many times when knocking on someone's door has resulted in convert baptisms.

The challenge with this method of finding investigators to teach is this: experience suggests that approximately a thousand people must be contacted in order to identify someone who is interested in hearing the message of the restored gospel. Clearly the more effective way of finding persons interested in the restored gospel is through member referrals, through investigators being taught in members' homes. I clearly remember very well tracting in western Massachusetts for many, many hours each day for several weeks. We had found no one to teach. I was feeling very discouraged, wondering seriously whether this was in fact the best way to spend my life. My companion and I came home to our apartment for lunch, he went into the kitchen to prepare the meal, and I loosened my tie and sat in a large chair in the small living room. I remember that my emotions were very close to the surface; this mission wasn't at all what I had imagined it would be.

I picked up my triple combination and placed it on my lap. Like you, I had heard marvelous stories of persons who were burdened or disappointed or in search of an answer picking up their scriptures and allowing them to simply open to a passage that either comforted or informed them. I had tried it a few times, but mostly I had found myself staring at the book of Leviticus or the gazetteer! Sensing, however, that I had nothing to lose, I decided to try it once more. In this case my scriptures opened to section 64 of the Doctrine and Covenants. I looked down more closely, and my eyes focused on the following:

"Wherefore, be not weary in well-doing, for ye are laying the foundation of a great work. And out of small things proceedeth that which is great" (Doctrine and Covenants 64:33). Tears came to my eyes, and a quiet comfort came into my mind and heart. It was what we call a tender mercy, a little thing with profound implications, a message that would serve me well again and again when I found myself in need of reassurance and recommitment.

Jeffrey R. Holland, then president of Brigham Young University, delivered an important address to faculty and staff. He spoke of a difficult time when, from his perspective, he felt that something "didn't seem quite right at the university, and found [himself] wondering if all the effort was really worth it." He wondered, for example, whether the Church really needed a university. "After all," he said, "the Church had disengaged from a number of operations, which included not only hospitals and hotels, but of far more interest to us, schools." Being physically and mentally exhausted, he decided to go to bed but realized that he had not spent time with the scriptures that day, something he always tried to do, even if he had time and energy for only one verse. President Holland decided to open the scriptures and attend to the first words he saw. He did so, and his eyes fell upon the following verse: "Behold, I say unto you, concerning the school in Zion, I, the Lord, am well pleased that *there should be a school in Zion*" (Doctrine and Covenants 97:3; emphasis added). "The words hit me like a jackhammer," he said. "I chilled and blushed and chilled again. I stood up and walked around the room. I'm not embarrassed to tell you I was emotional." President Holland concluded, "I got a pat on the backside that night that suggested I stop whining and go to work; there was an inheritance to be claimed."[1]

The Spirit can teach us, expand our understanding, strengthen our testimonies, and fortify us against sin and the wiles of the devil in

---

1. "School in Zion."

numerous ways. Because "true doctrine, understood, changes attitudes and behavior,"[2] the study of the doctrine found within holy writ can bring to pass remarkable changes in us, affecting profoundly how we feel about life, what we sense about the purposes of the Almighty, and what the Lord would direct us to do at that point in time. By reading of and pondering on great men and women of faith and righteous tenacity, we can have our own faith strengthened and our own spine stiffened. By exploring how God teaches, trains, empowers, chastens, and sanctifies noble souls in scripture who have since gone on to their glory, we come to better understand, by the enticing power of the Holy Ghost, the character, attributes, perfections, and holiness of the Father and the Son.

In a revelation given to Oliver Cowdery and David Whitmer in June 1829, Jesus Christ, in speaking of the words of modern revelation, declared: "These words are not of men nor of man, but of me; wherefore, you shall testify they are of me and not of man; for *it is my voice which speaketh them unto you; for they are given by my Spirit unto you,* and by my power [his Spirit] you can read them one to another; and save it were by my power you could not have them; wherefore, *you can testify that you have heard my voice,* and know my words" (Doctrine and Covenants 18:34–36; emphasis added). Could there be any greater motivation to search, ponder, and pray over the scriptures? When we read scripture, we are able to hear the Lord's words. Reading his word brings his Spirit, which is his voice. "Behold, that which you hear is as the voice of one crying in the wilderness—in the wilderness, because you cannot see him—my voice, because *my voice is Spirit*" (Doctrine and Covenants 88:66; emphasis added). In short, when we feel the Lord's Spirit operating in our lives, we are hearing his voice. It is a voice that whispers God's love, his approval, his acceptance of our offering.

And what is true of the words of Enoch and Abraham and Moses

---

2. Boyd K. Packer, "Little Children," *Ensign*, November 1986, 17.

and Peter and John—all former-day Saints—is equally true of the words of the latter-day prophets who have succeeded Joseph Smith. These are the living oracles of our day, and we have been charged to beware how we attend to their words, "lest they are accounted as a light thing, and are brought under condemnation thereby, and stumble and fall when the storms descend, and the winds blow, and the rains descend, and beat upon [our] house" (Doctrine and Covenants 90:5).

In an 1883 revelation received by President John Taylor, the Lord stated: "I will reveal unto you, from time to time, through the channels that I have appointed, everything that shall be necessary for the future development and perfection of my Church, for the adjustment and rolling forth of my kingdom."[3] The words of the prophets and seers must become our words, their witness our witness. "We often hear it said that the living oracles must be in the Church," President Brigham Young explained, "in order that the kingdom of God may be established and prosper on the earth. I will give another version of this sentiment. I say that the living oracles of God, or the Spirit of revelation must be in each and every individual, to know the plan of salvation and keep in the path that leads them to the presence of God."[4]

President Spencer W. Kimball offered priceless advice on how to increase our personal spirituality. "I find that when I get casual in my relationship with divinity," he explained, "and when it seems that no divine ear is listening and no divine voice is speaking, that I am far, far away. If I immerse myself in the scriptures the distance narrows and the spirituality returns. I find myself loving more intensely those whom I must love with all my heart and mind and strength, and loving them more, I find it easier to abide their counsel."[5] Notice what follows a sincere search of scripture: the distance between God and the individual

---

3. In *Messages of the First Presidency,* 2:354.
4. In *Journal of Discourses,* 9:279.
5. *Teachings of Spencer W. Kimball,* 135.

narrows; spirituality returns; there is an eagerness to love others more deeply; and, one feels an inclination to follow counsel.

One Christian leader put it this way: "Reading scripture, like praying and sharing in the sacraments [ordinances], is one of the means by which the life of heaven and the life of earth interlock. (This is what older writers were referring to when they spoke of 'the means of grace.' It isn't that we can control God's grace, but that there are, so to speak, places to go where God has promised to meet with his people.) . . . We read scripture in order to hear God addressing us—*us,* here and now, today."[6]

THROUGH OTHER PEOPLE

In the Book of Mormon we read of a tragic and poignant moment in the lives of King Mosiah and Alma. These two noble souls had given themselves to the gospel cause and laid their all on the altar of Christ. What might otherwise have been a joyful season in life was flawed by the disobedience and waywardness of their own sons. Alma the Younger and the sons of Mosiah were among the unbelievers who had actually begun to fight against the Church of Christ and to lead others astray. Of Alma the Younger, the account states that he "was a man of many words, and did speak much flattery to the people; therefore he led many of the people to do after the manner of his iniquities. And he became a great hinderment to the prosperity of the church of God; stealing away the hearts of the people; causing much dissension among the people; giving a chance for the enemy of God to exercise his power over them" (Mosiah 27:8–9).[7] One can only imagine the

---

6. Wright, *Simply Christian*, 188.

7. At a BYU devotional, Elder Bruce R. McConkie said about Alma the Younger: "He had been baptized in his youth, he had been promised the Holy Ghost, but he had never received it. He was too worldly-wise; he went off with the sons of Mosiah to destroy the Church and to do away with the teachings of his father, who in effect was President of the Church. He was fighting, and in opposition to the truth; he was like the college student who thinks he knows more than the Lord because he has learned a little science, and it does not seem to fit in

grief and perhaps embarrassment the king and president of the Church must have felt as they preached of the importance of love and fidelity to truth and the joys of family living while at the same time their own sons were actively leading people away from the Church.

Mormon wrote that "as they were going about rebelling against God, behold, the angel of the Lord appeared unto them; and he descended as it were in a cloud; and he spake as it were with a voice of thunder, which caused the earth to shake upon which they stood." The angel said unto Alma: "Behold, the Lord hath heard the prayers of his people, and also the prayers of his servant, Alma, who is thy father; for he has prayed with much faith concerning thee that thou mightest be brought to the knowledge of the truth; therefore, for this purpose have I come to convince thee of the power and authority of God, that the prayers of his servants might be answered according to their faith" (Mosiah 27:14).

Alma and the sons of Mosiah were stopped in their tracks, as it were, turned about and redirected. Alma underwent a spiritual transformation; he was justified and born again—changed from a carnal and fallen state to a state of righteousness (Mosiah 27:24–25). The sons of Mosiah—Ammon, Aaron, Omner, and Himni—underwent a similar transformation (Mosiah 28:3). Thereafter the sons of Mosiah devoted themselves wholly to the work of the Lord and were directly involved in the conversion of thousands of Lamanite souls to the gospel. Their conversion could not repair every damage and retrieve every apostate word, so Alma and the sons of Mosiah transferred their burden to God and yielded themselves to the work of the Master. They "labored without ceasing, that [they] might bring souls unto repentance; that [they]

---

to what his parents have been telling him about the plan of salvation. Alma was in this state, and then this occasion occurred when a new light came into his soul, when he was changed from his fallen and carnal state to a state of righteousness" (*Doctrines of the Restoration*, 137).

might bring them to taste of the exceeding joy of which [they] did taste; that they might also be born of God, and be filled with the Holy Ghost" (Alma 36:24).

This is a remarkable story, an inspiring narrative, one that yields significant lessons for life, lessons that span the chasm of time. The Spirit of the Lord touched these apostate wanderers in a way that changed not only them but also the course of Book of Mormon history. One important lesson of this story is that no one of us is beyond spiritual recovery, that "all are within the reach of pardoning mercy, who have not committed the unpardonable sin."[8] God can recognize goodness and potential within each of us, as he did with Saul of Tarsus, the infamous persecutor of the Christians. When Ananias hesitated to assist this enemy of the faith after Saul had been struck down on the road to Damascus, the Lord said boldly: "Go thy way: for [Saul] is a chosen vessel unto me, to bear my name before the Gentiles, and kings, and the children of Israel" (Acts 9:15).

Second, parents may find special comfort in this story, particularly parents of children who have wandered from the fold. From personal experience I know only too well that it is extremely difficult to keep going, to do all the right things, to keep one's head up and one's courage intact—it is extremely tough to stay on the covenant path ourselves when those we love the most forsake the faith and way of life to which we have dedicated and consecrated ourselves. And yet the promise is extended to all of us that "the effectual fervent prayer of a righteous man availeth much" (James 5:16) and that both in time and in eternity our God will wipe away all tears (Isaiah 25:8; Revelation 7:17; 21:4). Parents thus hope on, pray on, and trust in the power of the gospel covenant to restore, renew, and rekindle the flame of faith in the hearts of our children.

I have recounted this story because of a life-changing experience

---

8. *Joseph Smith* [manual], 76.

I had several years ago when I was instructed through the medium of memory while pondering on this grand Book of Mormon conversion story. About the time I turned eighteen years of age, I was deeply involved in the activities and programs of the Church. I was a stake missionary, had memorized some of the missionary discussions and scriptures, and worked closely and regularly with the full-time missionaries. I was so excited about serving a full-time mission that I couldn't wait for the time to pass when my bishop (who was also my dad) and I could begin the paperwork and interviews. All was well for several months, and then, without warning, my attitudes and my ideas began to change. I gradually began to think more and more about life at home, about friends and school, and about how long two years really was. In looking back now on that season of my life, there's no question but that Satan began to make subtle inroads into my resolve to serve a full-time mission.

I remember my father sitting down with me on a number of occasions at about the time of my nineteenth birthday and asking: "Well, son, shall we begin the process?"

My answer went something like, "I really do want to do this, but I just don't feel prepared yet. I'm not quite ready."

This conversation happened at least three times. The last time my dad heard those words about my lack of readiness he gently and lovingly said, in effect, "Robert, this is your decision. It's something you need to do on your own. You need to pray sincerely about it. Your mom and I will never pressure or push you to go on a mission." And then he added this pertinent comment: "But let me say one more thing. You're as ready as anyone I know. If you wait until you are perfectly prepared to go, you will never go." His words meant something to me, mainly because I had such a deep respect for my father and for his example of commitment to the kingdom. I didn't, however, make any progress toward beginning the process.

A few days after my interview with Dad there came a phone call for me. The person on the other end of the line said, "Is this you, Robert? This is Aunt Gladys. Do you have a few minutes?"

I asked her if she wanted to speak with my mother, but she quickly replied, "No, you're the one I want to speak to."

I thought it was a little odd that she should call me in the middle of the day, but she was one of my favorite people in the world. Her daughter (my cousin Linda) and I had always been close, and so Aunt Gladys was someone I dearly loved. There's one other thing that made her and my Uncle Joseph special: they had been a significant influence in reactivating our family just after I was baptized. Uncle Joseph had baptized me and my mother (who had been a Methodist) and had written my very first talk (which I memorized and delivered), a brief message on Joseph Smith's First Vision. It was clear from the way they lived and the things they valued that the gospel meant everything to them.

Aunt Gladys and I carried on a light conversation for quite a while, discussing such varied topics as football and college and my social life. Then my aunt surprised me with this question: "Listen, Robert, there are some other things I want to discuss with you. Do you have some time tomorrow?"

I thought and searched and finally admitted I had no plans. "Good," she said. "Why don't you come over and have lunch with me, and we can spend the afternoon together."

I should add here a very important point: Aunt Gladys was one who was close to the Source, one who had lived in tune with the Spirit of the Lord. She always made me slightly nervous when she said something like, "I had a dream the other night . . . ," or "I've been feeling lately as though I ought to . . . ," or as she said to me when she called that day on the phone, "You've been on my mind a lot lately." I had no question but that her impressions, feelings, and dreams were heaven-sent. My respect for her judgment and my awareness of her spirituality combined to cause me some nervousness about spending the afternoon with her, but I agreed to do so anyway.

The next afternoon the time slipped by rather quickly. There was an unusual spirit in her living room as we spoke, and my fears were banished by the wonderful feeling of love and peace I felt there. At the right moment, in a voice that shared her tender concern, she said, in essence, "Robert, I've been worried about you. I have known from the time you were a tiny boy that you should serve a mission and that your mission would chart the course for your life. I want you to know that your Uncle Joseph and I love you, just as if you were one of our own children. Maybe it's out of this love for you, and the deep affection I feel for your mom and dad, that I share with you some feelings I have had during the past few weeks. I feel that it's critical that you leave on a mission, and that you leave soon. If you do not, I'm afraid you will never go." Frankly, I had heard similar words previously from my father. Aunt Gladys's words, nevertheless, went into my heart and burned like fire. I knew that I must serve a mission, that that was what God wanted, and I knew that the time was short. The Lord needed me now. We embraced as I left, and I thanked her for being in tune with the Holy Ghost.

I left within weeks for the Eastern States Mission. As she predicted (and as I knew would be the case), my mission was a turning point in my life. I learned how to be obedient, to work hard, to set and achieve goals, to lead others, to take setbacks and deal productively with adversity, to love and appreciate people, and to acquire and cultivate the spirit of revelation. I developed a love for the scriptures that has never left me. I learned what things matter most in life, how critical it is to have an eye single to the glory of God, and how to consecrate my heart to the gospel cause. Every major decision in my life thereafter—including what kind of person I should marry and how I would know when I found her—has in some degree been made by virtue of what I learned and what I experienced on a mission. Other than my temple marriage, which is the most significant event in my life, the choice to serve a mission is without exception the most far-reaching and influential decision I have ever made.

Over the past few decades as I have rethought my experience with Aunt Gladys, it has become clear to me that although our Heavenly Father will force no man or woman to heaven, he *will* do everything he can to attract and entice us toward the Atonement of Jesus Christ and the fulness of gospel blessings. A zealous but misdirected Saul of Tarsus was redirected by the Lord Jesus himself (Acts 9). Alma's wayward course was interrupted by an angel, and his personal life and the Nephite narrative were never the same thereafter. The Lord Jesus didn't choose to come in person or send an angel from heaven to me, but he did send Aunt Gladys, and my life has not been the same since. Alma may have had his angel, but I had Gladys. And for me at least, the turnaround was just as important.

I am comforted by President Spencer W. Kimball's insight that "God does notice us, and he watches over us. But *it is usually through another mortal that he meets our needs.*"[9] I know that angels have and do and will yet minister to men and women on earth, "so long as time shall last, or the earth shall stand, or there shall be one man upon the face thereof to be saved" (Moroni 7:36). As Nephi taught, "angels"—heavenly messengers as well as inspired mortals—"speak by the power of the Holy Ghost; wherefore, they speak the words of Christ" (2 Nephi 32:3). In being open and receptive to divine direction, we just may have the opportunity to "entertain angels unawares" (Hebrews 13:2), both mortal and heavenly ones. The Almighty, who knows all things from beginning to end, has, does now, and will yet bring to pass great and important things through the sensitive intervention of attentive and caring men and women, men and women who have cultivated the gift and gifts of the Holy Ghost in their lives, who go and do what the Spirit directs.

---

9. *Teachings of Spencer W. Kimball*, 252; emphasis added.

CAREFUL STEWARDS OF WHAT WE RECEIVE

The Holy Ghost is a personal tutor. "The Comforter knoweth all things" (Doctrine and Covenants 42:17); he knows the hearts of every person and the readiness of individuals and congregations to be taught the things of God. Just as no one rushes into the presence of the Lord, so no one should be ushered prematurely into the realm of divine experience. Alma responded to Zeezrom's question concerning the resurrection by teaching a marvelous lesson: "And now Alma began to expound these things unto him, saying: It is given unto many to know the mysteries of God; nevertheless they are laid under a strict command that they shall not impart only according to the portion of the word which he doth grant unto the children of men, according to the heed and diligence which they give unto him.

"And therefore, he that will harden his heart, the same receiveth the lesser portion of the word; and he that will not harden his heart, to him is given the greater portion of the word, until it is given unto him to know the mysteries of God until he know them in full.

"And they that will harden their hearts, to them is given the lesser portion of the word until they know nothing concerning his mysteries; and then they are taken captive by the devil, and led by his will down to destruction. Now this is what is meant by the chains of hell" (Alma 12:9–11).

Those charged with proclaiming the gospel message must be sensitive to the Spirit, discerning enough to recognize that "portion of the word" suited to those being taught. Full-time missionaries, for example, are given specific commission to teach that portion of the word necessary to introduce sincere men and women to the message of the Restoration. They are not commissioned to teach doctrine that would be more easily understood and appreciated after baptism and the reception of the gift of the Holy Ghost. Their specific assignment is to "declare glad tidings"—the tidings that the Lord has spoken anew in our day through modern prophets (Doctrine and Covenants

31:3–4)—and to proclaim that the truthfulness of their message may be known through reading, pondering upon, and praying about the truthfulness of the Book of Mormon.

"And of tenets thou shalt not talk, but thou shalt declare repentance and faith on the Savior, and remission of sins by baptism, and by fire, yea, even the Holy Ghost" (Doctrine and Covenants 19:31). We are to teach those outside the Church how to get into the Church, and thereafter allow the Holy Spirit to teach the fulness of the gospel. "And this is my gospel—repentance and baptism by water, and then cometh the baptism of fire and the Holy Ghost, even the Comforter, which showeth all things, and teacheth the peaceable things of the kingdom" (Doctrine and Covenants 39:6). The Lord explained to Joseph Smith and Sidney Rigdon, "The time has verily come that it is necessary and expedient in me that you should open your mouths in proclaiming my gospel, the things of the kingdom, expounding the mysteries thereof out of the scriptures, according to that portion of Spirit and power which shall be given unto you, even as I will" (Doctrine and Covenants 71:1; compare 84:85).

In the meridian of time Jesus Christ was certainly cautious about how sacred matters were to be taught and distributed. We do not need to search the New Testament record very carefully to discover numerous occasions when the Savior instructed those closest to him to use care in speaking of things sacred. "Go ye into the world," he commanded his disciples, "saying unto all, Repent, for the kingdom of heaven has come nigh unto you. *And the mysteries of the kingdom ye shall keep within yourselves;* for it is not meet to give that which is holy unto the dogs; neither cast ye your pearls unto swine, lest they trample them under their feet. *For the world cannot receive that which ye, yourselves, are not able to bear;* wherefore ye shall not give your pearls unto them, lest they turn again and rend you" (JST, Matthew 7:9–11; emphasis added).

One reason Christ chose to speak in parables was to veil meaning and deeper content from those with spiritually insensitive souls, blind eyes, and deaf ears. "Why speakest thou unto them in parables?" the disciples asked. "He answered and said unto them, Because *it is given unto you to know the mysteries of the kingdom of heaven, but to them it is not given*" (Matthew 13:10–11; emphasis added).

The things of God are to be grasped through the Spirit of God, or they will be understood not at all (1 Corinthians 2:11–14). To present sacred teachings or ordinances to those lacking the gift of the Holy Ghost (and thus the lenses by which holy things are to be seen and grasped) is to risk immediate misunderstanding and subsequent misrepresentation. "*It is not always wise,*" taught Joseph Smith, "*to relate all the truth. Even Jesus, the Son of God, had to refrain from doing so,* and had to restrain His feelings many times for the safety of Himself and His followers, and had to conceal the righteous purposes of His heart in relation to many things pertaining to His Father's kingdom."[10]

Some truths and experiences are unlawful to be uttered in the sense that it is not *permitted* for those within the fold to share them with a doubting world; some special things are to be kept within the household of faith, among those who believe (Moses 1:42; 4:32). The Lord explained in a revelation given in August of 1831: "Remember that *that which cometh from above is sacred, and must be spoken with care, and by constraint of the Spirit; and in this there is no condemnation*" (Doctrine and Covenants 63:64; emphasis added). Members of the Church who have been endowed in the temple, for example, are under covenantal obligation to keep sacred some of the matters taught and revealed there.

Because there are ordinances and practices within the temples which are not public and thus not open for public review, enemies of the Church are eager to point out what they call the cultic nature of

---

10. Cited in Wheelock to George A. Smith, 29 December 1854, [13]–[19]; emphasis added.

the Church. If Latter-day Saints are cultists, then surely—for reasons we have already cited—Jesus of Nazareth was a cultist also, for there were matters which the Master chose to make known only to those willing and able to receive them. President Boyd K. Packer wrote: "Our reluctance to speak of the sacred temple ordinances is not in any way an attempt to make them seem more mysterious or to encourage an improper curiosity about them. The ordinances and ceremonies of the temple are simple. They are beautiful. They are sacred. They are kept confidential lest they be given to those who are unprepared. Curiosity is not a preparation. Deep interest itself is not preparation. Preparation for the ordinances includes preliminary steps: faith, repentance, baptism, confirmation, worthiness, a maturity and dignity worthy of one who comes invited as a guest into the house of the Lord."[11]

When we have received inspiration or divine direction, we must not treat these sacred communications lightly. They are not to be dispersed to the four winds, nor are they to be shouted from the housetops; rather, we must be wise in what we share, and especially careful in what we disclose. "Let us be faithful and silent," Joseph Smith exhorted the Saints, "and if God gives you a manifestation, keep it to yourselves; be watchful and prayerful, and you shall have a prelude of those joys that God will pour out on that day."[12]

And yet, condemnation is the consequence for speaking of that which is intended for our eyes and ears and hearts only. President Brigham Young explained simply that "the Lord has no confidence in those who reveal secrets, for He cannot safely reveal Himself to such persons."[13] In the words of President Marion G. Romney, "*I do not tell all I know;* I have never told my wife all I know, for I have found out that *if I talked too lightly of sacred things, thereafter the Lord would not trust me.*"[14]

11. *Holy Temple,* 26; see also 30.
12. Discourse, 12 November 1835.
13. In *Journal of Discourses,* 4:288.
14. Cited in Packer, "Candle of the Lord," *Ensign,* January 1983, 53; emphasis

Members of The Church of Jesus Christ of Latter-day Saints hold as a cardinal tenet of their faith that God does and will reveal himself, his Son, and the plan of salvation; he does make available to earnest and honest truth seekers a witness of the truthfulness of the message of the Restoration; and he does reveal his mind and will to the least and last Saint as quickly as they are prepared to receive it. Truly we believe that our Father will make known, through his Holy Spirit, "many great and important things pertaining to the kingdom of God" (Articles of Faith 1:9).

These blessings and spiritual endowments—all part of the marvelous flood of light and truth that is the Restoration of the gospel of Jesus Christ—are absolutely within our reach. This is a significant part of our religious heritage and will yet guide the destiny of this latter-day work, including the individual members of the Church. May we live in a state of spiritual readiness, a condition of worthiness, and always maintain a seeking and inquiring mind and heart. By so doing, we may be partakers of such sacred privileges and thereby continue to be partakers of the divine nature (2 Peter 1:4).

---

added.

Chapter 13

SPEAKING WITH THE
TONGUE OF ANGELS

ephi charged his people (and us) to follow the pattern of our great Exemplar, the Lord Jesus Christ, who sought to carry out the will of the Father and submitted to baptism at the hands of John the Baptist. Although Jesus was holy, wholly and completely free of any sin, he showed "unto the children of men that, according to the flesh he humbleth himself before the Father, and witnesseth unto the Father that he would be obedient unto him in keeping his commandments" (2 Nephi 31:7). Nephi added that once a genuine truth seeker has followed the Son "with full purpose of heart, acting no hypocrisy and no deception before God, but with real intent, repenting of your sins, witnessing unto the Father that ye are willing to take upon you the name of Christ, by baptism . . . then cometh the baptism of fire and of the Holy Ghost; and *then can ye speak with the tongue of angels,* and shout praises unto the Holy One of Israel" (2 Nephi 31:13; emphasis added).

THE WORDS OF CHRIST

In 2 Nephi 32 we are given fascinating and unique instructions concerning the tongue of angels. Nephi inquired: "How could ye speak with the tongue of angels save it were by the Holy Ghost? *Angels speak by the power of the Holy Ghost; wherefore, they speak the words of Christ*"

193

(vv. 2–3; emphasis added). If we grasp what Nephi is here striving to teach us, we understand that when a person receives the gift of the Holy Ghost—here equated with "the baptism by fire" (2 Nephi 31:13–14, 17)—he or she is able to speak with the tongue of angels, which Nephi defined as (1) speaking by the power of the Spirit, and thus (2) speaking the words of Christ. We are reminded that when Jesus met with his apostles at the Last Supper, he gave them powerful instructions concerning the Comforter, the Holy Spirit, whom the Father would send to them following the Savior's Crucifixion and Resurrection. Jesus explained that "when he, the Spirit of truth, is come, he will guide you into all truth: for *he shall not speak of himself; but whatsoever he shall hear* [from the Father and the Son], *that shall he speak:* and he will shew you things to come. He shall glorify me: for *he shall receive of mine, and shall shew it unto you*" (John 16:13–14; emphasis added).

One important truth we learn here is that the Holy Ghost, the third member of the Godhead, is not an independent revelator. He does not put forward his own views or his own point of view. Rather, he is the messenger of the first two members of the Godhead and is commissioned to deliver the mind, will, purposes, and words of God the Father and Christ the Son to God's children. And so, when Nephi informs us that those who receive the gift of the Holy Ghost—those who are baptized by fire—are enabled to speak with the tongue of angels, to speak the words of Christ, he is in essence unfolding to us the marvelous oneness of the Father, the Son, the Holy Ghost, and the angels of God. They speak with one and the same mind. That is, what an angel declares is what Jesus or the Father would have declared, and the message is delivered by the power of the Spirit.

Now, let's move from theologizing to practicality. Let's suppose that you have been assigned to speak in next week's sacrament meeting. The member of the bishopric did not mention a specific topic. By Tuesday you have managed to block out a period of time to organize your thoughts and put together a message that you think would edify.

Before you begin to sketch out your outline, however, you drop to your knees in prayer. What will you pray about? What will you request of the Father? What matters so much to you that you feel the need to seek the mind and divine assistance of God? For one thing, you might pray that your mind would be cleared and enlightened so that you will receive an impression, a direction, perhaps an idea of what topic the Lord might want addressed.

Now let's suppose you finish your prayer, get back into your chair, and spend several minutes in reflection, "listening" for what path you should pursue. In the midst of your pondering, you find yourself thinking of the importance of keeping the Sabbath day holy and making the Sabbath a delight. Okay, so now you have your subject. Now what? What's your next concern? You are probably concerned with how to approach this subject, what avenues to pursue, what direction you might take, what scriptures or prophetic statements you might include in the talk. After a few hours you arise from the table with a pretty good feeling for how to proceed and a fairly tight outline of your sermon on the Sabbath day. In the days following you find yourself returning to your outline, erasing one principle and adding another, shifting what you thought would be a good introductory statement to the conclusion, and so forth.

Now it's Sunday morning. You roll out of bed onto your knees and begin your morning prayer. After expressing thanks and seeking specific help for one of your children who is struggling, you find your mind quickly turning to the talk you will soon deliver. What do you pray for now? You find yourself asking for the Lord to bless you with his Spirit, to direct your thinking, to loosen your tongue, and to calm your nerves. Let's assume the sermon goes well and that it seems to have been just what the Lord wanted said.

Why so much pondering and prayer and mental stretching for a ten- or fifteen-minute message? Why sweat over so many details? Well, obviously you don't want to stand at the pulpit and have nothing to say. Nor do you want to stumble over your words because you didn't prepare properly. Those, however, are secondary concerns at best. As a member of the Church of Jesus Christ, as a person who knows how important it is for those who attend sacrament meeting to go away spiritually fed and strengthened, your deepest desire through the preparation and delivery of the message is that you will say what the Lord wants said, that the Saints of the Most High in that meeting will leave inspired, touched, instructed, and fortified in their resolve to keep the commandments, stay on the covenant path, and develop Christlike characteristics.

And so you strive with all your heart to be the Lord's agent, to represent him in a dignified and proper way, and to speak by the power of the Holy Spirit, because when you speak by that sacred power, you speak with the tongue of angels; you declare the words of Christ. Early in this dispensation the missionaries were commanded to "go forth *in the power of my Spirit, preaching my gospel,* two by two, in my name, lifting up your voices as with the sound of a trump, *declaring my word like unto angels of God*" (Doctrine and Covenants 42:6; emphasis added). Such holds true today for all of those on the Lord's errand.

"YE SHALL NOT TEACH"

We teach what we are. It is almost impossible to teach a gospel principle with spiritual power when we ourselves are not seeking to live the principle. If I am a Sunday School teacher, and I see that the next lesson deals with the blessings of living a chaste and moral life, I may have difficulty presenting the message very effectively if I spend most days harboring inappropriate sexual thoughts. If I am a Primary teacher who discovers that my next lesson is about the importance of living the Word of Wisdom, when in fact I have a smoking problem, the children in my class may not feel the power of the Spirit behind my words as they would if I *were* abiding by this commandment. Each of us struggles with something, and our Father in Heaven is remarkably patient with us. And no bishop or branch president throughout the Church has the luxury of always calling a perfectly faithful member to serve in the Church. And yet it is inevitably the case that a sermon or lesson on the value of daily scripture study will certainly have a greater spiritual impact if I am now doing my best, for example, to read and search the Book of Mormon and general conference addresses regularly.

In what might well be called the law of the teacher, the Lord in February 1831 counseled the Latter-day Saints that "the elders, priests and teachers of this church shall teach the principles of my gospel, which are in the Bible and the Book of Mormon, in the which is the fulness of the gospel. And they shall observe the covenants and church articles [the revelations and, particularly, what is taught in Doctrine and Covenants 20] to do them, and these shall be their teachings, as they shall be directed by the Spirit. And the Spirit shall be given unto you by the prayer of faith; and *if ye receive not the Spirit ye shall not teach*" (Doctrine and Covenants 42:12–14; emphasis added).

That last phrase can mean a number of things. The Lord could be saying, in essence, If you do not have the Spirit accompanying you when you speak or teach, your presentation may not be effective or may not accomplish what you hope to accomplish; your message may not be well received, nor will true spiritual learning take place. In the Lord's language, you may not really be teaching. In this sense, Doctrine and Covenants 42:14 seems to be a *prophecy* of what will or will not take place if the speaker does not have the Spirit with her.

Let's look at verse 14 from a different angle. Perhaps the Lord is saying, If the Holy Spirit does not attend you in your presentation, *you should not teach;* you really ought not plan to speak if the Spirit is not with you; or, don't try to press your message upon listeners if you are not spiritually prepared. From this perspective, verse 14 would be a *command,* a divine injunction. President Ezra Taft Benson put it this way: "This latter-day work is spiritual. It takes spirituality to comprehend it, to love it, and to discern it. Therefore, we should seek the Spirit in all we do. That is our challenge."[1]

In a revelation given to the Church through the Prophet Joseph Smith in May 1831, the members of the Church were invited to "reason together" with the Lord. Then came the question: "Unto what were ye ordained [or set apart or appointed]?" The reply: "To preach my gospel by the Spirit, even the Comforter which was sent forth to teach the truth. . . . Verily I say unto you, he that is ordained of me and sent forth to preach the word of truth by the Comforter, in the Spirit of truth, doth he preach it by the Spirit of truth or some other way? And if it be by some other way it is not of God." Now the attention turns to the recipient of the message, the listener, the student: "And again, he that receiveth the word of truth, doth he receive it by the Spirit of truth or some other way? If it be some other way it is not of God" (Doctrine and Covenants 50:10, 13–14, 17–20).

After quoting the preceding passage to religious educators, Elder Bruce R. McConkie commented: "It [the scripture] said, 'If it be by some other way it is not of God' (D&C 50:18). What is the antecedent of *it*? It is *the word of truth*. That is to say, if you teach the word of truth—now note, you're saying what is true, everything you say is accurate and right—by some other way than the Spirit, it is not of God. Now *what is the other way to teach than by the Spirit? Well, obviously, it is by the power of the intellect.*

"Suppose I came here tonight and delivered a great message on teaching, and I did it by the power of the intellect without any of the Spirit of God attending. Suppose that every word that I said is true, no error whatever, but it was an intellectual presentation. The revelation says: 'If it be by some other way it is not of God' (D&C 50:18).

"That is, *God did not present the message through me* because I used the power of the intellect instead of the power of the Spirit. Intellectual

---

1. *Come unto Christ*, 23.

things—reason and logic—can do some good, and they can prepare the way, and they can get the mind ready to receive the Spirit under certain circumstances. But *conversion comes and truth sinks into the hearts of people only when it is taught by the power of the Spirit*. . . .

"That is how you worship. Real, true, genuine, Spirit-borne worship, in a sacrament meeting for instance, comes when the speaker speaks by the power of the Holy Ghost, and when a congregation hears by the power of the Holy Ghost. So the speaker gives the word of the Lord, and the congregation receives the word of the Lord."[2]

THERE MUST BE SUBSTANCE

Many years ago I was asked to speak to a group of single adults. I chose the topic of doctrine from the Book of Mormon and focused most of the time on the nature of fallen humanity, the infinite Atonement of Jesus Christ, and the necessity of being born again, all themes that run through the book like doctrinal refrains. I spoke for a little over an hour and in general felt good about what I said. After I had shaken hands with many of those in attendance and was preparing to leave, the person in charge of the session walked up to me and said, "Brother Millet, thank you for taking the time to be with us, but we will probably not have you speak to this group again."

I was startled. "Why is that?"

His response still haunts me to this day. He said, "We're not into doctrine here. We focus on the Spirit."

I half-smiled, nodded, and walked to my car. I spent much of the rest of that night thinking through his rather unusual reprimand.

To suggest that we can enjoy the sweet influence of the Spirit, the convincing and convicting power of that Spirit, without there being something about which the Holy Ghost can testify, is foolish. Or to put that another way, the Holy Ghost bears witness of propositions,

2. *Doctrines of the Restoration*, 332–33; emphasis added.

of truths that have just been presented, of scriptural passages that have just been read and discussed, and of principles and precepts delivered to the Saints by the prophets and seers who guide the destiny of this Church.

In one of the most sobering statements I have encountered, President Joseph F. Smith scolded members of the Church for not preparing properly when called upon to speak or teach but instead relying solely on the bearing of testimony. "The sanctity of a true testimony," he explained, "should inspire a thoughtful care as to its use." He also taught that "the voicing of one's testimony, however eloquently phrased or beautifully expressed, is no fit or acceptable substitute for the needed discourse of instruction and counsel expected in a general gathering of the people. The man who professes a testimony as herein described, and who assumes that his testimony embraces all the knowledge he needs, and who therefore lives in indolence and ignorance shall surely discover his error to his own cost and loss." Finally, President Smith said, "Of those who speak in his name, the Lord requires humility, not ignorance."[3]

This is also why it is so important for the gospel of Jesus Christ to be taught plainly and truthfully in the various meetings of the Church. We need to provide something of substance that the Spirit can confirm, ratify, and upon which he can place his stamp of approval. A number of years ago, while I was serving as a stake president, there came one of those rare Sabbaths in which I was actually free to attend church with my wife and children. After sacrament meeting, which was uplifting and edifying, we made our way to the Sunday School Gospel Doctrine class. That year we were studying the New Testament. As we sat down, I looked up and saw the following notation written on the chalkboard: "Acts 19" on the upper left and "Galatians" on the upper right. I was thrilled. I reflected on the fact that Acts 19 was one of my favorite

---

3. *Gospel Doctrine*, 205–6.

chapters in the Acts of the Apostles and that Galatians, though a rather short epistle, is filled with exceptional doctrinal messages.

The instructor eventually walked into the room and called on someone to pray. He then said, in essence, "We have some exciting things to discuss today. Before we get to the book of Acts and the epistle to the Galatians, however, let me share with you a wonderful experience my family and I just had while on vacation in California. He then spoke at length about snorkeling, long afternoons and evenings on the beach, and great seafood. He added, "Oh, one other thing. My wife and I had the opportunity to attend a session at the Los Angeles temple." He then glanced at the clock on the wall (which showed there was one minute left in Sunday School), looked carefully at what he had written on the board, and asked, "Now, what does all of this have to do with the apostle Paul?" There was a long and sustained silence, indicating clearly and painfully that no one sitting in the room could manage to see even the slightest connection between his family's vacation and Paul's life and letter. He brought the silence to a close by calling on someone to offer the benediction. Profound silence prevailed.

At first I was extremely frustrated as we made our way to priesthood meeting and Relief Society. Then my frustration morphed into pain and disappointment. I knew every person in the class; I had served previously as their bishop. I also knew that each one in attendance was wrestling with something and that a few had very serious challenges in life. A precious opportunity was missed. Many had come to Sunday School hungry and had gone home largely unfed. I have no question but that even a brief conversation about Acts or Galatians could have strengthened someone's testimony, fortified their faith. Sadly, very little was said of which the Holy Spirit could bear testimony. There was no substance. Alma explained that "the word [has] a great tendency to lead the people to do that which [is] just—yea, it [has] had more powerful effect upon the minds of the people than the sword, or anything else."

Consequently, we must take every opportunity to "try the virtue of the word of God" (Alma 31:5).

"Inspired teaching must never become a lost art in the Church," Elder Jeffrey R. Holland counseled us, "and we must make certain that our quest for it does not become a lost tradition. . . .

"*When crises come in our lives—and they will—the philosophies of men interlaced with a few scriptures and poems just won't do.* Are we really nurturing our youth and our new members in a way that will sustain them when the stresses of life appear? Or are we giving them a kind of theological Twinkie—spiritually empty calories? President John Taylor once called such teaching 'fried froth,' the kind of thing you could eat all day and finish feeling totally unsatisfied. . . .

"Satan is certainly not subtle in his teachings," Elder Holland continued. "Why should we be? Whether we are instructing our children at home or standing before an audience in church, *let us never make our faith difficult to detect.* Remember—we are to be teachers 'come from God' [how Nicodemus characterized Jesus; John 3:2]. Never sow seeds of doubt. Avoid self-serving performance and vanity. *Prepare lessons well. Give scripturally based sermons. Teach the revealed doctrine.* Bear heartfelt testimony."[4]

As Elder Holland stated, the message we want to convey must never be "difficult to detect." That is, members of the class or the congregation should never be required to exhaust their mental capacity to discern what the instructor or speaker is attempting to teach. President James E. Faust once spoke to the young men of the Church about how best to prepare for full-time missions. He challenged them to "study, ponder, and teach from the scriptures, especially the Book of Mormon and the New Testament. *Know the truth so well that you can state it clearly.*" President Faust then quoted the following from Elder B. H. Roberts: "'To be known, the truth must be stated and the clearer and

---

4. "Teacher Come from God," *Ensign*, May 1998, 25–27; emphasis added.

more complete the statement is, the better the opportunity will the Holy Spirit have for testifying to the souls of men that the work is true."[5]

Oliver Wendell Holmes is reported to have made the following observation: "I would not give a fig for the simplicity [on] this side of complexity. But *I would give my life for the simplicity on the other side of complexity.*"[6] In commenting on Holmes's poignant remark, Bruce and Marie Hafen proposed a three-step model for growing in knowledge and understanding and thus being in a position to deal with some of the more difficult and sensitive challenges to the faith that Latter-day Saints may face. "Stage One of our model is the simplicity on this side of complexity, innocent and untested. Stage Two is complexity, the gap between the real and the ideal, where we struggle with conflicts and uncertainty. Stage Three is the simplicity beyond complexity, a settled and informed perspective that has been tempered and tested by time and experience."[7] Indeed, some of the most effective gospel teachers are those who have searched and wrestled and stretched to come to a clearer understanding of a deep doctrinal concept or a difficult scriptural or historical matter. Then, when they truly grasp what the prophet or teacher intended to convey, they are able to teach profound truth simply and clearly. They teach in such a way that they will not only be understood, but also that they will not be misunderstood.

In short, those who aspire to teach the gospel of Jesus Christ by the power of the Holy Ghost must have something to say; to *teach* the gospel most effectively, we need to *know* the gospel. Many years ago my friend Joseph Fielding McConkie, never shy about expressing his feelings, wrote: "Philosophy, ethics, and the wisdom of the world are not the only synthetics offered under a gospel label. Many inservice

5. "What I Want My Son to Know before He Leaves on His Mission," *Ensign*, May 1996, 41; emphasis added.

6. *Holmes-Pollock Letters*, 109; emphasis added.

7. *Faith Is Not Blind*, 11.

programs get lost in methodology and rarely concern themselves with what is being taught as long as it is being taught well. Teachers who are the products of such training often find themselves giving beautifully packaged gifts which when opened are of slight or passing worth. Might we ask of what value it is if a teacher has high involvement, good discipline, a neat and orderly classroom, but never really teaches anything? What is the value of a well-told story if it carries no message? If that which matters most is not to be at the mercy of that which matters least, the *how* of teaching cannot relegate the *what* of teaching to a place of secondary importance."[8]

Methods and various approaches to teaching—role playing, open-ended stories, quality questions, separating into small groups, discussion, etc.—can be extremely beneficial, especially when the scriptures or prophetic words have been read and gospel truth, diamond truth, has been taught. In the long run, however, the truth must be taught and then caught by those in the class or the congregation.

A dear price is associated with becoming a competent and inspired teacher in the Church, a cost in terms of personal searching and rigorous study, dues to be paid in terms of prayerful reflection, combined with faithfulness to one's covenants and loyalty to the restored gospel itself. Elder John A. Widtsoe described the price that the young Joseph Smith had to pay to learn and master the truths that were to be dispensed in these last days. Regarding Joseph's momentous quest to know where the truth was to be found and his accompanying wrestle with Satan, Elder Widtsoe explained: "It was his first realization of the fierce cost of truth. Knowledge does not come unsought or without effort on the part of the learner. Only by tremendous self-effort does great knowledge come. It required terrific effort to fight away the evil powers that sought to keep knowledge from him. It required an intense concentration of body and spirit to keep in tune with Divinity so that

---

8. *Teach and Reach*, 4; see also 32.

the heavenly message could be understood. Naturally, the boy was exhausted in body and in mind. But who would not gladly pay any price for such an experience?"[9]

AVOIDING THE SPIRITUAL ECLIPSE

Gospel teachers must avoid creating what might be called a spiritual eclipse. Stated another way, speakers and teachers must be careful that they do not point their students to themselves or draw the students to them as the teacher rather than to the Lord Jesus Christ. Those in our audience must never be so overwhelmed with the gospel knowledge, charisma, or teaching style of the presenter that they do not look to the Lord, from whom the message of salvation comes. Or, as renowned and beloved educator Parker J. Palmer put it, "Once I understand that I'm not the sun, I can get out of the sun's way and stop casting shadows. I can step aside to let the true sun shine on everyone and everything, making all things ripe with the glow of life."[10]

"Therefore, hold up your light that it may shine unto the world," the risen Redeemer taught the descendants of Lehi. "Behold *I am the light which ye shall hold up*—that which ye have seen me do" (3 Nephi 18:24; emphasis added). The presenter must never get in the way of the Light of the world, must never block the light that shines from the Christ. Jesus was and is the perfect Example in everything we might do, including teaching the gospel. As our perfect example, our Lord was forevermore pointing people to God the Father.

This counsel is very much linked with the scriptural injunction for us to have "an eye single to the glory of God" (Matthew 6:22; 3 Nephi 13:22; Doctrine and Covenants 88:67). To me this is the sobering reminder "it's not about me." Rather, it's all about God the Eternal Father and his Son Jesus Christ. The effective gospel teacher is not one

9. *Joseph Smith: Seeker after Truth*, 13–14.
10. *On the Brink of Everything*, 21.

who has students leaving and exclaiming, "Wow! Sister Atkinson is amazing!" or "I am blown away by how much Brother Hansen knows. His knowledge is staggering!" The sweet influence of the third member of the Godhead is much more likely to be felt if the teacher's greatest desire is that God—who knows all things, including the pains and sorrows and problems and challenges of every person in that room—will suit his tender mercies to each individual in the class.

Because I have had the opportunity for almost fifty years to teach the restored gospel, I have had hundreds of occasions where members of the Church have come up to the stand and expressed appreciation for my message. Those expressions have of course taken many forms. Some people say, "Good job." Others might remark, "Thanks for being with us. I learned a lot." I have generally been able to nod and thank them for their thank-you. The toughest situations for me, however, have been those where the individual tries to pay me a personal compliment, something along the lines of what students might say to Sister Atkinson or Brother Hansen. For years when individuals paid me such a flowery compliment, I would almost try to talk them out of it with, "Well, I don't think I did a very good job," or "Oh, I wasn't able even to get through my lesson," or "I didn't even get to the most important part." My wife, Shauna, who was often with me on such occasions, would sometimes comment after we were in the car and headed home, "Why don't you just thank the people and let it drop?" I began to do that and have been quite comfortable with the outcome.

Several years ago, a woman came to the stand, shook my hand, and said, "That was an unbelievable presentation." I found myself saying in reply, "Thank you. The Lord was good to us tonight, wasn't he?" On other occasions I have responded with, "We were blessed tonight, weren't we? There was a wonderful outpouring of the Spirit." Such replies have always made me feel better inside, because I was trying to deflect any light or accolade away from me and back to the Father, the

Son, or the Holy Ghost, the only ones truly responsible for any spiritually rewarding experience.

The Prophet Joseph Smith counseled the leaders of the Church that when they "stand before the congregations of the earth, and they preach in the power and demonstration of the Spirit of God, and the people are astonished and confounded at the doctrine and say, 'That man has preached a powerful discourse, a great sermon,' then *let that man or those men take care that they do not ascribe the glory unto themselves,* but be careful that they are humble, and ascribe the praise and glory to God and the Lamb; for *it is by the power of the Holy Priesthood and the Holy Ghost that they have power thus to speak.*"[11] Obedience to such counsel is both wise and safe. The one thing God does not need is for any person called or appointed to preach his gospel to become overly impressed with himself and thereafter begin to "read by the lamp of his own conceit."[12]

Truly, when a man or woman qualifies for the sustaining influence of the Holy Spirit, he or she is in a position to "speak with the tongue of angels," to speak the words of Christ, to speak under the influence of the Spirit (2 Nephi 32:2–3). To a very real extent, the words then spoken are not merely the words of the speaker, for the Lord has chosen to speak through that person. Nephi never spoke truer or more sublime words than when he taught us that "when a man speaketh by the power of the Holy Ghost the power of the Holy Ghost carrieth it unto the hearts of the children of men" (2 Nephi 33:1). Sister Virginia H. Pearce, formerly a counselor in the Young Women General Presidency, testified that "a teacher's goal is greater than just delivering a lecture about truth. It is to invite the Spirit and use techniques which will

---

11. Discourse, 2 July 1839; emphasis added.
12. Joseph F. Smith, *Gospel Doctrine,* 373.

enhance the possibility that the learner will discover the truth for herself and then be motivated to apply it."[13]

President Brigham Young once described the manner in which his heart was touched and his soul converted through simple testimony: "If all the talent, tact, wisdom, and refinement of the world had been sent to me with the Book of Mormon, and had declared, in the most exalted of earthly eloquence, the truth of it, undertaking to prove it by learning and worldly wisdom, they would have been to me like the smoke which arises only to vanish away. But when I saw a man without eloquence, or talents for public speaking, who could only say, 'I know, by the power of the Holy Ghost, that the Book of Mormon is true, that Joseph Smith is a prophet of the Lord,' *the Holy Ghost proceeding from that individual illuminated my understanding, . . . and I knew for myself that the testimony of the man was true. . . .* My own judgment, natural endowments, and education bowed to this simple, but mighty testimony."[14]

Like Jesus, who is our pattern and example in all things, especially teaching the gospel, we aspire to become "a teacher come from God" (John 3:2), a member of Christ's Church who teaches "as one having authority from God" (JST, Matthew 7:36), an authority that comes from the Holy Ghost (1 Nephi 10:22). And what more could any gospel teacher desire than for individuals to say of what they had been taught, "Did not our heart burn within us, while [Jesus] talked with us by the way, and while he opened to us the scriptures?" (Luke 24:32). Such moments happen more and more frequently as we pray earnestly, prepare properly, and then allow the Holy Spirit to assume his role as the true Teacher.

---

13. "Ordinary Classroom—A Powerful Place for Steady and Continued Growth," *Ensign,* November 1996, 12.

14. In *Journal of Discourses,* 1:90; emphasis added.

PART IV

Changed, Renewed, and Purified

Chapter 14

ENTRANCE INTO THE ROYAL
FAMILY OF JESUS CHRIST

To choose to follow Jesus Christ is to choose to change. Religion deals with things of eternal import, with things of the heart, with the change each of us must undergo to become more like our Savior and thereby become more serviceable in the kingdom of God.

Because he is a living God, the Lord Jehovah is forevermore involved in this matter of change. In the beginning he spoke, chaotic matter responded, and the heavens and the earth were formed. The placement of Adam and Eve and all forms of life on Earth thereby changed the nature of existence on this planet. Because of the Fall of our first parents and because individuals are often enticed to wander from the strait and narrow covenant path, the Father sent his Only Begotten Son to radically and redeemingly alter the course of events on Earth, even spiritual chaos. He came to bring order and to reverse what would otherwise continue as a movement toward dissolution and eternal disaster. The Savior lovingly and powerfully came into the world to change things, both cosmically and individually.

Spiritual change is about betterment. Refinement. Improvement. More specifically, it consists of the transformation of the human soul by and through the redeeming mercy and atoning power of Jesus Christ. It is a transformation that is accomplished through the singular work of the Holy Spirit. Our God is ever ready to extend his remarkable blessings to us in a variety of ways and thereby seeks to bring about a mighty change in us through several channels. In short, he who is omniscient and omnipotent is hardly limited to one avenue or course of action in bringing about spiritual change in our lives; such a change or conversion may take many forms. Perhaps one day, when we are able to look back on our own life and times, we will marvel at the manner in which the all-loving One orchestrated the events and worked his wonders in our lives in truly mysterious ways. We will then see even more clearly than we do now that although this change was made possible through the precious Atonement of our Savior, it was effected through the sublime ministry of the third member of the Godhead. President Heber C. Kimball explained that the kind of change about which we are speaking is "an improvement, or an advancement in the things of God. By some it is said to be the change and renovation of the soul by the Spirit and grace of God. Then, again, it is called the new birth."[1]

JESUS ENCOUNTERS NICODEMUS

There came to Jesus by night a man named Nicodemus, a "ruler of the Jews," presumably a member of the Sanhedrin, a man who was "a master of Israel," meaning a master teacher or acknowledged scholar among the Jews. He and others had been impressed with the miracles of Jesus. He said: "Rabbi, we know that thou art a teacher come from God: for no man can do these miracles that thou doest, except God be with him." It was as though Jesus then desired to do two things: (1) to point out to Nicodemus that more was required of him than a verbal recognition of Jesus as a miracle worker; and (2) to anticipate the question that must have lurked in the shadows of Nicodemus's mind but that went unasked, perhaps, "What must I do to inherit eternal life?" Jesus answered, "Except a man be born again, he cannot see the kingdom of God" (John 3:1–3; see also verse 10).

---

1. In *Journal of Discourses*, 10:77.

This was no new idea, no novel conception revealed for the first time, for the doctrine of rebirth was as old as the world. God spoke to Adam and Eve: "I give unto you a commandment, to teach these things freely unto your children, saying: That by reason of transgression cometh the fall, which fall bringeth death, and inasmuch as ye were born into the world by water, and blood, and the spirit, which I have made, and so became of dust a living soul, even so *ye must be born again into the kingdom of heaven, of water, and of the Spirit, and be cleansed by blood, even the blood of mine Only Begotten; that ye might be sanctified from all sin,* and enjoy the words of eternal life in this world, and eternal life in the world to come, even immortal glory" (Moses 6:58–59; emphasis added).

Jeremiah spoke of a time when the Lord would again propose a covenant to his covenant people, when He would "put [his] law in their inward parts, and write it in their hearts," and that Jehovah would truly be their God and Israel would be his people (Jeremiah 31:31–34). Likewise, the Lord had spoken through Ezekiel: "Then will I sprinkle clean water upon you, and ye shall be clean: from all your filthiness, and from all your idols, will I cleanse you. A new heart also will I give you, and a new spirit will I put within you: and I will take away the stony heart out of your flesh, and I will give you an heart of flesh" (Ezekiel 36:25–26). Even in the Book of Jubilees, an apocryphal work, the concept of a new birth was to be found: "But after this they will return to me in all uprightness and with all of their heart and soul. And I shall cut off the foreskin of their heart and the foreskin of the heart of their descendants. And I shall create for them a holy spirit, and I shall purify them so that they will not turn away from following me from that day and forever. And their souls will cleave to me and to all my commandments. And they will do my commandments. And I shall be a father to them, and they will be sons to me" (Jubilees 1:23–25).

Nicodemus asked, "How can a man be born when he is old? can he enter the second time into his mother's womb, and be born?" Jesus replied, "Except a man be born of water and of the Spirit, he cannot enter into the kingdom of God" (John 3:4–5). The Christian world is largely divided over this matter of the new birth. A large number of Christians today believe that being born again consists of having a personal spiritual experience with Jesus, whereas other Christians believe that being born again consists of receiving the sacraments (ordinances) of the church. And where are the Latter-day Saints? Where do we stand on this vital issue? Is it enough to receive the revelation that God lives, Jesus is the Christ, and that the gospel of Jesus Christ has been restored to earth through a modern prophet? Or is it sufficient to receive the proper ordinances? The Prophet Joseph Smith stated simply but powerfully that "being born again, comes by the Spirit of God through ordinances."[2]

This Choice Seer explained on another occasion that it is one thing to *see* the kingdom of God and another to *enter* into that kingdom. One must have "a change of heart" to see the kingdom; that is, he or she must be awakened spiritually to recognize the truth, recognize that the Church of Jesus Christ is the custodian of the truth and of the required ordinances, and recognize that the fulness of salvation is to be had through acceptance of those principles and ordinances. Further, the Prophet taught, persons must "subscribe the articles of adoption"—receive and enter into the first principles and ordinances of the gospel—before they can be saved.[3]

The first principles and ordinances of the gospel are the means whereby a person is adopted into the family of the Lord Jesus Christ. Orson Pratt explained that "Faith, repentance, baptism, and the laying on of hands are the *four rules of adoption*. Remission of sins, and the gift of the Holy Ghost, are the *two blessings of adoption* which are inseparably connected with obedience to the rules. Both the rules and the blessings of adoption are the same in all ages and dispensations of the gospel. No man or woman ever entered into the Church or kingdom

---

2. Discourse, between ca. 26 June and ca. 4 August 1839–A.

3. Journal, 15 October 1843; History, vol. E-1, 1755; see also *Words of Joseph Smith*, 256.

of God on this earth, and became a legal citizen thereof, without complying strictly with these rules. Indeed, it is the only door or entrance into the kingdom."[4] Acceptance of the truth is insufficient. Testimony is not enough. True conversion includes acting upon the revealed witness and submitting to those divine statutes that make it possible for us to be born again and thereby adopted into the family of the Lord Jesus Christ.

Daniel Tyler heard the Prophet Joseph explain that the birth spoken of in John 3:3—the birth to see the kingdom of God—"was not the gift of the Holy Ghost, which was promised after baptism, but was a portion of the spirit, which attended the preaching of the gospel by the elders of the Church. The people wondered why they had not previously understood the plain declarations of scripture, as explained by the elder, as they had read them hundreds of times. When they read the Bible [again] it was a new book to them. This was being born again, to see the Kingdom of God. They were not in it, but could see it from the outside, which they could not do until the Spirit of the Lord took the veil from before their eyes. *It was a change of heart, but not of state; they were converted, but were yet in their sins.* Although Cornelius [Acts 10] had seen an holy angel, and on the preaching of Peter the Holy Ghost was poured out upon him and his household, they were only born again to *see* the Kingdom of God. Had they not been baptized afterwards they would not have been saved."[5]

As we have said, although the new birth is made possible by the atoning sacrifice of our Savior, the Holy Ghost is vital in bringing about this change. The spiritual transformation of the individual that we know as the new birth is a movement from darkness to light, from death to life. "It is the spirit that quickeneth," Jesus taught. "The flesh profiteth nothing: the words that I speak unto you, they are spirit, and

---

4. *Orson Pratt's Works*, 48; emphasis added.

5. "Recollections of the Prophet Joseph Smith," *Juvenile Instructor*, vol. 27, no. 3 (1 February 1892): 93–94; emphasis added.

they are life" (John 6:63). Truly, "the Spirit giveth life" (2 Corinthians 3:6). This is the new life, the abundant life, the life in Christ.

FROM DARKNESS TO LIGHT

"Choose to put yourself in a position," Elder Robert D. Hales counseled us, "to have experiences with the Spirit of God through prayer, in scripture study, at Church meetings, in your home, and through wholesome interactions with others. *When you feel the influence of the Spirit, you are beginning to be cleansed and strengthened. The light is being turned on, and where that light shines, the darkness of evil cannot be.*"[6]

That journey from darkness to light is what spiritual rebirth is all about. We are born into a fallen world, a world of darkness. We grapple with the darkness and must decide if we are content to dwell in darkness or to walk toward the light. The Light of the world demands a decision. Either people will press toward him and partake of the light, or they will love and cling to the darkness because of their evil deeds (John 3:19). To come unto Christ is to forsake the darkness and to cleave unto light.

Not long ago, while rereading Lehi's dream as recorded in 1 Nephi 8, it occurred to me that what he saw in his dream represents the challenge of every person to come out of darkness into the light. Speaking to his sons, Lehi stated that he saw "a dark and dreary wilderness. And it came to pass that I saw a man, and he was dressed in a white robe; and he came and stood before me. And it came to pass that he spake unto me, and bade me follow him. And it came to pass that as I followed him I beheld myself that I was in a dark and dreary waste. And after I had traveled for the space of many hours in darkness, I began to pray unto the Lord that he would have mercy on me, according to the multitude of his tender mercies. And it came to pass after I had prayed unto the Lord I beheld a large and spacious field. And it came to pass that I beheld a tree, whose fruit was desirable to make one happy" (1 Nephi 8:4–10).

---

6. *Return*, 37–38; emphasis added.

It may be helpful to liken Lehi's experience to our own. As we traverse the roads of a darkened world, we receive the beckoning invitation to come out of the darkness unto Christ our Savior. As we have discussed, each of us is born with the Light of Christ, or Spirit of Jesus Christ, a moral monitor leading us directly toward greater light and truth; it helps us to reason, discern, and know right from wrong. If we will hearken to this light we will be led, either here or hereafter, to the covenant gospel and to the greater light of the gift of the Holy Ghost (Moroni 7:16–19; Doctrine and Covenants 84:45–48). Prayer and searching and pondering on things of substance lead us to Christ, of which the tree of life is a grand symbol (1 Nephi 11:7, 21–22, 25; Jeremiah 2:13). Partaking of the powers of the Savior cleanses our souls, lifts our burdens, and orients our minds toward eternity. We thereby become a peculiar, or purchased, people, those called out of darkness into his marvelous light (1 Peter 2:9). "That which is of God is light; and he that receiveth light, and continueth in God, receiveth more light; and that light groweth brighter and brighter until the perfect day" (Doctrine and Covenants 50:24).

Ammon taught the gospel to King Lamoni with great power and persuasion. Lamoni fell to the earth and "lay as if he were dead for the space of two days and two nights" (Alma 18:39–43). Ammon recognized what was taking place within Lamoni. Ammon and the other sons of Mosiah had previously undergone a spiritual transformation like unto Alma's, and so Ammon would likely understand very well what was going on within Lamoni's soul. Mormon's account indicates that Ammon "knew that king Lamoni was under the power of God; he knew that *the dark veil of unbelief was being cast away from his mind, and the light which did light up his mind,* which was the light of the glory of God, which was a marvelous light of his goodness—yea, *this light had infused such joy into his soul, the cloud of darkness having been dispelled, and that the light of everlasting life was lit up in his soul*" (Alma 19:6; emphasis added).

FROM BELIEF TO KNOWLEDGE

The Book of Mormon is filled with actual historical instances—experiences of real people in real time—that symbolize universal spiritual truths and focus on what each of us must do to be snatched, spared, sanctified, and saved. Occasionally we must sacrifice our worldly goods as did Lehi, be bold at difficult times as did Nephi, encounter anti-Christs as did Jacob, pray with great intensity as did Enos, and be born again as were Alma and the sons of Mosiah. First of all, "the dark veil of unbelief" must be cast away (Alma 19:6). Notice that one of the first things Nephi tells us about himself is that he had great desires to know the mysteries of God—those things that can only be known by the power of the Holy Ghost. "I did cry unto the Lord; and behold *he did visit me, and did soften my heart that I did believe all the words which had been spoken by my father;* wherefore, I did not rebel against him like unto my brothers" (1 Nephi 2:16; emphasis added).

The visitation of the Spirit leads to a softening of the heart, a malleability, a tenderness, an openness to the ways of the Master. One would suppose that Nephi's heart was soft before this experience, but it would appear that the closer we get to our Heavenly Father, the more open we are to his mind and will. Nephi's believing heart was at the foundation of his spiritual change and success; it made him what he was.

A believing heart is something for which a person should be deeply grateful. It is less and less common in today's world. Many in our day are like the rising generation who lived many years after the time of King Benjamin. These refused to believe the righteous traditions of their fathers. "They did not believe what had been said concerning the resurrection of the dead, neither did they believe concerning the coming of Christ." Now note these penetrating words: "And now *because of their unbelief they could not understand the word of God; and their hearts were hardened*" (Mosiah 26:1–3; emphasis added). There are some things that a skeptic will never make sense of. There are many things that a doubter, a naysayer, will never understand. Hardened hearts must be softened and, often, broken, before spiritual progress can be made. The things that really matter in this life can only be understood and appreciated by the power of the Holy Spirit. This comes about through a rebirth of the soul.

Believing is seeing. A person being born of the Spirit believes the words of inspired spokesmen (Mosiah 5:2; Alma 18:23; 22:7). Inquiries become more sincere (compare Alma 11:26–39 with 12:7–8). Whereas an unregenerated person is cynical, a spiritually reborn person is a believer. Whereas a worldly individual demands physical proof, the spiritual individual enjoys the measure of trust and divine patience that allows the Lord the prerogative to do his own work in his own time. The Lord calls us not to gullibility but to openness. The earnest seeker after truth must have a willing suspension of disbelief in order to have the truth confirmed in his or her heart. "Search diligently," the Redeemer implored in a modern revelation, "pray always, and be believing, and all things shall work together for your good, if ye walk uprightly and remember the covenant wherewith ye have covenanted one with another" (Doctrine and Covenants 90:24).

One group of people in the Book of Mormon spoke of their internal change as follows: "We, ourselves, . . . through the infinite goodness of God, and the manifestations of his Spirit, have great views of that which is to come; and were it expedient, we could prophesy of all things" (Mosiah 5:3). Theirs was a view of the truth, of things as they are, and as they were, and as they are to come (Doctrine and Covenants 93:24). Theirs was an elevated perspective, a glimpse of life and the plan of God not filtered through impure eyes or hearts. To be born again is to gain a heightened sensitivity to things that matter. In writing of the person who has been born of the Spirit, Elder Parley P. Pratt explained: "His mind is quickened, his intellectual faculties are aroused to intense activity. He is, as it were, illuminated. He learns more of divine truth in a few days, than he could have learned in a lifetime in the best merely human institutions in the world."[7]

For example, since the Lord works with members of the Church through their consciences, to be born again is to gain a deeper sensitivity to right and wrong, to enjoy greater manifestations of the gift of discernment, to develop more refined and educated desires. Since being born again consists in being adopted into the royal family and thus gaining godly attributes and qualities, experiencing the new birth entails feeling a deeper compassion and empathy for those who are poor, who mourn or suffer or reach out for succor. The quickening in the inner man peels away the film and facade of sin; makes unnecessary the rigors and taxing labors of duplicity; allows the spiritually initiated to see things clearly and sharply so as to sift and sort out the sordid or even the subsidiary. Those born of the Spirit have a spiritual priority and thus less inclination to labor in secondary causes and a consuming but patient passion to occupy themselves with that which brings light and life and love. They come to treasure the simple pleasures in life and rejoice in the goodness of their God. Joseph Smith taught that "the nearer man approaches perfection, the clearer are his views, and the greater his enjoyments, till he has overcome the evils of his life and lost every desire for sin."[8]

The Spirit brings certitude and conviction and banishes the darkness of doubt. It is not that those who are born of the Spirit never have questions or doubts; rather, they know for a certainty, by the power of the Holy Ghost, that the fundamental verities of the faith are true—that God is in his heaven, that the Church and kingdom of God have been restored to earth, with its keys and powers, and that those who have been chosen and anointed to lead the Church are divinely called. In many cases, questions and uncertainties are placed on the shelf. Spiritual stumbling blocks may not immediately disappear, but they do not disturb or divert. As President John Taylor explained, the Spirit "is

---

7. *Key to the Science of Theology*, 98.
8. Letter to the Church, ca. February 1834.

not something that affects the outward ear alone; it is not something that affects simply his judgment, but it affects his inner man; it affects the spirit that dwells within him; it is part of God imparted unto man, if you please, giving him an assurance that God lives."[9]

President Heber C. Kimball described what he experienced when he was confirmed a member of the Church: "Under the ordinances of baptism and the laying on of hands, I received the Holy Ghost, as the disciples did in ancient days, which was like a consuming fire. I felt as though I sat at the feet of Jesus, and was clothed in my right mind, although the people called me crazy.

"I continued in this way for many months, and it seemed as though my body would consume away; at the same time the scriptures were unfolded to my mind in such a wonderful manner that it appeared to me, at times, as if I had formerly been familiar with them."[10]

One may have been confirmed a member of the Church and yet never have enjoyed the supernal powers of the Spirit. Such was the case with President Lorenzo Snow. He wrote: "Some two or three weeks after I was baptized, one day while engaged in my studies, I began to reflect upon the fact that I had not obtained a *knowledge* of the truth of the work . . . and I began to feel very uneasy. . . . The spirit of prayer had departed and the heavens seemed like brass over my head." President Snow explained that he, "as a matter of formality, knelt as I was in the habit of doing, and in my accustomed retired place, but not feeling as I was wont to feel.

"I had no sooner opened my lips in an effort to pray, than I heard a sound, just above my head, like the rustling of silken robes, and immediately the Spirit of God descended upon me, . . . from the crown of my head to the soles of my feet, and O, the joy and happiness I felt! No language can describe the almost instantaneous transition from a

---

9. In *Journal of Discourses*, 11:23.
10. In Whitney, *Life of Heber C. Kimball*, 22–23.

dense cloud of mental and spiritual darkness into a refulgence of light and knowledge, as it was at that time imparted to my understanding. *I then received a perfect knowledge that God lives, that Jesus Christ is the Son of God, and of the restoration of the holy Priesthood, and the fulness of the Gospel.* It was a complete baptism—a tangible immersion in the heavenly principle or element, the Holy Ghost . . . *dispelling forever, so long as reason and memory last, all possibility of doubt or fear. . . .*

"On arising from my kneeling posture, with my heart swelling with gratitude to God, beyond the power of expression, I felt—I knew—that He had conferred on me what only an omnipotent being can confer— that which is of greater value than all the wealth and honors worlds can bestow. That night, as I retired to rest, the same wonderful manifestations were repeated, and continued to be for several successive nights. The sweet remembrance of those glorious experiences, from that time to the present, bring them fresh before me, imparting an inspiring influence which pervades my whole being, and I trust will to the close of my earthly existence."[11]

Clearly not all who receive the gift of the Holy Ghost, and who further receive a personal witness of Christ and of the restored gospel, will experience what Lorenzo Snow did. It is truly one of the great descriptions of rebirth in all our literature. All of us, however, who strive to keep the commandments and who seek to cultivate the gift and gifts of the Spirit can come to know just as he knew, can have the cloud of darkness dispelled just as it did for President Snow, and can come thereby to walk in the light of the Lord just as he walked.

IN PROCESS OF TIME

Must one's spiritual rebirth be dramatic? Is it not a true conversion unless I am knocked to the ground by an angel and given a startling and

---

11. In Snow, *Biography and Family Record of Lorenzo Snow*, 7–9; emphasis added.

immediate change of heart by God? Does a real baptism by fire require an extraordinary outpouring of the Spirit, circling flames of fire, blowing winds, and the ministry of angels? Is the rebirth something experienced only once in one's life? Must the mighty change be immediate, suddenly, in an instant, accompanied by great light and heavenly manifestations?

In my first year of teaching at Brigham Young University, a young woman in one of my classes came to my office to visit with me. The light of the gospel shone in her countenance, and her language, her demeanor, and her very manner bespoke an inner spiritual refinement.

"What can I do for you?" I asked.

She paused for about thirty seconds, bowed her head, and began to cry. "I'm so embarrassed," she said. "I'm ashamed of myself."

My first thought was that she had committed some serious sin that she needed to confess. "Would what you are about to say be better said to your bishop?" I gently inquired.

"Oh no," she said through her tears. "It's nothing like that." She went on. "I am embarrassed to say that although I grew up in the Church, attended four years of seminary, read the scriptures, and prayed continually, I have never been born again. As far as I can tell, I have never had an experience like Alma the Younger. You remember, Brother Millet, how he was turned around and changed, don't you? And Alma said that everyone must be born again. But I have never, ever had anything happen to me like Alma did. I feel like such a failure."

I sat there feeling helpless, wondering what would be appropriate to say to her. It occurred to me that one response might be, "Well, Susan, it is a serious matter that you have not yet been born again. You're absolutely right that you need to experience a mighty change of heart, and that change must come to you before you leave this life. Maybe you haven't been trying hard enough. Maybe your prayers aren't really sincere. You might try fasting more regularly until the change comes." Such an approach would no doubt have been devastating to

Susan. It would either depress her further or lead her to an excessive zeal that could in time result in spiritual instability.

Or I might be a bit more sensitive to her plight and say something like this, "Well, Susan, it's refreshing to find someone your age who is seriously concerned about this matter. Yes, we do need to be born again before we can be saved in the celestial kingdom. But you shouldn't be discouraged that an Alma-like experience hasn't come yet. You need to be patient. It'll come soon enough, just you watch."

Neither option seemed appropriate or helpful, and so I pondered for another moment. Without downplaying the importance of the mighty change (Mosiah 5:2), I carefully explained to Susan that she was already well on her way toward salvation. The light of the Spirit of God was with her. She was worthy, sensitive, and attentive. Her transformation might not have been as dramatic as Alma or Lamoni or Saul of Tarsus, but it was just as real.

In this regard, is the birth of the Spirit a single event, or is it a process? In a few cases people are born again suddenly, quickly, and their movement from darkness to light is rapid. In this sense, the rebirth is an event. Alma could rightly speak of having been born again during a specified three days in actual time. On the other hand—and this is important to emphasize—Alma's mighty change was far more extensive and lengthy than his experience with the angel and the three-day period of anguish, suffering, and forgiveness. Alma grew line upon line, precept upon precept, day by day, for the rest of his life, just as you and I do.

For example, how did Alma know of the truthfulness of the gospel and of the power of Christ to transform the souls of individuals? Was it because of his being struck down by the angel? That event obviously had a deep and lasting effect, to be sure. He spoke of it often (Alma 36:5–24; 38:6–8). Notice, however, that when Alma bore his testimony he did not say, "I know this work is true because an angel leveled me and sent me into a spiritual coma for three days." No, what he said is this: "Behold, I testify unto you that I do know that these things whereof I have spoken are true. And how do ye suppose that I know of their surety? Behold, I say unto you *they are made known unto me by the Holy Spirit of God. Behold, I have fasted and prayed many days that I might know these things of myself. And now I do know of myself that they are true; for the Lord God hath made them manifest unto me by his Holy Spirit;* and this is the spirit of revelation which is in me" (Alma 5:45–46; emphasis added).

In short, Alma came to know as we come to know—through personal prayer, searching, and inquiry, service to God and man, by the power of the Holy Ghost.

And even though it is true that our own rebirth may be a process, yet it is almost always the case that there was a moment in time—a vital moment or season in life that mattered—when we were touched, moved, motivated, and directed to turn our lives around or at least become better than we were. Besides, in a sense it is not the rebirth per se that is all-sufficient but rather the subsequent and changed life that flows therefrom. Just as there are critical days or months prior to the physical birth and many months and years that follow physical birth into maturity, so it is with the spiritual birth: many things prepare the soil before the time of birth and many things are done to harvest the fruit thereafter.

As Christian theologian John Stott observed, "It does not matter at all if, although you know you have turned to Christ, you do not know the date when you did so. Some do; others do not. What matters is not *when* but *whether* we have put our trust in Christ. Jesus called the beginning of our Christian life a second 'birth,' and the analogy is helpful in many ways. For example, we are not conscious of our physical birth taking place, and would never have known our birthday if our parents had not told us. The reason we know we were born, even though we do not remember it, is that we are enjoying a life today which we know must have begun at birth. It is much the same with the new birth."[12] As

---

12. *Authentic Christianity*, 203.

Paul explained to a group of Saints in the meridian of time, "now is our salvation nearer than when we [first] believed" (Romans 13:11).

President Ezra Taft Benson likewise taught: "The scriptures record remarkable accounts of men whose lives changed dramatically, in an instant, as it were: Alma the Younger, Paul on the road to Damascus, Enos praying far into the night, King Lamoni. Such astonishing examples of the power to change even those steeped in sin give confidence that the Atonement can reach even those deepest in despair.

"But we must be cautious as we discuss these remarkable examples. *Though they are real and powerful, they are the exception more than the rule.* For every Paul, for every Enos, and for every King Lamoni, there are hundreds and thousands of people who find the process of repentance much more subtle, much more imperceptible. Day by day they move closer to the Lord, little realizing they are building a godlike life. They live quiet lives of goodness, service, and commitment."[13]

In my own life, it seems as though I have been born again and again and again. That is, I feel as though there have been key moments or seasons of growth and transformation that I can point to as pivotal times, springboards to greater light and truth and conviction. Perhaps it was a general conference address, a poignant passage of scripture, or the singing of a hymn that jolted me into the stiff realization that I must climb higher. For me there does not seem to be one single event to which I can point as *the* time when my nature was changed. Rather, I can catalog several eras in my life when the Lord was attempting to get my attention, bolting me off a spiritual plateau, and moving me forward and upward to new vistas of understanding.

One cannot afford to coast spiritually, to live forevermore on past sacred moments; new ones must be sought for, treasured, and stored in our reservoir of faith. The Holy Spirit will not allow us to go stale if we attend to his promptings. There will always be stretchings and unlearning

---

13. "Mighty Change of Heart," *Ensign*, October 1989, 5; emphasis added.

and relearning and moments of divine discontent—subtle but serious reminders that it is time to move on. Alma inquired of his people, "And now behold, I say unto you, my brethren [and sisters], if ye have experienced a change of heart, and if ye have felt to sing the song of redeeming love, I would ask, can ye feel so now?" (Alma 5:26). Can you?

One who desires to become more like the Master cannot be resistant to change, especially spiritual change. This type of change must be sought for and then embraced. Alma the Younger explained that to be born of the Spirit is to be "changed from [our] carnal and fallen state, to a state of righteousness, being redeemed of God, becoming his sons and daughters; and thus [we] become new creatures; and unless [we] do this, [we] can in nowise inherit the kingdom of God" (Mosiah 27:25–26). "The conversion described in these verses," Elder David A. Bednar explained, "is mighty, not minor—a spiritual rebirth and fundamental change of what we feel and desire, what we think and do, and what we are. Indeed, the essence of the gospel of Jesus Christ entails a fundamental and permanent change in our very nature made possible through our reliance upon 'the merits, and mercy, and grace of the Holy Messiah' (2 Nephi 2:8)."[14]

Scriptural words like "mighty change" (Mosiah 5:2), "born again" (John 3:3), "born of the Spirit" (Mosiah 27:24), "new creatures" (2 Corinthians 5:17), or receiving Christ's "image in our countenances" (Alma 5:14)—these are but a few of the many, many ways of describing how Jesus Christ, by his atoning blood and through the medium of the Holy Spirit, accomplishes wonders and miracles in people's lives. Spiritually reborn people are simply different. They are guided by a higher light and have loftier ambitions. Their persistent noble deeds reflect their changed hearts.

---

14. "Ye Must Be Born Again," *Ensign*, May 2007, 20.

Chapter 15

TRANSFORMATION AND DEEP CONVERSION

⌐∽

aining a testimony—a divinely sent conviction of the living reality of the Father and the Son, as well as of the truthfulness of the restored gospel and this great latter-day work—is a remarkable thing. It is a miracle, an instance in which the Infinite impacts the finite, in which the heavens touch the earth, in which Spirit speaks to spirit, in which God manifests truth to mortals. To gain a testimony is to be reborn as to what we know and feel, what we understand and value (1 John 5:1). One who has received such a manifestation is becoming a new creature in Christ.

TESTIMONY AND CONVERSION

By the power of the Spirit we come to know the things of God, we gain a testimony and are charged to become a witness. By that same power we continue the process of *conversion*. In a sense, gaining a testimony is a form of conversion—from ignorance or unbelief to understanding and belief, from doubt to certitude. The process of conversion continues throughout our lives. "To become converted, according to the scriptures," President Harold B. Lee taught, "means having a change of heart and the moral character of a person turned from the controlled power of sin into a righteous life. . . . It means to overcome the tendencies to criticize and to strive continually to improve inward weaknesses and not merely the outward appearances."[1] A testimony of the gospel is thus a necessary but insufficient condition for salvation, for even the devils "believe and tremble" (James 2:19).

The importance of building upon one's testimony and thereafter becoming truly converted is illustrated quite dramatically in the life of Simon Peter. Peter was a humble man, a fisherman, when he was called by Jesus to the ministry. As a member of the meridian First Presidency, Peter was frequently alone with the Savior and privy to many of the moving spiritual experiences recorded in the New Testament (Matthew 14:28–29; 17:1–9; 26:37; Mark 5:35–43). There is little doubt that Peter was a good man with solid desires, one who had a testimony of the divinity of Jesus of Nazareth. At Caesarea Philippi some six months before the Crucifixion, Jesus asked the Twelve: "Whom do men say that I the Son of man am?" Answering for the Twelve, Simon said: "Thou art the Christ, the Son of the living God." Jesus assured this senior apostle that such a conviction came from God (Matthew 16:16–19).

After Jesus had preached his powerful bread of life sermon—in which he identified himself as the true Bread of Life and the Living Manna and also declared that only those who ate his flesh and drank his blood could have eternal life—many of the disciples were offended and "walked no more with him." Christ turned to the Twelve in that tender moment and asked, "Will ye also go away?" Peter responded in deep sincerity and conviction, speaking for the others of the Twelve: "Lord, to whom shall we go? thou hast the words of eternal life. And we believe and are sure that thou art that Christ, the Son of the living God" (John 6:66–69).

Although the New Testament attests to the fact that Peter had a testimony, it also affirms that he was weak—that he slipped and stumbled. Not infrequently he was chastened by his Master for his shortsightedness and impulsiveness. Almost immediately after his

---

1. *Stand Ye in Holy Places*, 354–55.

remarkable testimony at Caesarea Philippi, Jesus began to prepare his chosen Twelve for what lay ahead, including his arrest, passion, and death. "Then Peter took him, and began to rebuke him, saying, Be it far from thee, Lord: this shall not be unto thee. But [Jesus] turned, and said unto Peter, Get thee behind me, Satan: thou art an offence unto me; for thou savorest not the things that be of God, but those that be of men" (Matthew 16:21–23). Here we see that Cephas, the seer or stone (see JST, John 1:42), had, for a moment, become a potential stumbling block to others. And of course there was the most classic of Peter's blunders—his open denial of a knowledge of Jesus on the night the Savior was arrested (Matthew 26:69–74).

How could one who had a testimony fall short so often? How could one who knew as Peter knew slip as often as Peter did, even to the point of an outright denial? The answer to such questions seems to lie in a conversation between Jesus and Peter at the Last Supper. Jesus said: "Simon, Simon, behold, Satan hath desired to have you, that he may sift you as wheat: But I have prayed for thee, that thy faith fail not: and *when thou art converted, strengthen thy brethren*" (Luke 22:31–32; emphasis added). Though Peter had a testimony, he was not fully converted. Inasmuch as the full power and gifts of the Holy Ghost were not given until the day of Pentecost, Peter had enjoyed only flashes of inspiration. After the Resurrection of the Lord and after Pentecost and the accompanying baptism by fire, Peter and the Twelve walked in a new light. One only needs to read the opening chapters of the Acts of the Apostles to witness a remarkable transformation of the man Peter and his apostolic colleagues. He is bold and certain and solid in his ministry. The permanent and indelible impression was planted, and the Holy Ghost had made Peter into a new creation.

In speaking of this significant moment in Christian church history, Elder Kim B. Clark of the Seventy emphasized how the coming of the Spirit in a more powerful and constant manner "strengthened the Lord's disciples. Although the times they lived in were dangerous and confusing, they received the spiritual gift of eyes to see and ears to hear. By the power of the Holy Ghost, they began to see the truth of things as they really are, especially of the Lord Jesus Christ and His work among them. The Holy Ghost enlightened their understanding, and they heard the voice of the Lord more clearly. The gospel of Jesus Christ sank deep into their hearts (see Enos 1:3). They were steadfast and obedient (see Acts 2:42). They preached the gospel with boldness and power and built up the kingdom of God (see Acts 4:8–12). They had joy in the Lord Jesus Christ."[2]

Truly, one is converted "when he sees with his eyes what he ought to see; when he hears with his ears what he ought to hear; and when he understands with his heart what he ought to understand. And what he ought to see, hear, and understand is truth—eternal truth—and then practice it. That is conversion. . . . *When we understand more than we know with our minds, when we understand with our hearts, then we know that the Spirit of the Lord is working upon us.*"[3]

EXAMINING OURSELVES

In recent years we have been reminded by our leaders that a significant prophecy is being fulfilled in our day. The Lord said, "Behold, I will hasten my work in its time" (Doctrine and Covenants 88:73). To hasten is to urge on, to accelerate, to move or act quickly. Specifically, the Brethren have called upon the Latter-day Saints to hasten the work of (1) reaching out to those who may not now enjoy the blessings of the restored gospel; (2) extending the blessings of that gospel to those who have died without the opportunity to receive its requisite covenants and ordinances; and (3) searching out and caring for the poor and needy among us. These selfless acts—missionary service, temple service, and ministering—are part of what we are called upon to do

---

2. "Eyes to See and Ears to Hear," *Ensign*, November 2015, 124.
3. Lee, *Stand Ye in Holy Places*, 92; emphasis added.

as disciples of the Lord Jesus Christ. The apostle James, brother of our Lord, explained that this is what true Christians do; this is what he called "pure religion." But there was one more thing involved in pure religion—namely, keeping ourselves unspotted from the vices of the world (JST, James 1:27). This facet of the Christian faith has to do with personal spiritual refinement.

In addition to hearing much about hastening the work, we have been told how important it is to encourage and foster "real growth," that is, deep conversion, complete consecration to God and his Church and kingdom. At the October 2000 general conference, President Dallin H. Oaks delivered a stirring address entitled "The Challenge to Become." He emphasized that true righteousness is not just measured in what we do, although what we do may be an indicator of our inner righteousness. True righteousness is *what we have become, what we are, who we are!*

He pointed out that the process of becoming more like our Savior "requires far more than acquiring knowledge. It is not even enough for us to be *convinced* of the gospel; we must act and think so that we are *converted* by it. In contrast to the institutions of the world, which teach us to *know* something, the gospel of Jesus Christ challenges us to *become* something." President Oaks went on to say that "the Final Judgment is not just an evaluation of a sum total of good and evil acts—what we have *done.* It is an acknowledgment of the final effect of our acts and thoughts—what we have *become.*" He continued: "The commandments, ordinances, and covenants of the gospel are not a list of deposits required to be made in some heavenly account. The gospel of Jesus Christ is a plan that shows us how to become what our Heavenly Father desires us to become."[4]

While such growth is surely the product of consistent and sustained gospel living, what does it look like? How might we know if we

---

4. "Challenge to Become," *Ensign*, November 2000, 32.

are, through the years, experiencing real growth? What might we begin noticing in our own ministering and discipleship? How deep is our conversion? Here are a few thoughts to consider:

1. There begins to develop within our hearts *a desire to do more to further the work of the Lord and to be better people than we are.* This seems to be what Abraham felt when he wrote of how he had previously been a follower of righteousness but had felt the need "to be one who possessed great knowledge, and to be a greater follower of righteousness, and to possess a greater knowledge" (Abraham 1:2). That is, Abraham wanted to do more and be more.

As the Spirit of God becomes a more regular and consistent visitor, we begin feeling a growing sense of consecration—a desire to turn our lives over to God and allow him to use us as he will. President Boyd K. Packer taught a profound lesson many years ago. "I knew what agency was," he said, "and knew how important it was to be individual and to be independent, to be free. I somehow knew there was one thing the Lord would never take from me and that was my free agency. I would not surrender my agency to any being but to Him! I determined that I would *give* Him the one thing that He would never take—my agency. I decided, by myself, that from that time on I would do things His way." President Packer continued: "That was a great trial for me, for I thought I was giving away the most precious thing I possessed. I was not wise enough in my youth to know that because I exercised my agency and decided myself, I was not *losing* it. It was *strengthened!*"[5]

In a priesthood leadership meeting a number of years ago, President Packer spoke solemnly of the time in his life when he had determined to surrender his agency to God. He recommended to us that we consider doing the same. He then added, with unanticipated sternness, "But don't you monkey with this. This is serious business!" And indeed it is. We really should not offer something if we have no

---

5. "Spiritual Crocodiles," *Ensign*, May 1976, 32.

intention of letting it go. We really should not indicate to the Almighty that we intend to give him something when in fact we are prepared to give him only a small portion (see Acts 5).

In fact, what can we offer to God? Our savings accounts? Our properties? Our investments? No, for all of the world's goods are already his. "The earth is the Lord's, and the fulness thereof; the world, and they that dwell therein" (Psalm 24:1). As Elder Neal A. Maxwell pointed out, "The submission of one's will is really the only uniquely personal thing we have to place on God's altar. The many other things we 'give,' brothers and sisters, are actually the things He has already given or loaned to us. However, when you and I finally submit ourselves, by letting our individual wills be swallowed up in God's will, then we are really giving something to Him! It is the only possession which is truly ours to give! Consecration thus constitutes the only unconditional surrender which is also a total victory!"[6]

If we *in time* will seek to align ourselves with God's will, he will *in eternity* grant unto us whatsoever we ask, for our desires are then educated and our hearts purified of selfishness by the power of his Holy Spirit (Helaman 10:5). If we here submit, we shall there inherit. C. S. Lewis wisely and soberly observed, "There are only two kinds of people in the end: those who say to God, 'Thy will be done,' and those to whom God says, in the end, 'Thy will be done.'"[7]

Is there a better day than today to surrender to our Savior? Will there be a better time to change, a more appropriate or fitting occasion for refinement, conversion, or consecration? Or will we make today a moment that matters, an instant in eternity toward which we will look back with gratitude and thanksgiving for a decision that really counted?

2. We begin to view the Church as a place where we go to share, to give, to *contribute*. Realizing that the Church has need of every member

---

6. "Swallowed Up in the Will of the Father," *Ensign*, November 1995, 24.
7. *Great Divorce*, 72.

(Doctrine and Covenants 84:109–10; 1 Corinthians 12), we come to understand that each person, each member of the body of Christ, contributes to the ward or branch distinctive gifts and essential talents. It's not uncommon to hear someone say, "I just don't get anything out of church anymore," or "I go to church hungry and come home hungry. We read the same scriptures and hear the same messages over and over." The plain fact is, what we experience in our worship services or in our lessons is largely a matter of our own pre-worship preparation, our expectations, and the extent to which we choose to participate.

To begin with, let's discuss our preparation. What we do on Monday through Saturday in the home and with our family—personal and family scripture study, as well as personal reflection and family discussion on some of the materials prepared by the Church—will have a significant effect on what we experience in our meetings at church on the Sabbath. When we contemplate and think upon sacred things during the week (personal devotional time), then our Church experience (communal devotional time) becomes a spiritual capstone to a wonderfully well-spent week. When we earnestly seek the guidance and direction of the Holy Spirit on weekdays, then sacrament meeting, Sunday School, and priesthood or Relief Society meetings will be spiritually enriching and intellectually stimulating for us and others.

Now, our expectations. What do we expect to happen in a sermon or a lesson? Is it realistic to suppose that the speaker or teacher will consistently bring forth new doctrinal insights or formerly undiscovered historical details? Not really. Is it reasonable to suppose that we will spend most of our time in church dealing with the meat of the gospel of Jesus Christ? Probably not. In a church like ours, Brother and Sister Martinez, who joined the Church forty years ago, are frequently in the same chapel and in the same classroom with Brother and Sister Watson, who were baptized on Saturday. Because of the diversity of experience and gospel understanding within a given ward or branch, it will probably be the case that in Church meetings we will consistently teach the "milk" of the gospel, the fundamental principles and doctrine. Such teachings will stretch the recently baptized Watsons, will inspire them to search and pray and seek for deeper doctrinal understanding.

Whether longtime members Brother and Sister Martinez are edified depends largely on their *participation*. What might the Martinezes do to derive the most spiritual benefit from sacrament meeting or their classes? They could certainly, during the week, read the scriptural passages (or other lesson material) assigned for that day's lesson, study them carefully and prayerfully, and be prepared to make a contribution in class. Such a contribution may take the form of listening intently, thinking seriously, and praying for divine guidance in finding new meaning and new applications. Or, they might make helpful comments and observations throughout the lesson when it seems appropriate. They can also pray earnestly for the instructor that she or he will be comforted, guided, and inspired in teaching the truth and leading the class discussion. Frankly, no matter how much we know, no matter how much formal education we have, no matter how many scholarly works we have devoured, there is always room to learn and experience more at church. This, however, usually requires humility and openness on our part.

"Attitudes of apathy toward the Church and the gospel," President Russell M. Nelson warned, "are but symptoms—symptoms of an underlying *lack of conversion to the Lord*. Thus, the best way to combat apathy is to deepen one's conversion to God and His Beloved Son."[8]

3. We gradually begin to view commandments, laws, and Church directives differently, to no longer see them as guardrails, barricades, or hindrances to life's enjoyments, considering them to be helps, guides, and kind gestures of a benevolent Father in heaven. To those Saints who had begun to gather to the land of Missouri, those who had come out of the world and chosen the gospel path, the Savior promised that

---

8. *Teachings of Russell M. Nelson*, 67.

they would be "crowned with blessings from above, yea, and *with commandments not a few,* and with revelations in their time" (Doctrine and Covenants 59:4; emphasis added). We might well ask, Who wants more commandments? Yet we certainly cannot enjoy the blessings of living a law we do not keep or one of which we are ignorant. John the Beloved explained that "this is the love of God, that we keep his commandments: and *his commandments are not grievous* [burdensome, oppressive]" (1 John 5:3; emphasis added).

Sister Carole M. Stephens of the Relief Society General Presidency explained that "we can choose to see commandments as limitations. We may feel at times that God's laws restrict our personal freedom, take from us our agency, and limit our growth. But as we seek for greater understanding, as we allow our Father to teach us, we will begin to see that His laws are a manifestation of His love for us and obedience to His laws is an expression of our love for Him."[9]

4. The more earnestly we search the scriptures, the more often we begin to see patterns, connections, parallels, and principles closely related to our own experience. Holy writ becomes more and more relevant to everyday life. To borrow Nephi's words, we "liken the scriptures" to ourselves more often (1 Nephi 19:23). As a result and in our ever-changing circumstances, we begin to discover "new writing" (1 Nephi 16:29) in those frequently read scriptures, to uncover principles and precepts that we never really saw before. In my own life, as I found myself falling in love with scripture, the more I cross-referenced one scripture with another, the more I cross-referenced general conference addresses to scriptures, the more I heard myself quoting the words of Jesus and Paul and John or paraphrasing the words of Lehi or Abinadi or Moroni. Holy writ thereby becomes a part of us.

In a sense, the words of the prophets become our words. Many of us can still vividly remember the final sermon and testimony of Elder

9. "If Ye Love Me, Keep My Commandments," *Ensign*, November 2015, 119.

Bruce R. McConkie, delivered just days before his death. As he began to unfold the truths associated with Christ's atoning sacrifice, he said: "In speaking of these wondrous things I shall use my own words, though you may think they are the words of scripture, words spoken by other Apostles and prophets.

"True it is they were first proclaimed by others, but *they are now mine,* for the Holy Spirit of God has borne witness to me that they are true, and it is now as though the Lord had revealed them to me in the first instance. *I have thereby heard his voice and know his word.*"[10]

The scriptures are both timely and timeless: they may provide comfort, inspiration, or insight for a pressing problem, a current conundrum. And because they were spoken and written by the power of the Holy Spirit, their messages and lessons are everlastingly relevant. They never get old; they never expire or go out of date.

5. We begin to be more secure and settled in our faith, less troubled by unanswered questions. Our faith begins to be transformed into sure knowledge. This process, a lifetime endeavor, to be sure, is beautifully illustrated by the brother of Jared. Moroni explained that "there were many whose faith was so exceedingly strong, even before Christ came, who could not be kept from within the veil, but truly *saw with their eyes the things which they had beheld* [previously] *with an eye of faith,* and they were glad. And behold, we have seen in this record that one of these was the brother of Jared." Of his faith Moroni added that "*the Lord could not withhold anything from his sight;* wherefore he showed him all things, for he could no longer be kept without the veil" (Ether 12:19–21; emphasis added). In modern revelation, the Savior sets forth simply but powerfully a principle with a promise: "I, the Lord, am bound when ye do what I say; but when ye do not what I say, ye have no promise" (Doctrine and Covenants 82:10).

Sherem the anti-Christ "was learned, that he had a perfect

10. "Purifying Power of Gethsemane," *Ensign,* May 1985, 9; emphasis added.

knowledge of the language of the people; wherefore, he could use much flattery, and much power of speech, according to the power of the devil." Now note the words of Jacob: "And he had hope to shake me from the faith, *notwithstanding the many revelations and the many things which I had seen* concerning these things; for I truly had seen angels, and they had ministered unto me. And also, *I had heard the voice of the Lord speaking unto me in very word, from time to time; wherefore, I could not be shaken*" (Jacob 7:4–5; emphasis added).

Enos, the son of Jacob, knew very well the kind of man his father was. Enos knew of his goodness, his closeness to the Savior, his profound knowledge of the Savior's Atonement and the principles of the gospel. He no doubt recognized—and I suppose I am here reading between the lines—that his father had something he wanted, something most precious, something that brought strength and security and serenity into his life. And so Enos went into the woods ostensibly to hunt beasts, but in reality he went into solitude to hunt for the witness, the testimony, the sure knowledge that saves and satisfies the human soul. After many hours of stretching and pleading prayer, he heard the voice of the Lord saying, "Enos, *thy sins are forgiven thee,* and thou shalt be blessed." That gracious gift came to Enos, in the words of the Redeemer, "because of thy faith in Christ, whom thou hast never before heard nor seen. . . . Wherefore, go to, *thy faith hath made thee whole.*" Having poured out his heart in sublime supplication, having received the desire of his heart, his *"faith began to be unshaken in the Lord"* (Enos 1:1–11; emphasis added).

Unshaken faith in the work of the Lord. Isn't that what each one of us most desires in the midst of a world filled with snide cynicism and religious skepticism? Knowing the truth, and knowing that you know, bring peace and balance, certitude and calmness in a world gone mad.[11]

---

11. See Callister, "Knowing That We Know," *Ensign*, November 2007, 100–101.

"Certitude is certainty," President Gordon B. Hinckley pointed out. "It is conviction. It is the power of faith that approaches knowledge—yes, that even becomes knowledge. It evokes enthusiasm, and there is no asset comparable to enthusiasm in overcoming opposition, prejudice, and indifference."[12]

He continued: "If the Latter-day Saints, as individuals, ever lose that certitude, the Church will dwindle as so many other churches have. But I have no fear of that. I am confident that an ever-enlarging membership will seek for and find that personal conviction which we call testimony, which comes by the power of the Holy Ghost, and which can weather the storms of adversity."[13]

Cyprian, one of the great defenders of the faith after the apostolic period, described his own experience: "Into my heart, purified of all sin, there entered a light which came from on high, and then suddenly, and in a marvelous manner, I saw certainty succeed doubt."[14]

6. We begin to face our trials, our challenges—indeed, the vicissitudes of life—in a less defensive, angry way. We become much less inclined to cry out, "Why me?" We become less likely to blame God for our financial losses, our depression, or the death of a loved one. We become more accepting of the fact that we live in a fallen, mortal world, a world characterized not only by thorns and thistles and briars and noxious weeds but also by health challenges, emotional crises, and sins that disrupt marriages and families; these painful and poignant moments come with the turf of our second estate. We become more prone to ask God in prayer, "What would you have me learn from this? What would you have me do?"

Elder D. Todd Christofferson taught us a significant lesson when he stated that "the temptations and tribulations we experience, plus any testing that the Lord sees fit to impose, can lead to our full conversion

---

12. *Faith, the Essence of True Religion,* 1.
13. *Faith, the Essence of True Religion,* 5–6.
14. Cited in Lee, *Stand Ye in Holy Places,* 57.

and healing. But this happens if, and only if, we do not harden our hearts or stiffen our necks against Him. If we remain firm and steadfast, come what may, we achieve the conversion the Savior intended . . . , a conversion so complete that it cannot be undone."[15]

7. We begin to feel a deeper sense of love for and loyalty toward the apostles and prophets, those charged to guide the destiny of the kingdom of God. As the Lord explained in modern revelation (Doctrine and Covenants 1:38; 21:5), the words of the prophets, seers, and revelators truly are His words. Their counsel becomes His counsel. We cannot very well accept the word of the Savior and at the same time reject the word of those he has commissioned to lead us. In a revelation given to Thomas B. Marsh, who was serving as the President of the Quorum of the Twelve Apostles, Jesus Christ sounded this significant message: "Whosoever receiveth my word receiveth me, and *whosoever receiveth me, receiveth those, the First Presidency, whom I have sent*" (Doctrine and Covenants 112:20; emphasis added).

To say that another way, as the level of our love for and devotion toward the Father and the Son continues to rise, and as it begins to color and shine upon all we say and do, our loyalty to those men chosen to stand in the shoes of Joseph Smith and Oliver Cowdery and Brigham Young and Heber Kimball is driven deeper into the soil of faith and conversion. President Harold B. Lee was fond of teaching: "That [man or woman] is not truly converted unless he [or she] sees the power of God resting upon the leaders of this Church and [that witness] goes down into his [or her] heart like fire."[16] We begin to see and feel about world conditions and the state of society as the Brethren do, even and especially when what the prophets say is at variance with what the world would have us believe.

---

15. "Firm and Steadfast in the Faith of Christ," *Ensign*, November 2018, 33.
16. *Teachings of Harold B. Lee*, 520.

8. We come to accept the humbling fact that we are unable to identify and then correct our weaknesses on our own. We ask regularly, "Lord, what lack I yet?" (see Matthew 19:20). We need God's help. We need the power of his Holy Spirit to reach into the darkest corners of our souls, to penetrate to the depths of our being—to look for matters that are beneath the level of our consciousness—and then to reveal to us what specific areas are in need of change and improvement. Elder Larry L. Lawrence of the Seventy stated: "I knew a faithful mother who humbled herself and asked, 'What is keeping me from progressing?' In her case, the response from the Spirit came immediately: 'Stop complaining.' . . . In the days that followed, she became conscious of her habit of complaining. Grateful for the prompting to improve, she determined to count her blessings instead of her challenges. Within days, she felt the warm approval of the Spirit.

"A humble young man who couldn't seem to find the right young woman went to the Lord for help: 'What is keeping me from being the right man?' he asked. This answer came into his mind and heart: 'Clean up your language.' At that moment, he realized that several crude expressions had become part of his vocabulary, and he committed to change.

"A single sister bravely asked the question: 'What do I need to change?' and the Spirit whispered to her, 'Don't interrupt people when they are talking.' The Holy Ghost really does give customized counsel. He is a completely honest companion and will tell us things that no one else knows or has the courage to say."[17]

As members of the Lord's Church, we have been charged, like Simon Peter, to strengthen our brothers and sisters (Luke 22:31–32). The converted ones—those who have undergone the "mighty change"

---

17. "What Lack I Yet?" *Ensign*, November 2015, 33–34.

(Mosiah 5:2) associated with the new birth—are eager to reach down, extend a helping hand, and lift other souls, because they themselves are standing on higher ground.[18] In speaking of the Nephite nation after the transcendent visit of the resurrected Christ, Mormon records that "in the thirty and sixth year, the people were *all converted to the Lord,* upon all the face of the land, both Nephites and Lamanites, and there were no contentions and disputations among them, and every man did deal justly one with another." Further, there were not "rich and poor, bond and free, but *they were all made free, and partakers of the heavenly gift.*" Indeed, there was "no contention in the land, because of the love of God which did dwell in the hearts of the people" (4 Nephi 1:2, 3, 15; emphasis added).

It is Christ who changes the human heart; Christ who binds up the broken heart. He does so through the power of the Holy Ghost, that Spirit who bears witness of the Father and Son; that Spirit who plants a testimony in the soul; that Spirit who brings light and truth and clarity to the human mind; that Spirit who cleanses, purifies, and conforms the individual into the image of Christ; and that Spirit who seals one up unto eternal life. Conversion is to the Holy Messiah. It comes through applying his precious atoning blood and takes place through the mighty work of the third member of the Godhead.

---

18. See Lee, in Conference Report, April 1973, 178–79.

Chapter 16

LAYING HOLD ON
EVERY GOOD GIFT

~

*J*ust before the resurrected Lord ascended into heaven in the Old World, he gave a charge to his disciples. According to the Gospel of Mark, the Savior said, "Go ye into all the world, and preach the gospel to every creature. He that believeth and is baptized shall be saved; but he that believeth not shall be damned. And *these signs shall follow them that believe;* in my name shall they cast out devils; they shall speak with new tongues; they shall take up serpents; and if they drink any deadly thing, it shall not hurt them; they shall lay hands on the sick, and they shall recover" (Mark 16:15–18; emphasis added). The risen Lord issued that same charge to his American Hebrews (Mormon 9:22–24; see also Ether 4:18).

Let's reflect for a moment on this great commission that is at the heart of evangelism, or missionary work, in Christian churches throughout the world. Clearly, God desires that all of his children hear and receive the message of salvation. Our all-loving Father in heaven "will have all men to be saved, and to come unto the knowledge of the truth" (1 Timothy 2:4; see also 2 Peter 3:9). And perhaps the most effective way to accomplish this grand goal is to empower and commission those who have received the gospel to share it. Those who have received it are the ones who will have repented, been baptized by water and by the Spirit, and charted a course toward a whole new way of life, a "life in Christ" (Romans 8:2). Because they have received the Holy Ghost and are thereby spiritually filled and empowered, they strive to do the work of their Master, even as he did it.

Yes, they declare the words of truth and testify of their message—just as Jesus did. Their ministries are also characterized by the manifestations of the same supernal gifts and supernatural signs that Jesus and his apostles demonstrated—they have power over Satan and his unholy hosts; they speak with a tongue that has been touched by heaven; they are guarded, protected, and delivered from many of the roadblocks that inevitably cross the paths of true disciples; and they heal the sick by the laying on of hands, enjoying power in that holy priesthood with which they have been ordained. In short, faithful followers of Jesus Christ have, in the words of the apostle Peter, come out of the darkness of a decaying world into God's marvelous light (1 Peter 2:9). They become heirs of the gifts and fruit of the Spirit.

MANY, MANY GIFTS

It might well be the case that some of the most important doctrinal teachings are those that are dealt with again and again in scripture, making their way through both ancient and modern revelation like doctrinal refrains. How many times does John the Beloved, in his Gospel as well as in his epistles, mention that true Christians love and serve God and God's children? How often does Jesus warn his followers about being possessed by their possessions? How many times in the Book of Mormon does the prophet-editor Mormon warn us of the perils of the prosperity cycle and of the need to care for the poor and needy? How often does Jesus Christ call upon the Latter-day Saints to gather, to bring forth and establish the cause of Zion? Clearly these are matters dear to the heart of the Shepherd and his undershepherds.

And so it is with the gifts of the Spirit. We read of them in the twelfth, thirteenth, and fourteenth chapters of Paul's first epistle to the Corinthians. We encounter them again in Moroni 10 as the Book of

Mormon comes to a close. And we are reminded of the deep significance of those wonderful gifts in a modern revelation, Doctrine and Covenants 46.

First Corinthians 12 begins as follows: "Now concerning spiritual gifts, brethren [and sisters], I would not have you ignorant." In other words, Paul does not want the Saints to be in the dark or confused about this matter of spiritual gifts. Understanding them is a necessary, even a vital, part of our Christian ministry. Paul goes on: "Ye know that ye were Gentiles, carried away [led astray] unto these dumb idols, even as ye were led. Wherefore I give you to understand, that no man speaking by the Spirit of God calleth Jesus accursed: and that no man can say that Jesus is the Lord, but by the Holy Ghost" (1 Corinthians 12:1–3). Most of us would agree that no person who has within his or her soul the testimony that Jesus is the Christ can curse that very Christ. Or at least we might say that no person can do such a thing without serious spiritual consequences. I think we also would agree that anyone can *say* that Jesus is Lord; the devils can do that (Mark 1:34; Luke 4:41; James 2:19). Importantly, the Prophet Joseph Smith corrected that error in a sermon he delivered: "No man can *know* that Jesus is the Lord, but by the Holy Ghost."[1] As Paul teaches earlier in his epistle, the only way we can know anything pertaining to spiritual things is by the power of the Spirit of God (1 Corinthians 2:11–14). God and his plan of salvation are either revealed or remain forever unknown and little understood.

Paul then writes of the various gifts of the Spirit: wisdom, knowledge, faith, healing, the working of miracles, prophecy, discernment, tongues, and the interpretation of tongues. Moroni adds to this list the gifts of teaching wisdom, teaching knowledge, and beholding angels and ministering spirits. The Doctrine and Covenants adds the conviction that Jesus Christ is the Son of God and that he was crucified

---

1. *Words of Joseph Smith*, 115; emphasis added; see also "Gift of the Holy Ghost," *Times and Seasons* 3, no. 16 (15 June 1842): 823.

for the sins of the world (that is, the testimony of Jesus), the spiritual capacity to believe on the words of those who do know (the gift of a believing heart), and the faith to be healed.

Now what can we say about spiritual gifts that will provide a broader and deeper perspective?

1. Every person possesses at least one spiritual gift. "For all have not every gift given unto them; for there are many gifts, and to every man is given a gift by the Spirit of God" (Doctrine and Covenants 46:11). Early Latter-day Saint Amasa Potter recalled: "I remember the Prophet arising to preach to a large congregation in the grove west of the Temple in Nauvoo. He stated that he would preach on spiritual gifts. . . . Joseph stated that every Latter-day Saint had a gift, and by living a righteous life, and asking for it, the Holy Spirit would reveal it to him or her."[2]

2. The Holy Ghost draws upon the Light of Christ to dispense the gifts of the Spirit.[3] "And all these gifts come by the Spirit of Christ; and they come unto every man severally, according as he will" (Moroni 10:17).

3. It is perfectly appropriate for a disciple of Christ to pray for various spiritual gifts. Indeed, we are charged by the Lord to "seek ye earnestly the best gifts" (Doctrine and Covenants 46:8). It would seem that the best gifts would be the ones that would assist us most in blessing those with whom we have been called to serve and labor. They may be as different as our labors are different. We need, for example, persons who have musical talents, organizational abilities, discernment, knowledge, wisdom, the gift of healing, faith to be healed, and the gift of working miracles.

4. These gifts, as different as the people to whom they are given, assure that every member of the Church is divinely endowed to

---

2. *Joseph Smith* [manual], 117.
3. See McConkie, *New Witness for the Articles of Faith*, 258.

make special contributions to the "body of Christ," the Church (1 Corinthians 12:27). Thus all are benefited by and in their association with others who are part of the family, or community, of Saints.

5. When we choose not to attend church or associate with other members of the Church, we rob them of the encouragement and strength that would have come from the union of our gifts with theirs. In like manner, we forfeit all the richness and goodness we would have enjoyed through the gifts they have been given.

6. Spiritual gifts play a key role in keeping the doctrine and practices of the Church pure. Doctrine and Covenants 46 was given, at least in part, so that the Saints would not be "seduced by evil spirits, or doctrines of devils, or the commandments of men" (v. 7). Further, they have been given for the benefit of those who love the Lord and keep all the commandments, and, thank heaven, all that seek to do so (vv. 8–9).

7. Some gifts are noticeable; others may be invisible and quiet. That is not to say that one gift is of greater worth than another. In fact, the Prophet Joseph observed that the "greatest, the best, and the most useful gifts" might go unobserved.[4] One of the most noticeable gifts, one that many people have eagerly sought after, but one that is often counterfeited, is the gift of tongues. Joseph Smith actually gave more cautions than recommendations concerning this gift.[5]

8. Many spiritual gifts are described in scripture, but there is an almost infinite variety of gifts that the Lord can and will bestow upon his children. Elder Marvin J. Ashton taught: "Let us review some of these less-conspicuous gifts: the gift of asking; the gift of listening; the gift of hearing and using a still, small voice; the gift of being able to weep;

---

4. *Joseph Smith* [manual], 120–21.

5. The Prophet warned the Saints to be careful lest they be deceived; that it is not necessary for tongues to be taught to the Church; because the devil will often take advantage of the innocent and unwary, if anything is taught in the Church by the gift of tongues, it is not to be received as doctrine; it is the smallest gift of all but the one most sought after (*Joseph Smith* [manual], 383–84; "Gift of the Holy Ghost," *Times and Seasons* 3, no. 16 [15 June 1842]: 825).

the gift of avoiding contention; the gift of being agreeable; the gift of avoiding vain repetition; the gift of seeking that which is righteous; the gift of not passing judgment; the gift of looking to God for guidance; the gift of being a disciple; the gift of caring for others; the gift of being able to ponder; the gift of offering prayer; the gift of bearing a mighty testimony; and the gift of receiving the Holy Ghost."[6]

9. As to the governing and oversight of this multitude of gifts, the revelation declares that "the bishop of the Church" and all others God has called to preside over and look after the Church "are to have it given unto them to discern all those gifts lest there shall be any among you professing and yet be not of God" (Doctrine and Covenants 46:27). This gift of discernment functions in at least two ways. First, the presiding officer, the one holding priesthood keys, uses this gift to discern how to most effectively use the gifts of those who labor under his direction (that is, in which callings members should serve). Second, those possessing this gift are granted a special ability to discern when gifts are being used improperly and to detect those instances in which counterfeit gifts or false spirits are being used to manipulate, confuse, or deceive the Saints.

10. Wherever faithful members of the Church may be, there the gifts of the Spirit will be abundantly poured out upon the people of the covenant. On the other hand, where these gifts have ceased, "wo be unto the children of men, for it is because of unbelief, and all is vain" (Moroni 7:37). Moroni pleaded with his readers to "deny not the power of God; for he worketh by power, according to the faith of the children of men, the same today and tomorrow, and forever. And again, I exhort you, my brethren [and sisters], that ye deny not the gifts of God" (Moroni 10:7–8). The Lord himself reminds us: "I am God; and I am a God of miracles; and I will show unto the world that I am

---

6. "There Are Many Gifts," *Ensign*, November 1987, 20.

the same yesterday, today, and forever; and I work not among the children of men save it be according to their faith" (2 Nephi 27:23).

SEEKING THE GIFTS VERSUS SEEKING SIGNS

What is the difference between seeking for the gifts of the Spirit, which is commended, and seeking for signs, which is condemned? This is not as easy a question to answer as one might suppose. Jesus himself referred to the gifts of the Spirit as *signs*. They are also called *wonders*. You will recall the incident in the New Testament where the Pharisees came to Jesus requesting a sign that would affirm his divine Sonship. "But he answered and said unto them, An evil and adulterous generation seeketh after a sign; and there shall no sign be given to it, but the sign of the prophet Jonas: For as Jonas was three days and three nights in the whale's belly; so shall the Son of man be three days and three nights in the heart of the earth" (Matthew 12:38–40). That is to say, the Savior's death, burial, and resurrection from the dead would be the only sign he would provide to the faithless Pharisees.

Just how does a disposition to seek after signs relate to seeking after carnal pleasures? Simply stated, those who have given themselves up to their lusts—who desire that which will satisfy and satiate the flesh, who have exhausted their passions in their search for the sensual—also seek for physical manifestations of spiritual phenomena. Unable to recognize eternal certainties, they insist that the truths associated with the area with which they are least familiar—the spiritual—be manifested and translated into that realm they have come to know more surely than any other—the tangible or physical. They demand proof!

The adulterous are those who worship at the altar of appetite, whose thresholds for gratification are ever rising, and who thereby demand something extraordinary to establish the truthfulness of a religious claim. Ironically, such a claim may only be verified by the quiet and unobtrusive whisperings of the Spirit. Spiritual blindness and the spirit of adultery are thus common companions. The faithless demand signs as proof, when, ironically, *"faith cometh not by signs, but signs fol-low those that [already] believe"* (Doctrine and Covenants 63:9; empha-sis added).

"Show me Latter-day Saints who have to feed upon miracles, signs and visions in order to keep them steadfast in the Church," President Joseph F. Smith warned, "and I will show you members of the Church who are not in good standing before God, and who are walking in slip-pery paths. It is not by marvelous manifestations unto us that we shall be established in the truth, but it is by humility and faithful obedience to the commandments and laws of God." President Smith explained that when he was young he would often go to God in prayer and plead for grand and marvelous spiritual manifestations, so that he could gain a strong testimony. And then this holy and spiritually mature servant of God added: "But the Lord withheld marvels from me, and showed me the truth, line upon line, precept upon precept, here a little and there a little, until he made me to know the truth from the crown of my head to the soles of my feet, and until doubt and fear had been absolutely purged from me. He did not have to send an angel from the heavens to do this, nor did he have to speak with the trump of an archangel. *By the whisperings of the still small voice of the Spirit of the living God, he gave to me the testimony I possess. . . . And no amount of marvelous manifestations will ever accomplish this."*[7]

A little over three months before his unexpected death, President Harold B. Lee spoke to a large group of Latter-day Saint students. "As I pray for the guidance of the Spirit," he declared, "and seek to rise to the responsibility which has been given to me, I don't ask for any special endowment. I ask only to go where the Lord would have me go, and only to receive what the Lord would have me receive, knowing that more important than sight is the witness that one may have . . . of the Holy Ghost to his soul that things are so and that Jesus is the Christ,

---

7. *Gospel Doctrine*, 7; emphasis added.

a living personage. It is that which guides me through many of the experiences of life."[8]

THE FRUIT OF THE SPIRIT

One of the identifying marks of our discipleship, one of the significant evidences of our growth into this mighty change and new life in Christ, is the degree to which we have begun to enjoy the *fruit of the Spirit*. It is interesting that in 1 Corinthians 12 Paul suggests that the gifts of the Spirit are intended to enhance, build up, and make perfect the body of Christ, meaning the Church. They are for the good of the Church and kingdom. Certainly related to these gifts are the fruit of the Spirit. In Galatians, the apostle Paul teaches by contrast—by contrasting the works of the flesh with the fruit of the Spirit: "Now the works of the flesh are manifest [obvious, evident], which are these; adultery, fornication, uncleanness, lasciviousness, idolatry, witchcraft, hatred, variance, emulations, wrath, strife, seditions, heresies, envyings, murders, drunkenness, revellings, and such like: of the which I tell you before, . . . that they which do such things shall not inherit the kingdom of God" (Galatians 5:19–21). To say that another way, the works of the flesh are the attitudes and actions flowing from the heart of the natural man, the unredeemed man or woman who is shaping up to become a first-rate enemy of God (Mosiah 3:19; Alma 41:10–11).

For each of us there are two births—a natural birth and a spiritual birth. The natural birth comes automatically with mortality, and from the natural birth comes the natural man. The spiritual birth comes later. The natural birth has its own set of fruit, or works. Paul has just mentioned several of them. The spiritual man or woman—the one who has been cleansed by the atoning blood of Christ through the work of the Holy Spirit—brings forth his or her own fruit, namely, "love, joy, peace, longsuffering, gentleness, goodness, faith, meekness,

---

8. "Be Loyal to the Royal within You," 88.

temperance. . . . If we live in the Spirit, let us also walk in the Spirit" (Galatians 5:22–25).

It is interesting that Paul refers not to the *fruits* of the Spirit (plural) but rather to the *fruit* of the Spirit. One Pauline scholar, Ben Witherington III, offered a possible explanation: "This suggests the unity and unifying nature of these qualities, as opposed to the division and discord produced by works of the flesh. The singular also suggests that all these qualities should be manifest in any Christian's life. The term *fruit* also suggests that *we are not talking about natural virtues or personal attainments but character traits wrought in the believer's life by the work of the Spirit.* Believers must work out these qualities in their social interactions, but the Spirit is their source.

"*Love is the signature Christian quality* to which Paul refers here, as in 1 Corinthians 13. Romans 5:5 makes abundantly clear he is not talking about natural human feelings but rather about *love poured into the hearts of believers by the Spirit.*"[9]

The fruit of the Spirit appears to be associated largely with our relationship with other people—how we treat our fellow man. This is the strongest indication that we are becoming more Christlike. In that regard, President Henry B. Eyring taught that "we receive the Holy Spirit best when we are focused on serving others. . . . When we are engaged in service to others, we think less about ourselves, and the Holy Ghost

---

9. *Paul Quest*, 85; emphasis added. Professor N. T. Wright of St. Andrews University in Scotland made the astute observation that the fruit of the Spirit involves both divine grace and obedient discipleship. He explained that "Christian virtue, including the ninefold fruit of the Spirit, is *both* the gift of God *and* the result of the person of faith making conscious decisions to cultivate this way of life and these habits of heart and mind. In technical language, these things are both 'infused' and 'acquired'" (*After You Believe*, 197). Professor Wright also suggested that "Paul does not envisage that someone might cultivate one or two of these characteristics and reckon that she had enough of an orchard to be going on with. No: when the Spirit is at work, you will see all nine varieties of this fruit. Paul does not envisage specialization" (*After You Believe*, 195).

can more readily come to us and help us in our lifelong quest to have the gift of charity bestowed upon us."[10]

If, for example, people want to know what I'm really like, to know what kind of a person I really am, they can talk to my wife, Shauna, to our children, to my secretary, staff, or coworkers and learn how I treat them, whether I show respect to them, whether I make them feel appreciated and loved. In short, the fruit of the Spirit is the kind of thing that gradually begins to characterize men and women who are becoming more and more like the Savior, the true Prototype of a saved being.[11]

Elder Marion D. Hanks asked what I feel is a haunting question, one that strikes at the core of this matter: "If you were arrested and were to be tried for being a Christian, would there be enough evidence to convict you?"[12] It would be unfortunate if a member were to conclude, because he has been blessed to be a stimulating instructor, that his life is perfectly in order, that the Lord is pleased with his behavior. His gift of the Spirit allows him to help to move the kingdom of God toward its destined end, to broaden and deepen the understanding of the Saints. The Lord's barometer for righteousness, however, is the heart, and to the extent that we have come to value, even treasure the children of God, we are coming to approximate the life of the Savior and are thus on the path that leads to life eternal.

There are but few things upon which we may depend with absolute assurance. "Life has its share of some fear and some failure," said Elder Jeffrey R. Holland. "Sometimes things fall short, don't quite measure up. Sometimes in both personal and public life, we are seemingly left without strength to go on. Sometimes people fail us, or economies and circumstances fail us, and life with its hardship and heartache can leave us feeling very alone.

---

10. "Inspired Ministering," *Ensign*, May 2018, 64.
11. *Lectures on Faith*, 75–76.
12. Hanks, cited in Hartman Rector, Jr., "The Gospel."

"But when such difficult moments come to us, I testify that there is one thing which will never, ever fail us. One thing alone will stand the test of all time, of all tribulation, all trouble, and all transgression. One thing only never faileth—and that is the pure love of Christ. . . . Only the pure love of Christ will see us through. It is Christ's love which suffereth long, and is kind. It is Christ's love which is not puffed up nor easily provoked. Only his pure love enables him—and us—to bear all things, believe all things, hope all things, and endure all things (see Moroni 7:45)."[13]

No matter the depth of our knowledge, the efficiency of our administration, the charisma with which we influence and lead people—no matter how well we *do* what we do, of much greater significance in the eternal scheme of things is who we are, what we are becoming, and what we feel toward God and our fellowman. It is so easy to become distracted from what matters most, to focus on things—on goals, on excellence programs, on statistics—when in reality *it is people that count.* God and Christ are in the business of people (Moses 1:39), and so must we be.

Surely seeking for and acquiring the gifts and fruit of the Spirit is at least a part of what the apostle Peter had in mind when he wrote of the Saints becoming "partakers of the divine nature" (2 Peter 1:4). We partake of the divine nature—God's nature—as we become, through the sanctifying powers of the Holy Spirit, more and more Christlike each day, as we begin, be it ever so gradually, to think and feel and act as our blessed Redeemer and Exemplar thought, felt, and acted. We begin to partake of that holy nature when we separate ourselves from worldliness and waywardness, when we gradually wean ourselves

---

13. "He Loved Them unto the End," *Ensign*, November 1989, 26; see also *Christ and the New Covenant*, 336–37.

from matters of secondary importance, when we choose, as President George Albert Smith charged us, to stay on the Lord's side of the line.[14] The late Roman Catholic scholar Richard John Neuhaus observed: "The kind of people we are is more important than what we can do to improve the world; indeed, being the kind of people we should and can be is the best, and sometimes the only, way to improve the world."[15]

Oh the wonders and glories available to those who have repented of their sins, received baptism by water, been confirmed a member of The Church of Jesus Christ of Latter-day Saints, been extended the right to the constant companionship of the third member of the Godhead, and experienced the Spirit's gifts and fruit. In many ways, taught Elder Bruce R. McConkie, "true greatness, from an eternal standpoint, is measured not in worldly station nor in ecclesiastical office, but in the possession of the gifts of the Spirit and in the enjoyment of the things of God."[16] That we will seek for that kind and quality of greatness is my sincere hope.

---

14. See Smith, *Sharing the Gospel with Others*, 42–43.
15. Cited in Hafen, *Spiritually Anchored in Unsettled Times*, 121.
16. *Promised Messiah*, 574–75.

Chapter 17

PARDONED AND PURIFIED

⌇

*I*n his first epistle to his beloved Timothy, the apostle Paul declared, "This is a faithful saying, and worthy of all acceptation, that Christ Jesus came into the world to save sinners." Later in that same epistle, the apostle to the Gentiles wrote that God "is willing to have all men to be saved, and to come unto the knowledge of the truth which is in Christ Jesus, who is the Only Begotten Son of God, and ordained to be a Mediator between God and man; who is one God, and hath power over all men. For there is one God, and one mediator between God and men, the man Christ Jesus; who gave himself a ransom for all, to be testified in due time" (JST, 1 Timothy 1:15; 2:4–6).

Paul's message is both straightforward and central to the Christian faith: (1) Jesus Christ came to earth to save sinners; (2) God the Father desires to save all of his children; (3) there is but one mediator between an infinitely holy, perfect, resurrected Being and finite, fallen, and unholy mortals, and that Mediator is Jesus Christ; and (4) Jesus offers himself as a willing sacrifice, a ransom for our sins. Let us consider how individuals are both forgiven and purified—justified and sanctified—through the atoning work of the Savior and the cleansing power of the Holy Ghost. In all we say and do, we proceed in light of the grand hope that "if we walk in the light, as [God] is in the light, we have fellowship one with another, and the blood of Jesus Christ his Son cleanseth us from all sin" (1 John 1:7).

JUSTIFICATION BY FAITH THROUGH GRACE

Doctrine and Covenants 20, known in the early days of the Restoration as the "articles and covenants" of the Church (Doctrine and Covenants 33:14), is a marvelous and inspired collection of information on such matters as foundational doctrine, Church government, duties of those called to the Aaronic and Melchizedek Priesthoods, requirements for baptism, and the baptismal and sacramental prayers. Early in the revelation, we learn that the Book of Mormon "contains a record of a fallen people, and the fulness of the gospel of Jesus Christ" and that it has been given to prove "to the world that the holy scriptures are true, and that God does inspire men and call them to his holy work in this age and generation, as well as in generations of old" (Doctrine and Covenants 20:9–11).

A few verses later, after a divine witness of the truthfulness of the Book of Mormon, we are told that "by these things"—by means or because of our possession of this other testament of the Savior and the revelations received at that early date—"we know. . . ." Then follows a list of significant doctrinal themes found throughout Restoration scripture: there is a God in heaven; the Creation; that God the Father is the only true God, the One to whom our ultimate devotion and worship are directed; the fall of our first parents; the Atonement of Jesus Christ; the timelessness of that Atonement and the everlasting nature of the gospel; the oneness of the members of the Godhead; and we are to worship the Father in the name of the Son (Doctrine and Covenants 20:17–28).

Then comes the following: "And we know that justification through the grace of our Lord and Savior Jesus Christ is just and true; and we know also, that sanctification through the grace of our Lord and Savior Jesus Christ is just and true, to all those who love and serve God with all their mights, minds, and strength" (Doctrine and Covenants 20:30–31).

This is a fascinating statement. This verse seems to be saying that the teaching that individuals may be justified and sanctified is a true and essential doctrine, a vital part of the gospel of Jesus Christ.

For a person to be *justified* is for him or her to be forgiven of sin, to be pardoned, to be pronounced innocent or guiltless, to be placed once again in a proper relationship with Deity. Elder D. Todd Christofferson pointed out that "justification and sanctification are at the center of God's gracious plan of salvation." In speaking of justification, he wrote that "pardon comes by the grace of Him who has satisfied the demands of justice by His own suffering, 'the just for the unjust, that he might bring us to God' (1 Peter 3:18). He removes our condemnation without removing the law. We are pardoned and placed in a condition of righteousness with Him. We become, like Him, without sin. We are sustained and protected by the law, by justice. We are, in a word, *justified.* Thus, we may appropriately speak of one who is justified as pardoned, without sin, or guiltless."[1]

Elder Christofferson explained further that "to be sanctified through the blood of Christ is to become clean, pure, and holy. If justification removes the punishment for past sin, then sanctification removes the stain or effects of sin. . . . This marvelous pardon that relieves us of the punishment that justice would otherwise exact for disobedience and the purifying sanctification that follows are best described as gifts." That is, justification and sanctification come to us as an act of pure grace. "Given the magnitude of the gift of grace, we would never suppose, even with all the good we could possibly do in this life, that we had earned it. It is just too great."[2] In speaking of those who will inherit the highest heaven, the celestial glory, the Lord declared in the vision of the glories: "These are they who are *just men made perfect through Jesus the mediator of the new covenant,* who wrought out this

---

1. "Justification and Sanctification," *Ensign*, June 2001, 18, 20.
2. "Justification and Sanctification," *Ensign*, June 2001, 22.

perfect atonement through the shedding of his own blood" (Doctrine and Covenants 76:69; emphasis added).

The revelation recorded in Doctrine and Covenants 20 teaches, as did the apostle Paul, that justification comes not just through keeping the commandments of the Lord but as a gift of a gracious and loving God. In other words, while we seek our very best to keep God's laws and statutes, that is, to perform the works of righteousness, there should be no misunderstanding as to how one is justified: It is by the goodness and grace of the Lord.

Because no one of us—save Jesus only—will travel earth's paths without committing sin, we cannot be justified, or saved, by our works, that is, by our obedience to law. Our only hope is to hold tenaciously to and lean upon One who *did* keep God's law perfectly, the only person who could rightly be saved by law or by works. In other words, our only hope is to be justified *by faith in Christ.*

Elder Gerald N. Lund, formerly of the Seventy, wrote: "The Savior could effect the deliverance [from sin and death] for two important reasons. First, he met the demands of the law of justice for himself because *he kept the laws of God perfectly.* In other words, Christ *was* justified by his works. He avoided the debt [occasioned by sin] altogether and qualified himself to return to the Father—the only one of all mankind to do so. Secondly, he met the demands of the law for all of mankind. He himself owed no debt to the law, but he went before it and in essence said: 'I am perfect and therefore owe you no suffering. However, I will pay the debt for all mankind. I will undergo suffering that I might pay the price for every transgression and sin ever committed by any man.'" Elder Lund explained that "nothing man could do for himself could bring him past [God's] judgment bar successfully without such an Advocate [as Christ]. That is why eternal life is always a gift, and those who do so receive it by 'inheritance.' It is interesting to note," Elder Lund continued, "that the word *inherit* and its cognate words are used seventy-eight times in the Doctrine and Covenants, while the word *earned* and its related words are not used once."[3]

Mormon asked, "Wherefore, my beloved brethren [and sisters], have miracles ceased because Christ hath ascended into heaven, and hath sat down on the right hand of God, *to claim of the Father his rights of mercy which he hath upon the children of men?*" (Moroni 7:27; emphasis added).

The apostle Peter taught, "Humble yourselves therefore under the mighty hand of God, that he may exalt you in due time: *casting all your care upon him; for he careth for you*" (1 Peter 5:6–7; emphasis added). We can give away to him who is the Balm of Gilead our worries, our anxieties, our frettings, our fears, our awful and often unrealistic anticipations, knowing that he will lift our burdens, will care for us—he will not only love us but also, in many ways, *do the caring for us*. It is as though Peter is counseling us, "Quit worrying. Don't be so anxious. Stop wringing your hands. Let Jesus take the burden while you take the peace. Trust him." I once heard someone say, "Grace represents *God's acceptance of me.* Faith represents *my acceptance of God's acceptance of me.* Peace is *my acceptance of me.*" C. S. Lewis thus wrote that if "you have really handed yourself over to Him, it must follow that you are trying to obey Him. But *trying in a new way, a less worried way.*"[4]

An example early in the Book of Mormon of a person being justified by virtue of his faith is Enos, son of Jacob. Having gone into the forest to hunt beasts, he began to reflect on his father's teachings concerning "eternal life, and the joy of the saints." These words, he added, "sunk deep into my heart." In his hunger for greater spirituality, he cried out to God in prayer all day long and into the night. Then came the voice of the Spirit: "Enos, thy sins are forgiven thee, and thou shalt be blessed." He reported that his "guilt was swept away." When he asked God how this was done, he was told that it was accomplished

---

3. "Salvation: By Grace or by Works?" *Ensign*, April 1981, 20–22; see also Sperry, *Paul's Life and Letters*, 176.

4. *Mere Christianity*, 131; emphasis added.

"because of thy faith in Christ, whom thou hast never before heard nor seen" (Enos 1:3–8). Enos was justified by faith, pardoned, exonerated, placed once again in a proper relationship with God.

An illustration of a group being justified by faith is the account of the people of King Benjamin. Benjamin had just presented a message to his people that had recently been delivered to him by an angel—a remarkable and detailed prophecy of the coming of the Savior, his life and ministry, his mission and sufferings and death, his Resurrection, the salvation of little children, and the need to put off the natural man and put on Christ (Mosiah 3). What was the effect upon this assembled group? In Mosiah 4, we read that the people "viewed themselves in their own carnal state, even less than the dust of the earth," which is quite interesting, given that Benjamin had earlier described them as "a diligent people in keeping the commandments of God" (Mosiah 4:2; 1:11).

One sign that we are increasing in spirituality is a greater awareness of where we fall short, a keener sensitivity to our weaknesses. This "doesn't mean we are drifting away from Him," Elder Bruce Hafen pointed out. "It may well mean that we are drawing closer. Like a good coach, a good tutor will always help his students see and correct their mistakes. When we understand that, correction is motivating, not discouraging. For because of the [Lord's] Atonement, we can learn from our mistakes without being condemned by them."[5]

Notice the poignancy of the petition to God offered up by the people of Benjamin: "O have mercy, and apply the atoning blood of Christ that we may receive forgiveness of our sins, and our hearts may be purified; for we believe in Jesus Christ, the Son of God." As we discussed in chapter 15, "the Spirit of the Lord came upon them, and they were filled with joy, having received a remission of their sins, and having peace of conscience, because of the exceeding faith which they had in Jesus Christ" (Mosiah 4:2–3). The people were justified,

5. *Spiritually Anchored in Unsettled Times*, 29.

forgiven, and at peace. But how do we remain in a justified state? How do we remain free of sin? How can we enjoy that level of peace always? Obviously, we could refrain from sinning all the rest of our days on earth, but while such is theoretically possible, it is impossible in practical terms. So how do we remain in a justified state?

Elder David A. Bednar addressed that very question. "As members of the Lord's restored Church," he taught, "we are blessed both by our *initial cleansing from sin* associated with baptism and by the potential for an *ongoing cleansing from sin made possible through the companionship and power of the Holy Ghost—even the third member of the Godhead. . . .*

"That we might more fully keep ourselves unspotted from the world, we are commanded to go to the house of prayer and offer up our sacraments upon the Lord's holy day (Doctrine and Covenants 59:9). Please consider that the emblems of the Lord's body and blood, the bread and the water, are both blessed and sanctified. . . . To sanctify is to make pure and holy. The sacramental emblems are sanctified in remembrance of Christ's purity, of our total dependence upon His Atonement, and of our responsibility to so honor our ordinances and covenants that we can 'stand spotless before [Him] at the last day.'

"The ordinance of the sacrament is a holy and repeated invitation to repent sincerely and to be renewed spiritually. The act of partaking of the sacrament, in and of itself, does not remit sins. But as we prepare conscientiously and participate in this holy ordinance with a broken heart and a contrite spirit, then the promise is that we may *always* have the Spirit of the Lord to be with us. And *by the sanctifying power of the Holy Ghost as our constant companion, we can always retain a remission of our sins.*"[6] God taught Father Adam, "For by the water ye keep the commandment [to be baptized]; *by the Spirit ye are justified,* and by the blood ye are sanctified" (Moses 6:60; emphasis added).

---

6. "Always Retain a Remission of Your Sins," *Ensign*, May 2016, 61–62; emphasis added.

King Benjamin speaks of two additional means whereby we can retain a remission of sins and thus remain in a justified state. First, he charged his people to "remember, and always retain in remembrance, the greatness of God, and your own nothingness, and his goodness and long-suffering towards you, unworthy creatures, and humble yourselves even in the depths of humility." The righteous king then noted that "if ye do this ye shall always rejoice, and be filled with the love of God, and always retain a remission of your sins" (Mosiah 4:11–12). Here we are being challenged to live in a state of gratitude, thanksgiving, humility, a constant recognition of the hand of God in all things (Doctrine and Covenants 59:21), and an ever-present reminder that we can do nothing of worth without ongoing divine assistance (compare John 15:5).

Second, Benjamin closes his sermon with an appeal to this cleansed and purified people by emphasizing that as a sign to God, if they are indeed serious about remaining in good standing before Him, they should constantly look for opportunities to care for the poor and needy. He said, "For the sake of retaining a remission of your sins from day to day, that ye may walk guiltless before God—I would that ye should impart of your substance to the poor, every man according to that which he hath, . . . both spiritually and temporally, according to their wants" (Mosiah 4:26). Caring for other people, shifting our focus from ourselves to our brothers and sisters, and learning to live outside ourselves are the kinds of attitudes and actions that can shield us from sin and rivet us to righteousness. One of the ways we can serve God is through ministering to others (Matthew 25:40; Mosiah 2:17). Being personally and regularly involved in the work of the Master, the work of lifting and feeding and healing others, brings to us the blessings of the Master, including becoming like him.

This principle of caring for others reflects the timeless message of James, the brother of our Lord, who taught, "Religion that is pure and undefiled before God, the Father, is this: to visit orphans and widows in their affliction, and to keep oneself unstained from the world" (James

1:27, English Standard Version). Or, as another translation has it, "As far as God the father is concerned, pure, unsullied devotion works like this: you should visit orphans and widows in their sorrow, and prevent the world [from] leaving its dirty smudge on you."[7] The Prophet Joseph Smith made it clear that "to be justified before God we must love one another: we must overcome evil; we must visit the fatherless and the widow in their affliction, and we must keep ourselves unspotted from the world: for such virtues flow from the great fountain of pure religion. Strengthening our faith by adding every good quality that adorns the children of the blessed Jesus."[8]

SANCTIFICATION BY GRACE AND WORKS

Let's consider again the following scriptural passage: "And we know also, that sanctification through the grace of our Lord and Savior Jesus Christ is just and true, to all those who love and serve God with all their mights, minds, and strength" (Doctrine and Covenants 20:31). While a person may through repentance receive forgiveness of sin (be justified) on a particular day and at a specific time, sanctification is a process, a lifelong cleansing endeavor. The Prophet Joseph taught that when it comes to learning the principles of the gospel, "You must begin with the first, and go on until you learn all the principles of exaltation. But it will be a great while after you have passed through the veil [of death] before you will have learned them. It is not all to be comprehended in this world; it will be a great work to learn our salvation and exaltation even beyond the grave."[9]

So it is with being sanctified. To be sanctified is to be made pure and holy. If justification brings forgiveness of sin, exoneration, pardon, then sanctification entails the gradual removal of the *effects of sin.* Sanctification is a statement about one's state, one's nature. Elder

---

7. N. T. Wright, *The Kingdom New Testament,* 464.

8. Appendix 2: Letter to the Saints Scattered Abroad, June 1835, 137.

9. *Joseph Smith* [manual], 268.

Orson Hyde declared that sanctification "means a purification of, or a putting away from, us, as individuals, and as a community, everything that is evil, or that is not in accordance with the mind and will of our heavenly Father."[10] The Book of Mormon teaches that sanctification comes through yielding one's heart unto God (Helaman 3:35).

Let's return for a moment to the account of the people of King Benjamin. Notice the earnest plea and genuine request of the people after they have heard Benjamin's discourse: "O have mercy, and apply the atoning blood of Christ that we may receive *forgiveness of our sins* [justification], and *our hearts may be purified* [sanctification]; for we believe in Jesus Christ, the Son of God" (Mosiah 4:2; emphasis added).

In the beloved Christian hymn "Rock of Ages," we find these moving words, in which *wrath* refers to justification and *pure* speaks of sanctification:

> *Rock of Ages, cleft for me,*
> *Let me hide myself in thee;*
> *Let the water and the blood,*
> *From thy wounded side which flowed,*
> *Be of sin the double cure,*
> Save from wrath and make me pure.[11]

The apostle Paul testified that "being now justified by [Christ's] blood, we shall be saved from wrath through him" (Romans 5:9). Truly, the one who is worthy to ascend the hill of the Lord, worthy of the temple here and paradise hereafter, is "he that hath clean hands, *and a pure heart*" (Psalm 24:3–4; emphasis added). In the midst of his plea for forgiveness for his grievous sins, King David cried out, "Create in me a clean heart, O God; and renew a right spirit within me" (Psalm 51:10).

Salvation is the greatest of all the *gifts* of God (2 Nephi 26:23–27;

---

10. In *Journal of Discourses*, 1:71.
11. "Rock of Ages," *Hymns*, 1985, no. 111; emphasis added.

Mosiah 2:4; Doctrine and Covenants 6:13; 14:7) and comes through his mercy and grace. As the revelation states, sanctification also comes through the grace of God, but the sanctifying process entails also the performance of what we call the works of righteousness. Elder Christofferson put it this way: "Justification and sanctification are accomplished by the grace of Christ, which grace is a gift to man based on faith. But our moral agency is also a necessary element in this divine process. We must will to repent and act to repent. We must elect to be baptized and receive the Holy Ghost, and we must elect to remain loyal to our covenants thereafter. To receive the gift we must act in the manner He has ordained."[12]

We involve ourselves in good works not just because we have been commanded to do so but also because the works themselves become an important means by which our Christian character is formed, by which our hearts and minds are transformed.

We are sanctified because Jesus Christ suffered for us in Gethsemane and on Golgotha. His spilt blood makes sanctification possible. Truly, "it is the blood that maketh an atonement for the soul" (Leviticus 17:11). Indeed, it is "by the blood [we] are sanctified" (Moses 6:60). One of the most fascinating messages in scripture is that we must be "washed in the blood" of the Savior (1 Nephi 12:10; 3 Nephi 27:19; Ether 13:10). Alma taught that such ancient high priests as Melchizedek who had proven faithful to their covenants "were sanctified, and their garments were washed white through the blood of the Lamb" (Alma 13:11).

And yet the means, or medium, by which we are sanctified, or made pure, is God's Holy Spirit. Of those ancient high priests, Alma observed that "they, after being *sanctified by the Holy Ghost,* having their garments made white, being pure and spotless before God, could not look upon sin save it were with abhorrence" (Alma 13:11–12; emphasis added). When

---

12. "Justification and Sanctification," *Ensign,* June 2001, 23–24.

the resurrected Lord visited the Nephites after his death and ascension, he established the pattern by which persons are declared innocent and guiltless and also by which they may be purified. "And no unclean thing can enter into [the Father's] kingdom," he said. "Therefore nothing entereth into his rest save it be those who have *washed their garments in my blood*, because of their faith, and the repentance of all their sins, and their faithfulness unto the end. Now this is the commandment: Repent, all ye ends of the earth, and come unto me and be baptized in my name, that ye may be *sanctified by the reception of the Holy Ghost*, that ye may stand spotless before me at the last day" (3 Nephi 27:19–20; emphasis added).

It is one thing to simply stop doing wrong—which, of course, is of great importance—and another thing entirely to undergo the kind of spiritual metamorphosis in which the sinner is truly changed, his desires and longings and ambitions transformed, her inclinations and disposition altered. That is sanctification. Elder B. H. Roberts offered an excellent description of the work of the Holy Spirit in sanctifying the human soul. He pointed out that the forgiven soul may still continue to "feel the force of sinful habits bearing heavily upon him. . . .

"There is an absolute necessity for some additional sanctifying grace that will strengthen the poor human nature, not only to enable it to resist temptation, but also to root out from the heart concupiscence—the blind tendency or inclination to evil. The heart must be purified, every passion, every propensity made submissive to the will, and the will of man brought into subjection to the will of God.

"Man's natural powers are unequal to this task; so, I believe, all will testify who have made the experiment. Mankind stand in some need of a strength superior to any they possess of themselves, to accomplish this work of rendering pure our fallen nature. Such strength, such power, such a sanctifying grace is conferred on man in being born of the Spirit—in receiving the Holy Ghost. Such, in the main, is its office, its work."[13]

---

13. *Gospel and Man's Relationship to Deity*, 170.

C. S. Lewis wrote that as we begin to become new creatures in Christ, as we mature in the things of the Spirit, "we begin to notice, besides our particular sinful acts, our sinfulness; begin to be alarmed not only about what we do, but about what we are. This may sound rather difficult, so I will try to make it clear from my own case. When I come to my evening prayers and try to reckon up the sins of the day, nine times out of ten the most obvious one is some sin against charity; I have sulked or snapped or sneered or stormed. And the excuse that immediately springs to my mind is that the provocation [against me] was so sudden and unexpected: I was caught off my guard, I had not time to collect myself." He then pointed out that "surely what a man does when he is taken off his guard is the best evidence for what sort of man he is."

Lewis then offered a clever and memorable analogy: "If there are rats in a cellar you are most likely to see them if you go in very suddenly. But the suddenness does not create the rats: it only prevents them from hiding. In the same way the suddenness of the provocation [against me] does not make me an ill-tempered man: it only shows me what an ill-tempered man I am. . . . And if . . . what we are matters even more than what we do—if indeed, what we do matters chiefly as evidence of what we are—then it follows that *the change which I most need to undergo is a change that my own direct, voluntary efforts cannot bring about.* . . . I cannot, by direct moral effort, give myself new motives. After the first few steps in the Christian life we realise that everything which really needs to be done in our souls can be done only by God."[14]

As we strive daily to *imitate* the deeds of the only perfect Being to walk the earth, we also seek to *cultivate* the sacred influence that causes Christ to be "formed in us" and live in us (Galatians 2:20; 4:18–19), resulting in a Christlike nature as well as Christlike behavior. That

14. *Mere Christianity*, 165–66; emphasis added.

influence is, of course, the gift of the Holy Ghost. We are then in a position to *emulate* him who is the Captain of our salvation. Having forsaken the sins of this world, received the covenants and ordinances of salvation and exaltation, and complied faithfully with the terms of those covenants, we "are washed, . . . sanctified, . . . justified in the name of the Lord Jesus, and by the Spirit of our God" (1 Corinthians 6:11).

President Ezra Taft Benson offered profound counsel when he stated: "*The Lord works from the inside out. The world works from the outside in.* The world would take people out of the slums. Christ takes the slums out of people, and then they take themselves out of the slums. *The world would mold men by changing their environment. Christ changes men, who then change their environment.* The world would shape human behavior, but Christ can change human nature." President Benson said further: "Yes, Christ changes men, and changed men can change the world. Men changed for Christ will be captained by Christ. . . . Finally, men captained by Christ will be consumed in Christ."[15]

The call of Christ is not just a call to be good, a call to abstain from sinful deeds; it is a call to holiness, a call to be renewed in the spirit by the Spirit. His is not just a call for more grit and willpower but instead a call to submit to the cleansing and renovating powers of the Holy One of Israel, which powers are mediated to us by the third member of the Godhead. As we seek the Spirit always and strive to live in a manner that would allow the Holy Ghost to feel welcome, our lives become more joyous, more fulfilling, and more focused on righteousness. Being sanctified from sin, we become holy, just as God has called us to be (Leviticus 11:44; 1 Peter 1:15–16).

---

15. "Born of God," *Ensign*, November 1985, 6; emphasis added.

Chapter 18

HE WILL SEAL US HIS

he Spirit is the true teacher in any lesson or sermon. He is the one who plants a testimony, or a conviction, of God, Christ and his Atonement, and the restored gospel within human hearts. He is the one who reveals the mind and will of God—who points the way; who inspires and informs; who warns and cautions; who comforts and brings peace; who "speaks" through the still, small voice to the mind and heart; who makes things known through visions and dreams; who justifies and sanctifies individuals and thereby prepares them for life in a celestial realm hereafter. There is, however, another extremely important function or role that the Holy Ghost carries out, one that may well be the highest and holiest of all he performs. The third member of the Godhead is also a sealer, and in that role he operates as the Holy Spirit of Promise.[1]

---

1. In the dedicatory prayer of the Kirtland Temple we read: "And do thou grant, Holy Father, that all those who shall worship in this house may be taught words of wisdom out of the best books, and that they may seek learning even by study, and also by faith, as thou hast said; and that *they may grow up in thee, and receive a fulness of the Holy Ghost,* and be organized according to thy laws, and be prepared to obtain every needful thing" (Doctrine and Covenants 109:14–15; emphasis added).

THE EARNEST OF THE SPIRIT

Our faith and our hope are centered in Christ. Our hope cannot rest solely on mortal men and women, no matter how good or noble they may be. Because iniquity abounds in the world, those who are of the world live in despair (Moroni 10:22). Gospel hope is more than wishing, more than yearning for some eventuality or some possession. It is a solid and sure conviction. It is expectation. Anticipation. Assurance. The Saints of the Most High—those who have come out of the world, put off the natural man, and put on Christ—these are they who are entitled to a "more excellent hope" (Ether 12:32).

Hope flows from faith, faith in the Lord Jesus Christ. When we have faith in him, we believe him, in who he is, and in what he has done. Further, we believe he can do what he says he can do with us, which is to make us whole and pure before God the Father and make us happy, productive, and contributing members of his kingdom. Mormon taught: "And again, my beloved brethren [and sisters], I would speak unto you concerning hope. How is it that ye can attain unto faith, save ye shall have hope? And what is it that ye shall hope for? Behold I say unto you that ye shall have hope through the atonement of Christ and the power of his resurrection, to be raised unto life eternal, and this because of your faith in him according to the promise" (Moroni 7:40–41).

Truly, "whoso believeth in God might with surety hope for a better world, yea, even a place at the right hand of God, which hope cometh of faith, maketh an anchor to the souls of men, which would make them sure and steadfast, always abounding in good works, being led to glorify God" (Ether 12:4). Hope in Christ, which is a natural result of our saving faith in Christ, comes through spiritual reawakening, through rebirth. Because we have been born of the Spirit, we realize our place in the royal family and are warmed by this sweet family association. We know that if we can endure to the end—stay faithful to our covenants to the end of this mortal probation and thus true to the family name of Christ—we will enjoy the fulness of blessings of the family, which is the continuation of the family unit into eternity, and receive the fulness of the glory and power of our Heavenly Father (Doctrine and Covenants 76:56; 84:33–38; 132:19–20).

What is the indication and sign that we are on course? How do we know we are spiritually on track? John the Beloved provided a simple answer, one that has profound implications: "Hereby know we that we dwell in him, and he in us, because he hath given us of his Spirit" (1 John 4:13). The presence of God's Holy Spirit is the attestation, the divine assurance, that we are headed in the right direction. It is God's seal, his anointing, his unction to us that our lives are in order (1 John 2:20). "A seal is a mark of ownership . . . and God's seal, by which he brands us as belonging for ever to him, is the Holy Spirit himself. The Holy Spirit is the identity tag of the Christian."[2]

I can recall vividly the fear and anxiety that my wife, Shauna, and I felt when we decided to purchase our first home. We had very little money in savings and only a steady job that did not, at that time, result in what was required to survive. Yet we knew that we needed to get started sometime if we ever hoped to become homeowners. We determined to start slowly. A dear friend of ours, a fellow seminary teacher, located a home for us in his neighborhood. Another seminary teacher offered to lend us the down payment. We made a good will payment to the owner of the home, a small amount, to be sure, but an amount sufficient to evidence our seriousness about purchasing the place. That amount was a good faith deposit and was called the *earnest money.* It was a token payment, a gesture indicating our desire to acquire that home, a promissory note of sorts. The good faith deposit, or earnest money, was a token or gesture of our intention to be bound by contract and thereafter follow through to the purchase of the house.

In a similar way, our Father in Heaven communicates to us that

---

2. Stott, *Authentic Christianity,* 81.

we are following a proper course by sending his Sprit. The Holy Ghost thus represents God's earnest money and down payment on us, his commitment (even obligation; Doctrine and Covenants 82:10) that he is serious about saving us and that one day he will own us and claim us fully as his own. "Now he which stablisheth us with you in Christ, and hath anointed us, is God; who hath also sealed us, and given *the earnest of the Spirit in our hearts*" (2 Corinthians 1:21–22; emphasis added). "Now he that hath wrought us for the selfsame thing is God, who also hath given us *the earnest of the Spirit*" (2 Corinthians 5:5; emphasis added). The apostle Paul wrote that the Saints had trusted in Christ, "after that ye heard the word of truth, the gospel of your salvation: in whom also after that ye believed, ye were sealed with *that holy Spirit of promise,* which *is the earnest of our inheritance* until the redemption of the purchased possession, unto the praise of his glory" (Ephesians 1:13–14; emphasis added). In short, the same Spirit that eventually seals us up unto eternal life stamps a seal of approval upon our lives now and later. Though the fulness of the blessings of eternal life are not available until the world to come, the peace and rest and hope that are harbingers of those unspeakably sweet blessings can and should be ours in this world (Doctrine and Covenants 59:23).

There is, then, a sense in which we can know our standing with the Lord. If we are living in such a way that the Holy Ghost can dwell in and with us, then we are on the covenant path, on course, and, as both Paul and John would say, "in Christ" (2 Corinthians 5:17; 1 John 4:13). If we are doing all we can to cultivate the gift and gifts of the Spirit, we are living in what might be called *a saved condition.* President David O. McKay observed that "the gospel of Jesus Christ, as revealed to the Prophet Joseph Smith, is in very deed, in every way, the power of God unto salvation. It is salvation *here*—here and now. It gives to every man the perfect life, here and now, as well as hereafter."[3] President Brigham

---

3. *Gospel Ideals,* 6.

Young stated: "It is present salvation and the present influence of the Holy Ghost that we need every day to keep us on saving ground. . . .

"I want present salvation. I preach, comparatively, but little about the eternities and Gods, and their wonderful works in eternity; and do not tell who first made them, nor how they were made; for I know nothing about that. Life is for us, and it is for us to receive it today, and not wait for the millennium. Let us take a course to be saved today, and, when evening comes, review the acts of the day, repent of our sins, if we have any to repent of, and say our prayers; then we can lie down and sleep in peace until the morning, arise with gratitude to God, commence the labors of another day, and strive to live the whole day to God and nobody else."[4]

"I am in the hands of the Lord," President Young pointed out, "and never trouble myself about my salvation, or what the Lord will do with me hereafter."[5] He said on another occasion that our work "is a work of the present. *The salvation we are seeking is for the present, and, sought correctly, it can be obtained, and be continually enjoyed.* If it continues today, it is upon the same principle that it will continue tomorrow, the next day, the next week, or the next year, and we might say, the next eternity."[6]

Though we dare not face life with pride or immoderate self-assurance, we must also avoid false modesty and doubt, which are antithetical to faith. The early Saints of this dispensation were taught that doubt—including a constant worry about our standing before God or our capacity to go where Christ is—cannot coexist with saving faith.[7] "If we are saved," President Young declared, "we are happy, we are filled with light, glory, intelligence, and we pursue a course to enjoy the blessings that the Lord has in store for us. If we continue to pursue that

---

4. In *Journal of Discourses*, 8:124–25.

5. In *Journal of Discourses*, 6:276.

6. In *Journal of Discourses*, 1:131; emphasis added.

7. *Lectures on Faith*, 42, 52–53, 71.

course, it produces just the thing we want, that is, to be saved at this present moment. And this will lay the foundation to be saved forever and forever, which will amount to an eternal salvation."[8]

We cannot overcome the world if we are worldly. We cannot overcome the world if our trust is in the arm of flesh (2 Nephi 4:34). And we cannot overcome the world if we live in constant spiritual insecurity. Satan, the arch deceiver, is versatile, observant, and terribly attentive. As surely as the day follows the night, he will strike at our sense of insecurity before God if we do not acquire the hope or assurance that comes by and through the Holy Spirit. As President Benson taught, we overcome the world though Christ—through being changed by Christ, captained by Christ, and consumed in Christ.[9] In his Last Supper, Jesus declared to his disciples, "These things I have spoken unto you, that in me ye might have peace. In the world ye shall have tribulation: but be of good cheer; I have overcome the world" (John 16:33).

We need not be possessed of an intemperate zeal in order to be saved; we need only to be constant and dependable. God is the other party with us in the gospel covenant, a sacred promise that places us on the covenant path. He is the senior Partner. He lets us know, through the influence of the Holy Ghost, that the everlasting covenant is intact and his supernal promises are sure. President Marion G. Romney taught that "the fulness of eternal life is not attainable in mortality, but the peace which is its harbinger and which comes as a result of making one's calling and election sure is attainable in this life. The Lord has promised that 'he who doeth the works of righteousness shall receive his reward, even peace in this world and eternal life in the world to come' (D&C 59:23)."[10]

Peace. Hope. Assurance. These blessings come to us by virtue of the atoning blood of Jesus Christ and as a natural result of the mighty change, the new creation in Him by the Holy Spirit.

---

8. In *Journal of Discourses*, 1:131.
9. "Born of God," *Ensign*, November 1985, 5–7.
10. *Look to God and Live*, 125–26.

EFFICACY, VIRTUE, AND FORCE HEREAFTER

In the revelation on eternal marriage, the new and everlasting covenant of marriage, we find a lengthy and weighty verse that sets forth what might be called the law of justification: "All covenants, contracts, bonds, obligations, oaths, vows, performances, connections, associations, or expectations, that are not made and entered into and sealed by the Holy Spirit of promise, of him who is anointed, both as well for time and for all eternity . . . are of no efficacy, virtue, or force in and after the resurrection from the dead; for all contracts that are not made unto this end have an end when men are dead" (Doctrine and Covenants 132:7).

The Holy Spirit of Promise is the Holy Ghost, the Holy Spirit promised to the faithful. Because he is a member of the eternal Godhead, "the Comforter knoweth all things" (Doctrine and Covenants 42:17; compare Moses 6:61). Thus in this capacity he is able to search the hearts of all persons (Romans 8:27), certify that persons are justified before God, and seal an exaltation upon them. In the language of holy scripture, such persons will have received the more sure word of prophecy—the knowledge that they are "sealed up unto eternal life, by revelation and the spirit of prophecy, through the power of the Holy Priesthood" (2 Peter 1:10–11; Doctrine and Covenants 131:5). They will thereby have made sure their calling and election to eternal life (2 Peter 1:10–11, 16–19; Doctrine and Covenants 131:5).

This seems to have been the case with Book of Mormon prophets Enos (Enos 1:27), Alma the Elder (Mosiah 26:20), and Nephi, son of Helaman (Helaman 10:5–7). It was also the case with the Prophet Joseph Smith, to whom the Savior said, "I am the Lord thy God, and will be with thee even unto the end of the world, and through all eternity; for verily I seal upon you your exaltation, and prepare a throne for you in the kingdom of my Father, with Abraham your father" (Doctrine and Covenants 132:49).

In the spring of 1839, at the time that Joseph Smith and five other brethren were confined in Liberty Jail, Heber C. Kimball sought to do all he could to care for the Saints and work to free Joseph and his associates. Adding to his feelings of sorrow was the fact that his family had been gone for two months, sent with other families out of Missouri for their protection, and he had received no word from them. "The following words came to my mind," Heber said, "and the Spirit said unto me, 'write,' which I did by taking a piece of paper and writing on my knee as follows: 'A word from the Spirit of the Lord to my servant, Heber C. Kimball:

"'Verily I say unto my servant Heber, thou art my son, in whom I am well pleased; for thou art careful to hearken to my words, and not transgress my law, nor rebel against my servant Joseph Smith, for thou hast a respect to the words of mine anointed, even from the least to the greatest of them; therefore *thy name is written in heaven, no more to be blotted out for ever, because of these things; and this Spirit and blessing shall rest down upon thy posterity for ever and ever.*'"[11]

William Clayton's journal indicates that on 16 May 1843 Joseph the Prophet visited in Ramus, Illinois, with Benjamin F. Johnson and his family. The journal contains the following from the Prophet: "Before retiring, I gave Brother and Sister Johnson some instructions on the priesthood; and putting my hand on the knee of William Clayton, I said: 'Your life is hid with Christ in God, and so are many others. Nothing but the unpardonable sin can prevent you from inheriting eternal life for you are sealed up by the power of the Priesthood unto eternal life, having taken the step necessary for that purpose.'"[12]

TWO COMFORTERS

At the Last Supper Jesus delivered some of the most profound teachings of his ministry, especially as that instruction is recorded in

---

11. Kimball, cited in Whitney, *Life of Heber C. Kimball*, 241; emphasis added.
12. Journal, 16 May 1843.

the Gospel of John. In the fourteenth chapter Jesus taught the apostles that in his Father's house are many mansions; that he is the Way, the Truth, and the Life; that if they have seen Jesus, they have seen the Father; and that he was in the Father and the Father in him. He provided a test for evaluating the depth of one's love for him: "If ye love me, keep my commandments." He then began his instruction relative to the two Comforters. "And I will pray the Father, and he shall give you another Comforter, that he may abide with you for ever; even the Spirit of truth; whom the world cannot receive, because it seeth him not, neither knoweth him; but ye know him; for he dwelleth with you, and shall be in you" (John 14:15–17).

The Greek word translated in the King James Version as *comforter* may also be rendered as *helper* or *advocate*. "Another" helper means "another of the same kind, i.e., someone like Jesus himself who will take his place and do his work. The Spirit . . . is the third person of the [Godhead], having the same essence of deity as Jesus and as perfectly one with him as he is with the Father." The Greek term for *helper* means "one called alongside to help, and has the idea of someone who encourages and exhorts."[13] Jesus also explained that "the Comforter, which is the Holy Ghost, whom the Father will send in my name, he shall teach you all things, and bring all things to your remembrance, whatsoever I have said unto you" (John 14:26).

Within the same chapter of John we find these words: "*I will not leave you comfortless* [orphans]: *I will come to you*"; "He that hath my commandments, and keepeth them, he it is that loveth me: and he that loveth me shall be loved of my Father, and *I will love him, and will manifest myself to him*"; "If a man love me, he will keep my words: and my Father will love him, and *we will come unto him, and make our abode with him*" (John 14:18, 21, 23; emphasis added). "After a person has faith in Christ," Joseph Smith explained, "repents of his sins and

---

13. *MacArthur Study Bible*, 1572.

is baptized for the remission of his sins and receives the Holy Ghost (by the laying on of hands), which is the first Comforter, then let him continue to humble himself before God, hungering and thirsting after righteousness, and living by every word of God, and the Lord will soon say unto him, Son, thou shalt be exalted. When the Lord has thoroughly proved him, and finds that the man is determined to serve Him at all hazards, then the man will find his calling and his election made sure, then it will be his privilege to receive the other Comforter, which the Lord hath promised the Saints, as is recorded in the testimony of St. John, in the fourteenth chapter. . . .

"Now what is this other [Second] Comforter? It is no more nor less than the Lord Jesus Christ Himself; and this is the sum and substance of the whole matter; that when any man obtains this last Comforter, he will have the personage of Jesus Christ to attend him, or appear unto him from time to time, and even He will manifest the Father unto him, and they will take up their abode with him, and the visions of the heavens will be opened unto him, and the Lord will teach him face to face, and he may have a perfect knowledge of the mysteries of the kingdom of God."[14]

God our Father expects us to continue to climb and grow and expand spiritually all our days; this is a vital part of what it means to endure faithfully to the end. Even those who have received the assurance of eternal life must reach and stretch themselves, striving for greater light and deeper understanding. Elder Bruce R. McConkie pointed out that "there are, of course, those whose callings and election have been made sure who have never exercised the faith nor exhibited the righteousness which would enable them to commune with the Lord on the promised basis," that is, face to face. "There are even those who neither believe nor know that it is possible to see the Lord in this day, and they

---

14. Discourse, between ca. 26 June and ca. 2 July 1839; see also *Words of Joseph Smith*, 5.

therefore are without the personal incentive that would urge them on-
ward in the pursuit of this consummation so devoutly desired by those
with spiritual insight."[15]

Let's be perfectly clear on this matter. The Holy Spirit of Promise
is not the Second Comforter. The Holy Spirit of Promise is the Holy
Ghost, the third member of the Godhead, whose role it is to place
his stamp of approval upon all ordinances we have received, as well as
upon our very lives. The Second Comforter is Jesus Christ himself.[16]

We have learned that the unpardonable sin is to deny the Holy
Ghost and defy the Lord's Church and its prophetic leaders, after having
had the heavens opened, received significant light and knowledge, come
to know God, and then sinned against that knowledge. What about
a person who has received the Second Comforter, the presence of the
Savior, and then denied and defied him? President Joseph Fielding Smith
explained that such a person "would also have the knowledge of the First
Comforter and should he turn away, his sin would be unpardonable."[17]

Can we appreciate the singular role of God's Holy Spirit in this
greatest of all spiritual attainments? Latter-day Saints search the scriptures, ponder over them, lift their voices heavenward in prayer frequently and consistently, are involved in the ordinances and instruction found in our meetinghouses and our temples, and seek to minister
to the poor and lift the heavy burdens of those within their sphere of
influence. And through all of this, they plead with the first member of
the Godhead, in the name of the second member of the Godhead, to
bless them with the gifts and influence and power of the third member of the Godhead. All of these facets and functions of Christian discipleship are motivated, quickened, empowered, and inspired by the
Holy Ghost, and it will be so in mortality until we pass through the
veil of death and take up residence in the postmortal spirit world. The

---

15. *Promised Messiah*, 586.
16. See Joseph Fielding Smith, *Doctrines of Salvation*, 1:55.
17. *Doctrines of Salvation*, 1:55.

Prophet of the Restoration summarized things in few but tender words when he taught that the Holy Spirit "shall bring all things to remembrance, whatsoever things I have said unto you. *He shall teach you until you come to me and my Father.*"[18]

~~~~~

The very title Holy Spirit of Promise clearly reminds us that we are a people who have received, as Peter said, "exceeding great and precious promises: that by these [we] might be partakers of the divine nature, having escaped the corruption that is in the world through lust" (2 Peter 1:4). "One of the great challenges each of us faces every day," Elder David A. Bednar declared, "is to not allow the concerns of this world to so dominate our time and energy that we neglect the eternal things that matter most. We can be too easily diverted from remembering and focusing upon essential spiritual priorities because of our many responsibilities and busy schedules. Sometimes we try to run so fast that we may forget where we are going and why we are running. . . .

"We easily can be overcome by the routine and mundane matters of mortality. Sleeping, eating, dressing, working, playing, exercising, and many other customary activities are necessary and important. But *ultimately, what we become is the result of our knowledge of and willingness to learn from the Father, the Son, and the Holy Ghost;* it is not merely the sum total of our daily pursuits over the course of a lifetime."[19]

---

18. *Words of Joseph Smith*, 14–15. Elder D. Todd Christofferson noted: "In the Kirtland Temple dedicatory prayer . . . , the Prophet petitioned, 'And do thou grant, Holy Father, that all who shall worship in this house . . . may grow up in thee, and receive a fulness of the Holy Ghost' (D&C 109:14–15). The 'fulness of the Holy Ghost' includes what Jesus described as 'the promise which I give unto you of eternal life, even the glory of the celestial kingdom; which glory is that of the church of the Firstborn, even of God, the holiest of all, through Jesus Christ his Son' (D&C 88:4–5)" ("Power of Covenants," *Ensign*, May 2009, 23n5).

19. "Exceeding Great and Precious Promises," *Ensign*, November 2017, 90, 93; emphasis added.

What wise counsel could a Latter-day Saint mother and father give to their beautiful daughter or their handsome son as the child leaves home and makes his or her way to the university or the mission field? What gems of truth or wisdom would be appropriate to convey to one in whom so much of Mom and Dad's time and energy and resources and prayers have been expended? Certainly the child could be counseled to "remember who you are and act accordingly." Or they could be reminded of the Savior's golden rule—always treat others as you would want to be treated. I am persuaded that somewhere in that amalgam of advice we would also be well advised to suggest lovingly that the child seek the Spirit and always strive to live worthy of his companionship. It is a grand key to genuine success in this life, a key that opens the door to peace and happiness in this world and eternal glory in the world to come.

Chapter 19

SWEET COMMUNION AND CONSTANT COMPANIONSHIP

We receive the gift of the Holy Ghost following baptism at the time of confirmation through the laying on of hands by those holding the Melchizedek Priesthood. The gift of the Holy Ghost is the right to enjoy the constant companionship of the Spirit if we are worthy. It is a sobering responsibility and a lifetime quest to live such that we are able to maintain that companionship.

THE COMPANIONSHIP OF THE SPIRIT

"The companionship of the Holy Ghost," President Henry B. Eyring taught, "makes what is good more attractive and temptation less compelling. That alone should be enough to make us determined to qualify for the Spirit to be with us always." This is one of the ways that we are "enticed" by the Holy Ghost (Mosiah 3:19). "Just as the Holy Ghost strengthens us against evil," he continues, "He also gives us the power to discern truth from falsehood. The truth that matters most is verified only by revelation from God. *Our human reason and the use of our physical senses will not be enough. We live in a time when even the wisest will be hard-pressed to distinguish truth from clever deception. . . .* Confirmation of truth comes to a son or daughter of God who has claimed the right to receive the Holy Ghost. . . . So, for many reasons, we need the constant companionship of the Holy Ghost. We desire it, yet we know from experience that it is not easy to maintain."[1]

While members of the Church throughout the world are far from perfect, many have charted their course and given their heart to the Lord and his gospel. They have gladly consecrated themselves to the Church and the establishment of the kingdom of God. They earnestly strive to keep God's commandments and continue on the Savior's covenant path, knowing with a sweet certainty that the restored gospel is true, that The Church of Jesus Christ of Latter-day Saints is divinely led, and that the "marvelous work and a wonder" foreseen by Isaiah will eventually triumph in the earth.

If, however, we speak honestly and humbly, we admit that we do *not* always feel the Spirit the same way from moment to moment or from day to day. Many of you have had a magnificent and uplifting Sabbath, closed that holy day on a spiritual high, only to awaken the next day with a very different feeling—you did not feel the same Spirit you enjoyed only hours before. What happened? Where did it go? Perhaps you ask, what did I do wrong?

Each one of us has had our spiritual lows, not necessarily caused by negligence or willful sin, by a negative attitude or a critical or murmuring disposition, or by anything we may have done wrong. What's going on? A part of the answer is contained in the conversation between Jesus and Nicodemus, as recorded in the New Testament. The Savior had just testified of the importance of the new birth, the spiritual birth that every man and women must undergo in order to enter into the abundant life. "The wind bloweth where it listeth," Jesus said, "and thou hearest the sound thereof, but canst not tell whence it cometh, and whither it goeth: so is every one that is born of the Spirit" (John 3:8). It's a rather odd and unusual, even enigmatic passage, isn't it? Do we

---

1. "The Holy Ghost as Your Companion," *Ensign*, November 2015, 104–5; emphasis added.

grasp what the Master was attempting to teach this brilliant Pharisee who was somehow drawn to the Master?

The word translated here as *wind* is the Greek word *pneuma,* which may also (as in Hebrew) be rendered as *breath* or *spirit.* It is as if Jesus had said, "The Spirit goes where it will, and you can hear the sound [also rendered as *voice*] but you cannot always tell where it came from or where it is going." The Spirit of God is not totally under our control. It cannot be called here or sent there according to human whims or wishes. It cannot be compelled, elicited, or commanded whenever we as humans desire to do so. We can certainly set the stage: we can prepare properly, listen to uplifting music, search the scriptures, pray, and plead humbly for its intervention or manifestation, but we cannot presume upon the motions or movement of this sacred spiritual endowment.

Obviously we will not enjoy the Spirit's prompting or peace if we are guilty of unrepentant sin, if we continue to pause indefinitely on spiritual plateaus, or if we persist in living well beneath our spiritual privileges. Surely all of us understand this. What is not so readily understood is that the power of the Holy Ghost may come and go, in terms of its intensity and its evident involvement in our lives. This means that we should take heart when we do not feel the presence of the Holy Ghost with the same magnitude on a regular, continuous basis.

SOMETIMES WE KNOW IT NOT

In October 2000 I experienced something I had never undergone before—I went into a deep depression for several months. Oh, I had had a bad day here and there, had known frustration and disillusionment like everyone else, but I had never been trapped by the tentacles of clinical depression so severely that I simply could not be comforted or convinced, either by others or myself, that there was a light at the end of the tunnel. For days at a time I wanted only to sleep or gaze at the walls or be alone. For weeks I felt as though I was in a closed casket, a prison cell that allowed no light or sound whatever. I prayed. Oh, how I prayed for deliverance. I sought for and received priesthood blessings. I counseled with friends who knew of my pain and my feelings of alienation.

A physician described my condition as depletion depression, a time in my life when my body, my emotions, and my mind had chosen—whether I liked it or not—to take a vacation from normalcy. I had been driven for too long and could no longer live on adrenaline. I clung to my wife and children. I read the Liberty Jail letter (Doctrine and Covenants 121–23) over and over, holding tenaciously to the words, "Thine adversities and thine afflictions shall be but a small moment" (121:7). Again and again I pleaded with my Heavenly Father, in the name of the Prince of Peace, to lift the pall, chase the darkness away, and draw me back into the light.

During those weeks of suffering I had great difficulty feeling the Spirit. In my head I knew that I was "worthy," in the sense that I was striving to live in harmony with the teachings of the Savior, but I simply did not *feel* the peace and joy and divine approbation that I had come to expect and cherish. I was serving as a stake president at the time, and my Area Presidency and the First Presidency tenderly and kindly encouraged me to turn everything over to my counselors for a time, take the needed break, and follow the doctor's orders, including using medication if prescribed. Let me see if I can state this more accurately: I knew *in my mind* that the Lord was pleased with my life, but I did not *feel* close to God as I had felt only days and weeks before. In other words, there is a mental or intellectual component to spiritual living that is in many ways just as important as the affective, or emotional, component. Sometimes God tells us in our minds, sometimes in our hearts, and sometimes in both (Doctrine and Covenants 8:2–3; 128:1).

It is one thing to *have* the Spirit of the Lord with us, even the constant companionship of that member of the Godhead, and another to *feel* that influence in the same way at all times. Many, if not most, times that the Spirit is enlightening us, we feel it. Many, if not most, times that we are being divinely led, we are very much aware of it. But there are occasions when the Holy Ghost empowers our words or directs our paths and we, like the Lamanites who had been taught by Helaman's sons Nephi and Lehi and enjoyed a mighty spiritual rebirth, know it not (3 Nephi 9:20).

In speaking of those moments in life when we simply *must* have an answer from God to a pressing dilemma but in which that answer is slow in coming, Elder Richard G. Scott taught: "Be thankful that sometimes God lets you struggle for a long time before that answer comes. Your character will grow; your faith will increase. . . . You may want to express thanks when that occurs, for it is an evidence of His trust."[2] In short, said Elder Robert D. Hales, "revelation comes on the Lord's timetable, which often means we must move forward in faith, even though we haven't received all the answers we desire."[3] President Joseph F. Smith observed that "the presentation or 'gift' of the Holy Ghost simply confers upon a man the right to receive at any time, when he is worthy of it or desires it, the power and light of truth of the Holy Ghost, *although he may often be left to his own spirit and judgment.*"[4]

Elder Bruce R. McConkie pointed out that "we are cleansed from sin and are born again and become converted to truth when we get the constant companionship of that member of the Godhead, that is, get the *right* to constant companionship. *Nobody actually has that companionship all the time, because no one is perfect, no one lives in the ideal and perfect state. We do the best we can, and get sufficient of the companionship to have our sins burned out of us as though by fire.* And that is what is

---

2. "Using the Supernal Gift of Prayer," *Ensign*, May 2007, 9–10.

3. "Personal Revelation: The Teachings and Examples of the Prophets," *Ensign*, November 2007, 87.

4. *Gospel Doctrine*, 60–61; emphasis added.

involved when we use this expression, the baptism of fire, meaning the baptism of the Holy Ghost."[5]

PRACTICE AND OPENNESS

While I was serving as a bishop, I attended a regional priesthood leadership meeting. That day our visitors were Elders Boyd K. Packer and Russell M. Nelson of the Quorum of the Twelve Apostles and Elder John H. Groberg of the Seventy. Somewhere in the middle of his presentation, Elder Packer began to speak of the importance of priesthood leaders being guided in their ministry by the power of the Holy Ghost.

One of the local leaders raised his hand. "Elder Packer," he asked, "How do we come to know the difference between our own thoughts and feelings and the impressions of the Spirit?"

Elder Packer paused for about ten or fifteen seconds and replied, "Oh, that's easy."

The questioner followed up: "What do you mean when you say that it's easy?"

The apostle smiled and said, "You learn by practice."

I was somewhat disappointed with his reply until later in the day, when I reflected on what he was really saying. Like any other spiritual labor or gift, we grow in understanding by having repeated experience with that labor or gift. As the years have passed since that occasion, I have come to appreciate the value of Elder Packer's counsel. I cannot expect to recognize the Holy Spirit's promptings if I am regularly ignoring feelings from my conscience, if I continue to act contrary to what the Light of Christ is attempting to teach me. I cannot expect to become the recipient of great and significant revelation from God if I am not recognizing, noting, and responding affirmatively to small and gentle spiritual nudges from the Spirit throughout the day.

---

5. *Doctrines of the Restoration*, 136; emphasis added.

When I do make the effort to listen attentively to any and all direction from the Spirit—no matter how small it may seem to be—I will be a little better prepared to recognize the voice of the Lord the next time he speaks through his Spirit. It will be with us as it was with the servants in the parable of the talents who chose wisely, to build upon and multiply that which had been given to them by their Lord: "Well done, thou good and faithful servant: *thou hast been faithful over a few things, I will make thee ruler over many things:* enter thou into the joy of thy Lord" (Matthew 25:21; emphasis added).

"Consider the scripture study we've been taught to incorporate into our daily lives," President Dallin H. Oaks declared. "Or consider the personal prayers or kneeling family prayers that are regular practices for faithful Latter-day Saints. Consider attendance at seminary for youth or institute classes for young adults. *Though each of these practices may seem to be small and simple, over time they result in powerful spiritual uplift and growth. This occurs because each of these small and simple things invites the companionship of the Holy Ghost,* the Testifier who enlightens us and guides us into truth."[6]

While I was serving as a stake president, it became necessary for me to select and call two new bishops. There are, of course, many outstanding Latter-day Saint men in my area of the country, noble and faithful and experienced souls who could serve worthily and well. It matters very much, however, that the right man be called, that the Lord recommend and approve him, and that the entire stake presidency feel that comforting assurance. We had discussed several names over a period of months, all of whom were wonderful men. We wanted to know, however, what the Lord felt about the matter, and so we continued to talk regularly and pray periodically.

For some reason, I just couldn't get settled on two specific names. It seemed like I was always racing here or there, running to and fro in the

---

6. "Small and Simple Things," *Ensign*, May 2018, 90; emphasis added.

earth—doing good things, serving righteous causes, but not pausing long enough to learn the will of God. Shauna and I traveled with some friends to England on a British Isles tour. About halfway through the trip, we learned that the next day would be spent in restful activities—visiting recreational areas, shopping, and so forth—and that nothing of any historical significance would be covered. I knew only too well that time was running out and that I needed to focus on the bishops to be called. I asked the group if they would mind if I stayed behind and spent the day at the hotel. They were perfectly fine with that.

Fortunately, the hotel was located in a rural area, a few miles from a small town. When the group had left the next day, I took my scriptures, a notebook, and a bottle of water and walked for about half an hour until I found a beautiful, hilly area. I climbed to the top of a hill, marveled at the loveliness of the location, and sat quietly for a few hours. I read some chapters in the Book of Mormon, prayed earnestly for direction about who should be called as bishop, roamed about the top of the hill, and sat and listened for some time. There, in the quiet and beauty of the English countryside, all alone with my thoughts and my God, I received strong impressions about who should serve where. The still, small voice was heard; it was all very clear, very simple, very powerful. The calls were extended, the same witness of the Spirit that initiated the call accompanied us in the interviews, and some great and good things took place in the months and years that followed.

Clearly one need not travel to England or drive to a farm or climb a mountain to commune more regularly with the Lord. But we do need time, and silence, and the personal discipline associated with pondering, meditation, and meaningful reflection. On an earlier trip to England, several Brigham Young University colleagues and I spent a number of days at Oxford University and retraced the steps of C. S. Lewis. Having studied most of his writings and read a number of biographies of his most unusual life, we wanted to get a better sense of this man who had such fascinating insights into the Savior and His

Atonement. We stayed at Magdalen College, ate and slept in the same quarters and pubs where Lewis had been, and conversed in some of the rooms where he had held tutorials with small groups of students. In addition, we took strolls behind the college on a pathway that Lewis had traversed hundreds of times. On the flight home, I reflected on Lewis's life—his studies, his scholarship, his conversion to Christianity, and his lasting effect on the Christian world. The thought that weighed upon me was that at least as important as Lewis's broad academic training was his contemplative and prayerful mind, his desire to walk and think and analyze and synthesize and distill truth.

President David O. McKay related to the General Authorities a story of Bishop John Wells, a member of the Presiding Bishopric, a story that pointed up the need for times when we put aside our cares, shelve our worries, and open ourselves to divine direction. President Harold B. Lee, who heard President McKay tell the story, later recounted : "A son of Bishop Wells was killed in Emigration Canyon on a railroad track. Brother John Wells was a great detail man and prepared many of the reports we are following up now. His boy was run over by a freight train. Sister Wells was inconsolable. She mourned during the three days prior to the funeral, received no comfort at the funeral, and was in a rather serious state of mind.

"One day soon after the funeral services while she was lying on her bed relaxed, still mourning, her son appeared to her and said, 'Mother, do not mourn, do not cry. I am all right.' He . . . explained that he had given the signal to the engineer to move on, and then made the usual effort to catch the railing on the freight train; but as he attempted to do so his foot caught on a root and he failed to catch the handrail, and his body fell under the train. It was clearly an accident.

"Now, listen. He said that as soon as he realized that he was in another environment he tried to see his father, *but couldn't reach him. His father was so busy with the duties in his office he could not respond to his call.* Therefore he had come to his mother. He said to her, 'You tell father that all is well with me, and I want you not to mourn anymore.'

"Then [President McKay] made the statement that the point he had in mind was that when we are relaxed in a private room we are more susceptible to those things; and that so far as he was concerned, his best thoughts come after he gets up in the morning and is relaxed and thinking about the duties of the day; that impressions come more clearly, as if it were to hear a voice. Those impressions are right."[7] I am haunted by this story, which I first heard almost fifty years ago, for it illustrates the vital need for each one of us to seek the Spirit always and to make room in our schedule or our complex lives for the Spirit to prompt or guide us.

WALKING IN MEEKNESS

In a revelation given to Martin Harris, the Savior implored: "Learn of me, and listen to my words; *walk in the meekness of my Spirit,* and you shall have peace in me" (Doctrine and Covenants 19:23; emphasis added). What, by the way, is meant by the word *meekness?* While meekness is a quality that is certainly related to the quality of *humility,* the two words do not have exactly the same meaning. Unfortunately, many people suppose that a person who is meek is a docile pushover, a weak and spineless individual, one who lacks courage and is regularly dominated by the more assertive of the world. Many years ago, L. Elmer Peterson, a religious educator, wrote that "to be meek one must be mild of temper, patient under injuries, long suffering. The meek will not be quick to anger. . . . Therefore meekness is the spirit of one who is not easily provoked [see 1 Corinthians 13:5; Moroni 7:45], but keeps under control the natural instinct to assert oneself and to retaliate. It is the quality of patient and calm endurance under affliction and persecution."

---

7. *Teachings of Harold B. Lee*, 415; emphasis in original.

Interestingly, "meekness is the only personality characteristic which [Jesus] calls attention to in himself [Matthew 11:29]."[8]

As a cousin to humility, meekness in a person allows him or her to acknowledge both their needs and their possibilities. "Those of us who fail in one way or another," Elder Neal A. Maxwell pointed out, "almost always do so because we carry unnecessary and heavy baggage. Thus overloaded, we then feel sorry for ourselves. We need not carry such baggage, but when we are not meek, we resist the informing voice of conscience and feedback from leaders, family members, and friends. Whether from preoccupation or pride, the warning signals go unnoticed and unheeded." On the other hand, "if we have sufficient meekness, we will have help to jettison unneeded burdens and keep from becoming mired in the ooze of self-pity."[9]

Similarly, Elder David A. Bednar taught that "meekness is a defining attribute of the Redeemer and is distinguished by righteous responsiveness, willing submissiveness, and strong self-restraint." Further, "whereas humility generally denotes dependence upon God and the constant need for His guidance and support, a distinguishing characteristic of meekness is *a particular spiritual receptivity to learning both from the Holy Ghost and from people who may seem less capable, experienced, or educated, who may not hold important positions, or who otherwise may not appear to have much to contribute.*" Finally, "the consistency of the Lord's willing submission and strong self-restraint is both awe-inspiring and instructive for us all."[10]

Meekness is certainly a first cousin to humility. The Torah teaches that "the man Moses was very meek, above all the men which were upon the face of the earth" (Numbers 12:3). Jesus described himself as "meek and lowly in heart" (Matthew 11:29). Consequently, "none is acceptable before God, save the meek and lowly in heart" (Moroni

---

8. *Beatitudes,* 42–43.
9. *Meek and Lowly,* 6.
10. "Meek and Lowly of Heart," *Ensign,* May 2018, 32–33; emphasis added.

7:44). In short, the meek shall inherit the celestialized earth (Matthew 5:5; 3 Nephi 12:5). "In a world too preoccupied with winning through intimidation and seeking to be number one," President Howard W. Hunter observed, "no large crowd of folk is standing in line to buy books that call for mere meekness. But *the meek shall inherit the earth, a pretty impressive corporate takeover—and done without intimidation!* Sooner or later, and we pray sooner than later, everyone will acknowledge that Christ's way is not only the right way, but ultimately the only way to hope and joy. Every knee shall bow and every tongue will confess that *gentleness is better than brutality, that kindness is greater than coercion, that the soft voice turneth away wrath.* In the end, and sooner than that whenever possible, we must be more like him."[11]

The Holy Ghost "is not merely a line on an organizational chart or part of a procedural checklist," Elder Maxwell wrote. "Nor is He someone with whom we can be content to have merely a nodding acquaintance, or consider an object of periodic contemplation, or reduce to a bumper-sticker. *He is actually involved with all that really matters.* If we cultivate this Gift, we access the powers of the universe. No wonder we are to 'stir up' and 'quench not' that 'great gift' (2 Timothy 1:6; 1 Thessalonians 5:19)."[12]

In the Prophet Joseph Smith's letter from Liberty Jail, he charged the Saints to minister to one another through persuasion, long-suffering, gentleness and meekness, love unfeigned, kindness, pure knowledge, heaven-inspired reproof, virtue, and charity. Then came the supernal promise that their "confidence [would] wax strong in the presence of God. . . . *The Holy Ghost shall be thy constant companion*"

11. "Jesus, the Very Thought of Thee," *Ensign*, May 1993, 64–65; emphasis added.

12. *Moving in His Majesty and Power*, 70–71; emphasis added.

(Doctrine and Covenants 121:41–46; emphasis added). Few things could be promised that are of more surpassing worth than the right to enjoy a close and ongoing association with the third member of the Godhead. Our mood is brighter when the Spirit is with us. Our temperament is kinder and gentler. Our mind is sharper and our decisions wiser. Our speaking and teaching are more powerful and insightful. Our perspective is loftier. Our ministry is higher and holier. In short, the more closely we can approximate a constant companionship with the Holy Spirit in our lives, the more we approximate that perfect life to which our blessed Savior and Redeemer has called us (Matthew 5:48; 3 Nephi 12:48; Moroni 10:32–33).

Conclusion

THE SPIRIT—FOREVER
WORTHY OF OUR TRUST

*E*arly in this dispensation, in May 1829, Hyrum Smith was called upon to "put your trust in that Spirit which leadeth to do good—yea, to do justly, to walk humbly, to judge righteously; and this is my Spirit" (Doctrine and Covenants 11:12). Fascinating instructions. Hyrum (and you and I, by extension) was charged to trust the Holy Ghost. Why? Because it is the Spirit of God that prompts people to be faithful and true, to be good. Because it is the Spirit of God that inspires, even impels, the disciples of the Lord Jesus Christ to treat others with respect, to be fair and equitable, to be just. Because it is the Spirit of God that makes known unto us our weakness, our absolute dependence upon a Person and a power greater and wiser than ourselves, so that we may be humble. Because it is the Spirit of God that grants to us the wisdom and discernment to "judge not unrighteously, that [we] be not judged; but judge righteous judgment" (JST, Matthew 7:1–2). This is why we should put our trust in the third member of the Godhead—he points us in the right direction, opens our eyes to see things as they really are, and softens our hearts to love and serve our brothers and sisters.

Many years ago on a Sunday morning I opened the door and reached down to pick up the morning newspaper. Beside the paper was a plastic bag containing a paperback book. I brought both inside and laid the newspaper aside as I browsed the paperback. On the cover was a lovely picture of a mountain stream, but the title of the book revealed to me what in fact the book was all about—it was a book attacking the restored gospel. Many of the arguments in the book against The Church of Jesus Christ of Latter-day Saints were old and worn-out ones, dead horses that have been beaten since the days of E. D. Howe, arguments to which Latter-day Saints have provided responsible replies many, many times.

One section of the book, however, proved to be of some interest to me. Let me paraphrase what was said a little over a hundred pages into the text. The author, formerly a member of The Church of Jesus Christ of Latter-day Saints himself, pointed out that eventually two of our missionaries would come to the reader's door. If they do come, he pleaded, don't let them in. If, however, you do let them in, then don't listen to them. If they are allowed to tell you about their message, about Joseph Smith and angels and gold plates, they will ask you to kneel and pray about the truthfulness of these things. Whatever you do, don't pray! The writer then made this strange and absolutely perplexing observation: In determining the truthfulness of a religious claim, there are three things a person can never trust: (1) their thoughts; (2) their feelings; and (3) their prayers.

I was at full attention at this point, wondering how we could ever know *anything* if we couldn't trust our thoughts, feelings, or prayers. I didn't have to wait long, for the writer then noted that the only thing that could be trusted was the Holy Bible. I shook my head and felt a deep sense of sadness for the author, for I wondered how a person could know of the truthfulness of the Bible if he or she could not think, feel, or pray. It was obvious that the author could not see the blatant inconsistency and irrationality of his own words. I tried to put myself in the place of a reader who was not a Latter-day Saint and wondered how I might feel upon reading such things. To be honest, I would feel insulted, having been told that I could not be trusted enough in my pursuit of truth to rely upon my mind, my heart, or even the most tried and true method of obtaining divine direction—prayer to my Heavenly Father, who knows the truthfulness of all things.

Now the reason we cannot trust ourselves in our search for truth, the author added, is that we are a fallen and depraved race. Our souls are bent, our hearts are corrupt, and we are absolutely clueless when it comes to knowing the things of God. I almost spoke aloud to the author: "Shame on you, a man schooled and trained to lead people to Jesus. And yet you tell readers that they cannot even trust their prayers." I immediately thought of the words of Nephi at the close of his second book: "If ye would hearken unto *the Spirit* which *teacheth a man to pray* ye would know that ye must pray; for *the evil spirit teacheth not a man to pray, but teacheth him that he must not pray*" (2 Nephi 32:8; emphasis added; see also Doctrine and Covenants 10:21).

I attest that God is ever ready to respond to our heartfelt requests, that, in the words of James, "the effectual fervent prayer of a righteous man [or woman] availeth much" (James 5:16). I testify further that James spoke the truth when he wrote: "If any of you lack wisdom, let him ask of God, that giveth to all men liberally, and upbraideth [reproaches, censures] not; and it shall be given him" (James 1:5). I know that Jesus the Christ meant what he said when he beckoned: "Ask, and it shall be given you; seek, and ye shall find; knock, and it shall be opened unto you" (Matthew 7:7). In short, we can trust God. We can trust the Son of God. And we can trust the Holy Spirit of God. We can confidently put our trust in them, for they want only our best. Our peace and joy in this life, and our eternal glory in the world to come— these are the greatest desires of the members of the Godhead.

Not long after I joined the Religious Education faculty at Brigham Young University, I was asked by the people at Continuing Education if I would travel to a particular part of the country to assist the Latter-day Saints in the area in dealing with opposition to the Church. An announcement had been made that a temple would be built in that area, and, as is so often the case, critics and naysayers came out of the woodwork. Latter-day Saint high school students had even opened their school lockers to find within them stacks of scurrilous pamphlets and videos attacking our faith and way of life. I spoke in one town on Thursday evening and all went well. On Friday night I delivered the same message to members of the Church in a nearby city, and I felt good about the meeting. On Saturday morning I slept in a bit, then arose, went for a nice walk, and returned to the hotel. I read and worked on a few projects for several hours that day. An early dinner was followed by a glance at the television to check on sports scores.

After getting dressed, I knelt beside the bed and prayed. I thanked the Lord for the good experiences we had had the two preceding nights and asked for his help one more time. I then heard myself say: "Father, I want to do what's right and what thou wouldst have done. Tell me *what to say*, and I will say it. Tell me *what not to say*, and I won't say it." I thought the words were a bit unusual, but they were quickly forgotten.

Within ten or fifteen minutes, a local member of the Church picked me up, and we drove to the stake center. While sitting on the stand and as the time to deliver my message drew closer, I felt a deep discomfort begin to settle over me. When I thought about my topic, I felt ill at ease. During the special musical number, I leaned over to the stake president and said, "President, I have a problem."

"What's the matter," he asked.

I told him that I felt extremely uncomfortable about speaking on the subject I'd been given. Yet I knew that this lecture had been advertised for several months, and I didn't want to disappoint the Saints (there were perhaps five hundred people in attendance). I asked him what I should do.

He smiled and said gently, "Brother Millet, I think you should tell the people what the Lord wants you to say."

I felt a few seconds' comfort, for part one of my problem was now solved. I knew clearly what I *was not* to say. Then I stood at the pulpit and realized that my next task was to find out what I *was* to say.

A speaker can take only so long telling the congregation how lovely it is to be there, how beautiful the natural surroundings are, and how delightful it is to participate in the Know Your Religion program. At the same time, I prayed intently to know what to do and what to say. I had no private agenda, no favorite subject I was longing to discuss. After about ten minutes of my feeling my way through the darkness, the light came on. It was clear to me that I was, for some unknown reason, to speak on what modern prophets and the scriptures of the Restoration have taught us concerning life after death. I glanced at my briefcase near my feet. It was filled with information about how to respond graciously but effectively to opposition to the Church. All that I had to assist me in this new undertaking were my scriptures and a copy of *Teachings of the Prophet Joseph Smith.* And, of course, there was also the Spirit of the Lord.

This was one of those occasions that may come rarely in one's life. For well over an hour I spoke on this subject with no notes, no quotations from Church leaders before me, nothing but the earnest desire of my heart to do this subject justice. I learned a great deal that night from what I had to say, and I sensed the congregation did, as well.[1] My tongue was loosened, and I enjoyed a fluency of speech I had seldom before experienced. The words and writings and teachings of Church leaders flooded into my mind, and I spoke them.

When I sat down I looked over at the stake president. He was very sober, and I feared that perhaps I had disappointed him or that my inclination not to address the advertised subject had been out of line. After the closing prayer, and as the members of the Church began to come to the stand to shake hands, the stake president said that he

---

1. See Marion G. Romney, cited in Packer, *Teach Ye Diligently*, 304.

would like to speak briefly with me after everyone was gone. Finally, when no one else was on the stand, the president and I sat together.

He asked, "Do you know why you chose to speak on life after death?"

I said no.

He replied, "Brother Millet, one of the members of our stake died a few days ago. It was a tragic death, what many felt to be an untimely passing, one that raised many questions among members of the stake. A funeral was held for the young man in this chapel this afternoon. After the services, even after all was said, many people went home deeply distressed, spiritually troubled, filled with questions. Brother Millet, you addressed most of those questions in your talk. Thank you."

A few more members came up to me after the president and I had finished our chat and asked if I would like to join them for a late snack. I thanked them for offering but indicated that I was very tired and needed to get some rest. Actually, what I wanted to do most right then was to return to the hotel, kneel beside my bed once again, and thank a gracious Lord for allowing me to be a part of something that might well have made a difference in people's lives.

God Almighty is in charge—this is his work, and it must be done in his own way and according to his will. We are weak, ever so weak, when it comes to speaking the words of truth, but I know, as Ammon humbly affirmed, that "in [God's] strength I can do all things" (Alma 26:12; compare Philippians 4:13). Our task is to repent and improve and read and study and prepare and pray and plead for divine assistance. And when the time is right, God will work through us, by the power of his Holy Spirit, to bless his children.

"Our time is a dangerous time," Elder Kim B. Clark pointed out, "a time of great evil and temptation, a time of confusion and commotion. . . . *Whatever level of spirituality or faith or obedience we now have, it will not be sufficient for the work that lies ahead. We need greater spiritual light and power.* We need eyes to see more clearly the Savior working in our lives and ears to hear His voice more deeply in our hearts. . . .

"If we will look to Christ and open our eyes and our ears, the Holy Ghost will bless us to see the Lord Jesus Christ working in our lives, strengthening our faith in Him with assurance and evidence. We increasingly will see all of our brothers and sisters the way God sees them, with love and compassion. We will hear the Savior's voice in the scriptures, in the whisperings of the Spirit, and in the words of the living prophets. . . . We will see and understand ourselves and the world around us the way the Savior does. We will come to have what the apostle Paul called 'the mind of Christ' (1 Corinthians 2:16). We will have eyes to see and ears to hear, and we will build the kingdom of God."[2]

I have never spoken or written on the power and blessing of the Holy Ghost without referring to the marvelous message the Prophet Joseph Smith delivered to Brigham Young almost three years after Brother Joseph's death. "Joseph stepped toward me," Brigham said, "and looking very earnestly, yet pleasantly said, 'Tell the people to be humble and faithful, and be sure to keep the Spirit of the Lord and it will lead them right. Be careful and not turn away the small still voice; it will teach you what to do and where to go; it will yield the fruits of the kingdom. Tell the brethren to keep their hearts open to conviction, so that when the Holy Ghost comes to them, their hearts will be ready to receive it. They can tell the Spirit of the Lord from all other spirits; it will whisper peace and joy to their souls; it will take malice, hatred, strife and all evil from their hearts; and their whole desire will be to do good, bring forth righteousness and build up the kingdom of God. . . .' Joseph again said, 'Tell the people to be sure to keep the Spirit of the Lord and follow it, and it will lead them just right.'"[3]

---

2. "Eyes to See and Ears to Hear," *Ensign*, November 2015, 124–25; emphasis added.

3. Young, Journal History, 23 February 1847.

No summary of all we have discussed here could be more comprehensive nor more enlightening and heartwarming than the words of the Prophet of the Restoration. Of all the things Joseph might have explained to Brigham Young—principles of priesthood government, succession in the presidency of the Church, how to organize the exodus from Nauvoo to the Great Basin, and how to set up the restored kingdom of God in the West—the Prophet instructed his prophetic successor to plead with the Latter-day Saints to seek for, obtain, cherish, and follow the divine guidance of the third member of the Godhead. What a lesson for you and me! Could there be any message today that would be of more importance? Is there anything members of The Church of Jesus Christ of Latter-day Saints could do that would have more immediate and everlasting relevance and impact than simply to seek and maintain the Spirit in our lives?

Just before my late friend and colleague Joseph Fielding McConkie and his wife, Brenda, left to preside over a mission in Edinburgh, Scotland, my wife, Shauna, and I had dinner with them. Joseph explained to me that he had been doing a great deal of thinking about how to lead and inspire their missionaries. He had read carefully the handbooks and procedures and felt the need somehow to distil for his missionaries a kind of mission motto, a simple and memorable expression that would keep the elders and sisters on task and motivate them to be their very best. What he came up with was this: "I will never do anything that would cost me the influence of the Spirit of God." How much more spiritually rich our lives would be if each one of us could live by that simple but profound, succinct but comprehensive maxim. It says it all. "The pure in heart shall see God," Elder Marion D. Hanks reminded us. "Those who become the manner of man [Christ] was, *who walk in the Spirit,* will see him, and will be his."[4]

In a world where we are surrounded by loud, discordant, and

---

4. *Gift of Self,* 19; emphasis added.

competing voices emanating from the great and spacious building, all seeking to confuse and distract us from our highest and holiest priorities, may we, like Lehi and Nephi, heed them not (1 Nephi 8:33). Rather, may we listen attentively to that voice which is still and small but eternally significant, the voice of God that is mediated through his Holy Spirit. "I do not care how learned a man may be," President John Taylor declared, "or how extensively he may have traveled. I do not care what his talent, intellect, or genius may be, at what college he may have studied, how comprehensive his views or what his judgment may be on other matters, he cannot understand certain things without the Spirit of God."[5]

"Our Savior and Redeemer, Jesus Christ, will perform some of His mightiest works between now and when He comes again," President Russell M. Nelson stated. "We will see miraculous indications that God the Father and His Son, Jesus Christ, preside over this Church in majesty and glory. But in coming days, it will not be possible to survive spiritually without the guiding, directing, comforting, and constant influence of the Holy Ghost. My beloved brothers and sisters, I plead with you to increase your spiritual capacity to receive revelation."[6]

I close on a note of testimony. I have a conviction deep within my soul that God our Heavenly Father lives; that Jesus Christ is the Son of God, and that he was crucified for the sins of the world; and that the Holy Ghost, the third member of the Godhead, is the messenger of the Father and the Son, the means by which we come to know the things of God; have testimonies burned into our souls as though by fire; and have our hearts and minds sanctified from sin.

If we live our lives in a manner that we constantly strive never to do anything that would cost us the influence of the Spirit of God, we will in this life enjoy the peace that passes all understanding (Philippians

---

5. *John Taylor* [manual], 157.
6. *Teachings of Russell M. Nelson*, 335.

4:7), the rest of God associated with knowing that our course in life is pleasing to the Father and the Son. We will also, as we pass through the veil of death, be welcomed joyously into paradise and eventually enjoy, with our families, exaltation in the highest degree of the celestial kingdom.

At the time of the dedication of the temple, the Kirtland Saints sang with gusto the words of a hymn written by W. W. Phelps:

> *The Spirit of God like a fire is burning!*
> *The latter-day glory begins to come forth;*
> *The visions and blessings of old are returning,*
> *And angels are coming to visit the earth.*[7]

My great desire is that the same Holy Spirit that ignited the souls of so many of the early Saints will burn always and forever in our hearts, bringing forth visions, blessings, and spiritual manifestations. God grant that we will live worthy of those precious privileges, for that is the destiny and will be the legacy of the Latter-day Saints.

---

7. "The Spirit of God," *Hymns*, 1985, no. 2.

SOURCES CITED

The Ante-Nicene Fathers. Edited by Alexander Roberts and James Donaldson. 10 vols. Peabody, MA: Hendrickson Publishers, 2012.

Ashton, Marvin J. "There Are Many Gifts." *Ensign*, November 1987.

Ballard, M. Russell. "Questions and Answers: An Apostle Comes to Campus for a Grandfatherly Chat with the BYU Student Body." *BYU Magazine,* Spring 2018.

"Baptism." *Times and Seasons* 3, no. 21 (1 September 1842): 903–5.

Beck, Julie B. "And upon the Handmaids in Those Days Will I Pour Out My Spirit." *Ensign,* May 2010.

Bednar, David A. "Always Retain a Remission of Your Sins." *Ensign*, May 2016.

———. "Exceeding Great and Precious Promises." *Ensign*, November 2017.

———. "Meek and Lowly of Heart." *Ensign*, May 2018.

———. "Ye Must Be Born Again." *Ensign*, May 2007.

Benson, Ezra Taft. "Born of God." *Ensign*, November 1985.

———. *Come unto Christ.* Salt Lake City: Deseret Book, 1983.

———. "A Mighty Change of Heart." *Ensign*, October 1989.

———. "What I Hope You Will Teach Your Children about the Temple." *Ensign*, August 1985.

Bushman, Richard Lyman. *On the Road with Joseph Smith: An Author's Diary.* Salt Lake City: Greg Kofford Books, 2007.

Bytheway, John. *Moroni's Guide to Surviving Turbulent Times.* Salt Lake City: Deseret Book, 2017.

Callister, Douglas L. "Knowing That We Know." *Ensign*, November 2007.

Cannon, George Q. *Gospel Truth: Discourses and Writings of George Q. Cannon.* Compiled by Jerreld L. Newquist. 2 vols. in 1. Salt Lake City: Deseret Book, 1987.

Caussé, Gérald. "For When I Am Weak, Then Am I Strong." Devotional address delivered at Brigham Young University, Provo, Utah, 3 December 2013.

Christofferson, D. Todd. "Firm and Steadfast in the Faith of Christ." *Ensign*, November 2018.

———. "Justification and Sanctification." *Ensign*, June 2001.

———. "The Power of Covenants." *Ensign*, May 2009.

Clark, J. Reuben, Jr. "The Charted Course of the Church in Education." In *J. Reuben Clark: Selected Papers*. Edited by David H. Yarn. Provo, UT: Brigham Young University Press, 1984.

Clark, Kim B. "Eyes to See and Ears to Hear." *Ensign*, November 2015.

Clayton, William. Journal, 16 May 1843, josephsmithpapers.org.

Covey, Stephen R. "An Educated Conscience." *1975 BYU Speeches of the Year*. Provo, UT: Brigham Young University Press, 1976.

———. *Spiritual Roots of Human Relations*. Salt Lake City: Deseret Book, 1970.

Craig, Michelle D. "Divine Discontent." *Ensign*, November 2018.

Dew, Sheri L. *Go Forward with Faith: The Biography of Gordon B. Hinckley*. Salt Lake City: Deseret Book, 1996.

———. "Knowing Who You Are—and Who You Have Always Been." *Ensign*, July 2018.

"The Elders of the Church in Kirtland, to Their Brethren Abroad." *The Evening and the Morning Star*, vol. 2, no. 19 (April 1834): 152.

English Standard Version Study Bible. Wheaton, Ill.: Crossway Bibles, 2008.

Eyring, Henry B. *Because He First Loved Us*. Salt Lake City: Deseret Book, 2002.

———. "Finding Safety in Counsel." *Ensign*, May 1997.

———. "His Spirit to Be with You." *Ensign*, May 2018.

———. "The Holy Ghost as Your Companion." *Ensign*, November 2015.

———. "Inspired Ministering." *Ensign*, May 2018.

Faust, James E. "What I Want My Son to Know before He Leaves on His Mission." *Ensign*, May 1996.

"Gift of the Holy Ghost." *Times and Seasons* 3, no. 16 (15 June 1842): 823–25.

Hafen, Bruce C. *Spiritually Anchored in Unsettled Times*. Salt Lake City: Deseret Book, 2009.

Hafen, Bruce C., and Marie K. Hafen. *Faith Is Not Blind*. Salt Lake City: Deseret Book, 2018.

Hales, Robert D. "Holy Scriptures: The Power of God unto Our Salvation." *Ensign*, November 2006.

———. "Personal Revelation: The Teachings and Examples of the Prophets." *Ensign*, November 2007.

———. *Return: Four Phases of Our Mortal Journey Home*. Salt Lake City: Deseret Book, 2010.

Hanks, Marion D. *The Gift of Self*. Salt Lake City: Bookcraft, 1974.

Harper, Steven C. *Joseph Smith's First Vision: A Guide to the Historical Accounts*. Salt Lake City: Deseret Book, 2012.

Hinckley, Gordon B. *Faith, the Essence of True Religion.* Salt Lake City: Deseret Book, 1989.

———. *Teachings of Gordon B. Hinckley.* Salt Lake City: Deseret Book, 1997.

———. "Till We Meet Again." *Ensign,* November 2001.

Holland, Jeffrey R. *Christ and the New Covenant: The Messianic Message of the Book of Mormon.* Salt Lake City: Deseret Book, 1997.

———. "He Loved Them unto the End." *Ensign,* November 1989.

———. "None Were with Him." *Ensign,* May 2009.

———. "Of Souls, Symbols, and Sacraments." Devotional address delivered at Brigham Young University, Provo, UT, 12 January 1988.

———. "Personal Purity." *Ensign,* November 1998.

———. "A School in Zion." Address to conference of faculty and staff, Brigham Young University, Provo, UT, August 1988.

———. "A Teacher Come from God." *Ensign,* May 1998.

Holland, Jeffrey R., and Patricia T. Holland. *On Earth as It Is in Heaven.* Salt Lake City: Deseret Book, 1989.

Holmes-Pollock Letters: The Correspondence of Mr. Justice Holmes and Sir Frederick Pollock, 1874–1932. Cambridge, MA: Harvard Belknap Press, 1961.

Hunter, Howard W. "Being a Righteous Husband and Father." *Ensign,* November 1994.

———. "Eternal Investments." Address to educators in the Church Educational System, Salt Lake City, UT, 10 February 1989.

———. "Jesus, the Very Thought of Thee." *Ensign,* May 1993.

Hymns of The Church of Jesus Christ of Latter-day Saints. Salt Lake City: The Church of Jesus Christ of Latter-day Saints, 1985.

Journal of Discourses. 26 vols. Liverpool: F. D. Richards & Sons, 1851–86.

Kimball, Spencer W. *The Miracle of Forgiveness.* Salt Lake City: Bookcraft, 1969.

———. *Teachings of Spencer W. Kimball.* Edited by Edward L. Kimball. Salt Lake City: Bookcraft, 1982.

Lawrence, Larry L. "What Lack I Yet?" *Ensign,* November 2015.

Lectures on Faith. Salt Lake City: Deseret Book, 1985.

Lee, Harold B. "Be Loyal to the Royal within You." *1973 BYU Speeches of the Year.* Provo, UT: BYU Publications, 1974.

———. In Conference Report, April 1973, 178–79.

———. *Harold B. Lee.* Teachings of Presidents of the Church series. Salt Lake City, Utah: The Church of Jesus Christ of Latter-day Saints, 2000.

———. *Stand Ye in Holy Places.* Salt Lake City: Deseret Book, 1974.

———. *Teachings of Harold B. Lee.* Edited by Clyde J. Williams. Salt Lake City: Bookcraft, 1996.

———. *Ye Are the Light of the World.* Salt Lake City: Deseret Book, 1974.

Lewis, C. S. *The Great Divorce.* New York: Touchstone, 1996.

————. *Letters to Malcolm, Chiefly on Prayer.* New York: Harcourt, Brace & Company, 1992.

————. *Mere Christianity.* New York: Touchstone, 1996.

Lund, Gerald N. "Salvation: By Grace or by Works?" *Ensign*, April 1981.

Lundwall, N. B., comp. *Discourses on the Holy Ghost.* Salt Lake City: Bookcraft, 1959.

MacArthur, John, ed. *The MacArthur Study Bible.* Wheaton, IL: Crossway, 2010.

Madsen, Truman G. *Eternal Man.* Salt Lake City: Deseret Book, 1966.

Maxwell, Neal A. *Meek and Lowly.* Salt Lake City: Deseret Book, 1987.

————. "Meeting the Challenges of Today." *1978 BYU Devotional Speeches of the Year.* Provo, UT: BYU Press, 1979.

————. *Men and Women of Christ.* Salt Lake City: Bookcraft, 1991.

————. *A More Excellent Way: Essays on Leadership for Latter-day Saints.* Salt Lake City: Deseret Book, 1967.

————. *Moving in His Majesty and Power.* Salt Lake City: Deseret Book, 2004.

————. "Out of Obscurity." *Ensign*, November 1984.

————. *Plain and Precious Things.* Salt Lake City: Deseret Book, 1983.

————. "Swallowed Up in the Will of the Father." *Ensign*, November 1995.

————. "What Should We Pray For?" In *Prayer.* Salt Lake City: Deseret Book, 1978.

McConkie, Bruce R. *Doctrinal New Testament Commentary.* 3 vols. Salt Lake City: Bookcraft, 1965–73.

————. *Doctrines of the Restoration: Sermons and Writings of Bruce R. McConkie.* Edited by Mark L. McConkie. Salt Lake City: Bookcraft, 1989.

————. "The Foolishness of Teaching." Address to educators in the Church Educational System, Salt Lake City, UT, February 1981.

————. "Jesus Christ and Him Crucified." *1976 BYU Speeches of the Year.* Provo, UT: BYU Press, 1977.

————. *The Mortal Messiah: From Bethlehem to Calvary.* 4 vols. Salt Lake City: Deseret Book, 1979–81.

————. *A New Witness for the Articles of Faith.* Salt Lake City: Deseret Book, 1985.

————. *The Promised Messiah: The First Coming of Christ.* Salt Lake City: Deseret Book, 1978.

————. "The Purifying Power of Gethsemane." *Ensign*, May 1985.

McConkie, Joseph Fielding. *Prophets and Prophecy.* Salt Lake City: Bookcraft, 1988.

————. *Teach and Reach.* Salt Lake City: Bookcraft, 1975.

McConkie, Oscar W. *The Holy Ghost.* Salt Lake City: Deseret Book, 1944.

McKay, David O. *Gospel Ideals: Selections from the Discourses of David O. McKay.* Salt Lake City: The Improvement Era, 1953.

Messages of the First Presidency of The Church of Jesus Christ of Latter-day Saints. Edited by James R. Clark. 6 vols. Salt Lake City: Bookcraft, 1965–75.

Miller, Adam. *An Early Resurrection: Life in Christ before You Die.* Salt Lake City: Deseret Book and the Neal A. Maxwell Institute for Religious Scholarship, 2018.

Monson, Thomas S. "The Spirit Giveth Life." *Ensign*, May 1985.

Montgomery, John W. *History and Christianity.* San Bernardino, CA: Here's Life Publications, 1983.

Nelson, Russell M. "Drawing the Power of Jesus Christ into Our Lives." *Ensign*, May 2017.

———. "Revelation for the Church, Revelation for Our Lives." *Ensign*, May 2018.

———. *Teachings of Russell M. Nelson.* Salt Lake City: Deseret Book, 2018.

Neuhaus, Richard John. *Death on a Friday Afternoon: Meditations on the Last Words of Jesus from the Cross.* New York: Basic Books, 2000.

Nibley, Hugh. "Funeral Address." In *Approaching Zion.* Vol. 9 of the Collected Works of Hugh Nibley. Salt Lake City: Deseret Book and the Foundation for Ancient Research and Mormon Studies, 1989.

———. *The World and the Prophets.* Vol. 3 of the Collected Works of Hugh Nibley. Salt Lake City: Deseret Book and Foundation for Ancient Research and Mormon Studies, 1987.

Oaks, Dallin H. "Alternate Voices." *Ensign*, May 1989.

———. "The Challenge to Become." *Ensign*, November 2000.

———. "Good, Better, Best." *Ensign*, November 2007.

———. "Judge Not and Judging." *Ensign*, August 1999.

———. "Small and Simple Things." *Ensign*, May 2018.

———. "Things They're Saying." *New Era*, February 1974.

———. "Truth and the Plan." *Ensign*, November 2018.

———. *With Full Purpose of Heart.* Salt Lake City: Deseret Book, 2002.

Olson, Roger E., and Christopher A. Hall. *The Trinity.* Grand Rapids, MI: Eerdmans, 2002.

Packer, Boyd K. "Atonement, Agency, Accountability." *Ensign*, May 1988.

———. "The Candle of the Lord." *Ensign*, January 1983.

———. *The Holy Temple.* Salt Lake City: Bookcraft, 1980.

———. "Little Children." *Ensign*, November 1986.

———. *Mine Errand from the Lord: Selections from the Sermons and Writings of Boyd K. Packer.* Salt Lake City: Deseret Book, 2008.

———. "Prayers and Answers." *Ensign*, November 1979.

———. "Reverence Invites Revelation." *Ensign*, November 1991.

———. "Spiritual Crocodiles." *Ensign*, May 1976.

———. *Teach Ye Diligently.* Salt Lake City: Deseret Book, 1975.

———. *That All May Be Edified.* Salt Lake City: Bookcraft, 1982.

Palmer, Parker. *On the Brink of Everything.* Oakland, CA: Berrett-Koehler Publishers, 2018.

Pearce, Virginia H. "The Ordinary Classroom—A Powerful Place for Steady and Continued Growth." *Ensign*, November 1996.

Peterson, Eugene H. *The Message: The Bible in Contemporary Language.* Carol Stream, IL: NavPress, 2016.

Peterson, L. Elmer. *The Beatitudes.* Salt Lake City: Deseret Book, 1964.

Pratt, Orson. *Orson Pratt's Works on the Doctrines of the Gospel.* Salt Lake City: Deseret News Press, 1945.

Pratt, Parley P. *Key to the Science of Theology.* Classics in Mormon Literature series. Salt Lake City: Deseret Book, 1978.

The Random House College Dictionary, rev. ed. New York: Random House, 1988.

Rasband, Ronald A. *Led by Divine Design: Seeking for and Recognizing the Spirit.* Salt Lake City: Deseret Book, 2018.

Rector, Hartman, Jr. "The Gospel." BYU devotional, 29 September 1985, speeches .byu.edu.

Roberts, B. H. *Defense of the Faith and the Saints.* 2 vols. Salt Lake City: Deseret News, 1907.

———. *The Gospel and Man's Relationship to Deity.* Salt Lake City: Deseret Book, 1966.

———. *The Seventy's Course in Theology.* Vol. 5. Salt Lake City: Deseret News, 1912.

Romney, Marion G. *Look to God and Live.* Salt Lake City: Deseret Book, 1971.

———. "The Holy Ghost." *Ensign,* May 1974.

Scott, Richard G. *21 Principles: Divine Truths to Help You Live by the Spirit.* Salt Lake City: Deseret Book, 2013.

———. "Using the Supernal Gift of Prayer." *Ensign,* May 2007.

Smith, George Albert. *George Albert Smith.* Teachings of Presidents of the Church series. Salt Lake City: The Church of Jesus Christ of Latter-day Saints, 2011.

———. *Sharing the Gospel with Others.* Selected by Preston Nibley. Salt Lake City: Deseret Book, 1948.

———. *The Teachings of George Albert Smith.* Edited by Robert and Susan McIntosh. Salt Lake City: Bookcraft, 1996.

Smith, Joseph. Account of Meeting and Discourse, 5 January 1841, josephsmith papers.org.

———. Answers to Queries to Brother Phelps's Letter of June 4th, josephsmith papers.org.

———. Appendix 2: Letter to the Saints Scattered Abroad, June 1835, joseph smithpapers.org.

———. Discourse, 12 November 1835, josephsmithpapers.org.

———. Discourse, 6 April 1837, josephsmithpapers.org.

———. Discourse, between ca. 26 June and ca. 2 July 1839, josephsmithpapers .org.

———. Discourse, 2 July 1839, josephsmithpapers.org.

———. Discourse, between ca. 26 June and ca. 4 August 1839–A, josephsmith papers.org.

———. Discourse, 16 May 1841, josephsmithpapers.org.

———. Discourse, 7 April 1844, josephsmithpapers.org.

———. History, 1838–1856, volume C-1 [2 November 1838–31 July 1842], josephsmithpapers.org.

———. *Joseph Smith.* Teachings of Presidents of the Church series. Salt Lake City: The Church of Jesus Christ of Latter-day Saints, 2007.

———. Journal, 2 February 1843, josephsmithpapers.org.

———. Journal, 27 August 1843; "Remarks by President Joseph Smith on Sunday Morning August 27th 1843," josephsmithpapers.org.

———. Journal, 15 October 1843; Joseph Smith History, Volume E-1, 1755, josephsmithpapers.org.

———. Letter to Church Leaders in Jackson County, Missouri, 25 June 1833, josephsmithpapers.org.

———. Letter to John S. Carter, 13 April 1833, josephsmithpapers.org.

———. Letter to the Church, ca. February 1834, josephsmithpapers.org.

———. *Personal Writings of Joseph Smith.* Edited by Dean C. Jessee. Rev. ed. Salt Lake City: Deseret Book, 2002.

———. *The Words of Joseph Smith: The Contemporary Accounts of the Nauvoo Discourses of the Prophet Joseph.* Edited by Andrew F. Ehat and Lyndon W. Cook. Provo, UT: BYU Religious Studies Center, 1980.

Smith, Joseph F. *Gospel Doctrine.* Salt Lake City: Deseret Book, 1971.

Smith, Joseph Fielding. In Conference Report, April 1970, 113–14.

———. *Doctrines of Salvation.* Compiled by Bruce R. McConkie. 3 vols. Salt Lake City: Bookcraft, 1954–56.

———. "The Sin Against the Holy Ghost." *Improvement Era,* July 1955, 494–95, 542–43.

Smith, Lucy Mack. *History of Joseph Smith by His Mother.* Edited by Preston Nibley. Salt Lake City: Bookcraft, n.d.

Snow, Eliza R. *Biography and Family Record of Lorenzo Snow.* Salt Lake City: Deseret News Company, 1884.

Sperry, Sidney B. *Paul's Life and Letters.* Salt Lake City: Bookcraft, 1955.

Staheli, Donald L. "Obedience—Life's Great Challenge." *Ensign,* May 1998.

Stephens, Carole M. "If Ye Love Me, Keep My Commandments." *Ensign,* November 2015.

Stott, John. *Authentic Christianity from the Writings of John Stott.* Edited by Timothy Dudley-Smith. Downers Grove, IL: InterVarsity Press, 1995.

———. *Life in Christ.* Wheaton, IL: Tyndale House Publishers, 1991.

Talmage, James E. *The Articles of Faith.* Salt Lake City: The Church of Jesus Christ of Latter-day Saints, 1961.

Tanner, N. Eldon. "Obedience." *Ensign,* January 1974.

Taylor, John. *John Taylor.* Teachings of Presidents of the Church series. Salt Lake City: The Church of Jesus Christ of Latter-day Saints, 2001.

"Try the Spirits." *Times and Seasons* 3, no. 11 (1 April 1842): 743–48.

Tyler, Daniel. "Recollections of the Prophet Joseph Smith." *Juvenile Instructor* 27, no. 3 (1 February 1892): 93–95.

Uchtdorf, Dieter F. "Bearers of Heavenly Light." *Ensign*, November 2017.

———. "Of Regrets and Resolutions." *Ensign*, November 2012.

Webster's 1828 Dictionary of the English Language. American Christian History Series, facsimile ed. San Francisco, Calif.: Foundation for American Christian Education, 1985.

Welch, John W. "The Role of Evidence in Religious Discussion." In *No Weapon Shall Prosper: New Light on Sensitive Issues.* Edited by Robert L. Millet. Provo, UT, BYU Religious Studies Center and Deseret Book, 2011.

Wheelock, Cyrus. Letter written in London, England, to George A. Smith, 29 December 1854, [13]–[19], Historians' Office, Joseph Smith History Documents, 1839–1860, Church History Library, Salt Lake City, Utah, or josephsmithpapers.org.

Whitney, Orson F. *Life of Heber C. Kimball.* 4th ed. Salt Lake City: Bookcraft, 1973.

Widtsoe, John A. *Joseph Smith: Seeker after Truth, Prophet of God.* Salt Lake City: Bookcraft, 1951.

Wilkin, Robert Louis. *The First Thousand Years: A Global History of Christianity.* New Haven, CT: Yale University Press, 2012.

Witherington, Ben, III. *The Paul Quest: The Renewed Search for the Jew of Tarsus.* Downers Grove, IL: InterVarsity Press, 1998.

Woodruff, Wilford. *Wilford Woodruff.* Teachings of Presidents of the Church series. Salt Lake City: The Church of Jesus Christ of Latter-day Saints, 2004.

Wright, N. T. *After You Believe: Why Christian Character Matters.* New York: HarperOne, 2012.

———. *The Kingdom New Testament: A Contemporary Translation.* New York: HarperOne, 2011.

———. *Simply Christian: Why Christianity Makes Sense.* San Francisco: Harper-Collins, 2006.

Young, Brigham. Discourse, 29 August 1852, Church History Department, Church History Department, Salt Lake City, UT.

———. Journal History, 23 February 1847, Church History Library, Salt Lake City, UT.

———. Minutes, *Deseret News* Extra, 14 September 1852, Church History Library, Salt Lake City, UT.

———. Office Journal, 28 January 1857, Church History Library, Salt Lake City, UT.

Young, Joseph. "Vocal Music." In *History of the Organization of the Seventies.* Salt Lake City: Deseret Steam Printing Establishment, 1878.

SCRIPTURE INDEX

OLD TESTAMENT

Genesis
37:5–11, p. 164
40:1–19, p. 164
41:1–8, p. 164
41:14–38, p. 164

Exodus
33:11, p. 171

Leviticus
11, p. 50
11:44, p. 270
17:11, p. 267

Numbers
11: 24–29,
pp. 10–11
11:16–17, p. 10
12:3, pp. 171, 294
12:6–8, p. 171

1 Samuel
3:10, p. 174n21

1 Kings
18:21, p. 96
19:4–12, pp. 166–167

Psalms
23:1–6, pp. 151–152
24:1, p. 234
24:3–4, p. 266
46:10, pp. 119, 170
51:10, p. 266
139:7–8, p. 40

Isaiah
5:20, p. 63
9:6, p. 31
25:8, p. 183
48:22, p. 112
57:20–21, p. 112
63:3, p. 28

Jeremiah
2:13, p. 217
31:31–34, p. 213

Ezekiel
36:25–26, p. 213

Daniel
2, p. 164

Joel
2:28, p. 160
2:28–29, p. 36

NEW TESTAMENT

Matthew
3:15, p. 145
3:24–26 (JST), p. 148
3:45–46 (JST), p. 15
5:5, p. 295
5–7, p. 24
5:27–28, p. 92
5:48, p. 296
6:22, p. 205
6:38 (JST), p. 158
7:1–2 (JST), p. 297
7:7, p. 299
7:9–11 (JST), p. 189

7:13–14, pp. 63, 92
7:36 (JST), p. 208
10:5–6, p. 49
11:29, p. 294
12:31–32, p. 100
12:38–40, p. 250
13:10–11, p. 190
14:28–29, p. 229
15:24, p. 49
16:16–19, p. 229
16:21–23, p. 230
17:1–9, p. 229
18:10, p. 116
25:21, p. 290
25:40, p. 264
26:37, p. 229
26:69–74, p. 230
27:54 (JST), p. 29
28:19–20, p. 49

Mark
1:5–6 (JST), p. 24
1:6–8 (JST), p. 9
1:34, p. 246
5:35–43, p. 229
16:15–18, pp. 49, 244

Luke
3:28–29 (JST), p. 15
4:41, p. 246
11:1–3, p. 59
22:31–32, pp. 114, 230, 242
24:13–32, p. 149
24:32, pp. 115, 208

John
1:1–3, p. 21
1:9, p. 33
1:11–12, p. 100n18
1:37–39, p. 92
3:1–3, p. 212
3:2, pp. 202, 208
3:3, pp. 215, 227
3:3–5, p. 145
3:4–5, p. 213
3:8, p. 285
3:19, p. 216
3:34 (JST), p. 27
5:26–27, p. 25
6:56, p. 30
6:63, p. 215
6:66–69, p. 229
7:37–39 (JST), p. 22
10:17–18, p. 26
14, pp. 278–279
14:2, pp. 1–2, 173
14:9, p. 117
14:15–17, pp. 278–279
14:18, p. 279
14:21, p. 279
14:23, p. 279
14:26, pp. 3, 149, 150, 279
15:5, p. 264
16:7, p. 3
16:13–14, pp. 17, 194
16:33, p. 276

17:12, p. 106
17:20–21, p. 30

Acts
2:2–4, p. 10
2:14–18, p. 36
2:42, p. 231
4:8–12, p. 231
5, p. 234
5:3, p. 18
5:3–4, p. 16
5:4, p. 18
5:9, p. 18
8, p. 46
8:9, p. 52
8:14–23, p. 52
8:16–20, p. 46
9, p. 187
9:15, p. 183
10, pp. 50, 215
10:11, p. 50
10:15, p. 50
10:28, p. 50
10:34–35, p. 51
10:38, p. 62
10:43, p. 51
10:44–48, p. 51
19, pp. 52,
   200–201
19:1–6, p. 46
19:2–6, p. 52
22:15–16, p. 45

Romans
1:1–3, p. 33
5:5, p. 253
5:9, p. 266
6:6, p. 29
8:2, p. 245
8:26–27, p. 118
8:27, p. 277
13:11, p. 225

1 Corinthians
2:11–12 (JST),
   p. 125
2:11–14, pp. 73,
   190, 246
2:16, pp. 14–15,
   303
2:16 (JST), p. 125
3:16–17, p. 86
4:1, p. 130
6:11, p. 270
6:19–20, p. 86
11:26–27, p. 27
11:29–30, p. 27

12, pp. 234, 246,
   252
12:1–3, p. 246
12:27, p. 248
13, p. 253
13:5, p. 293
13:12, p. 141
14:40, p. 74
15:22, p. 107

2 Corinthians
1:21–22, p. 274
3:6, p. 215
5:5, p. 274
5:7, p. 141
5:17, pp. 25, 30,
   54, 227, 274
5:21, p. 28
12:2, pp. 161–162
12:4, pp. 161–162

Galatians
2:20, pp. 30, 269
3:13, p. 28
4:18–19, p. 269
5:19–21, p. 252
5:22–25, pp. 252–
   253
6:15, p. 25

Ephesians
1:13–14, p. 274
2:20, p. 57
3:9, p. 21
4:8, p. 34
4:8–10, p. 28
4:12–13, p. 56
6:4, p. 38

Philippians
4:7, pp. 305–306
4:13, p. 302

Colossians
3:5, p. 25

1 Thessalonians
5:16–21, p. 84
5:19, p. 295
5:22, p. 64

1 Timothy
1:15 (JST), p. 257
2:4, p. 244
2:4–6 (JST), p. 257

2 Timothy
1:6, pp. 46, 295

Hebrews
1:1–2, pp. 21–22
2:17, p. 25

3:1, p. 157
4:16, p. 118
6:4–6, p. 102
10:29, p. 102
10:31, p. 102
13:2, pp. 176, 187

James
1:5, p. 299
1:8, p. 64
1:17, p. 33
1:27, pp. 264–265
1:27 (JST), pp. 62,
   232
2:19, pp. 229, 246
4:3, p. 120
5:16, pp. 115, 183,
   299

1 Peter
1:15–16, p. 270
2:9, pp. 163, 217,
   245
3:18, p. 259
3:18–20, p. 162
4:6, p. 162
5:6–7, p. 261

2 Peter
1:4, pp. 68, 192,
   255, 282
1:10–11, p. 277
1:16–19, p. 277
1:20–21, p. 11
1:21, p. 82
2:20–21, p. 109
3:9, p. 244

1 John
1:5, p. 33
1:7, pp. 257–258
2:5, p. 30
2:20, p. 273
2:24, p. 54
2:27, p. 148
4:1, p. 72
4:13, pp. 30, 54,
   273, 274
4:15, p. 30
5:1, p. 228
5:3, p. 237
5:6–7, p. 32
5:14–15, p. 99
5:16–17, p. 99

Revelation
3:20, p. 39
5:6, p. 33
7:17, p. 183

13:8, p. 33
21:4, p. 183

**BOOK OF
MORMON**

1 Nephi
1:1, p. 154
2:16, p. 218
3:7, p. 153
8, pp. 164, 216
8:4–10, p. 216
8:33, p. 305
10:9, p. 130
10:17–19, pp. xi,
   53
10:18–19, p. 163
10:21, p. 85
10:22, p. 208
11:7, p. 217
11:11, p. 13
11–14, p. 164
11:21–22, p. 217
11:25, p. 217
12:10, p. 267
15:33, p. 85
16:29, p. 237
17:3, p. 153
17:45, p. 174
19:23, p. 237
19:24, p. x
22:2, p. 125

2 Nephi
2:8, pp. 26, 67, 227
2:10–16, pp.
   150–151
4:34, p. 276
9:13, p. 107
9:16, p. 108
9:39, p. 151
9:41, p. 92
15:20, p. 63
25:12, p. 21
26:23–27, p. 266
27:23, pp. 249–250
31:2, pp. 144–145
31:3, p. 159
31:5–6, p. 145
31:7, p. 193
31:7–9, p. 145
31:13, pp. 145, 193
31:13–14, p. 194
31:17, pp. 45, 194
31:21, pp. 16,
   144–145

32, p. 145
32:2–3, pp. 145,
  193–194, 207
32:3, p. 187
32:5, p. 145
32:8, p. 299
33:1, p. 207

Jacob
4:8, pp. 125,
  154–155
6:5, p. 84
6:8, p. 84
7:4–5, p. 239
7:7, p. 97
7:9, p. 97
7:13, p. 97
7:19, p. 97

Enos
1:1, p. 38
1:1–11, p. 239
1:3, p. 231
1:3–8, pp. 261–262
1:27, p. 277

Jarom
1:4, p. 158

Mosiah
1:11, p. 262
2:4, p. 267
2:17, p. 264
2:36, p. 28
2:37, p. 85
3, p. 262
3:7, p. 25
3:8, p. 21
3:19, pp. 151, 252,
  284
4, p. 262
4:1–3, p. 26
4:2, pp. 262, 266
4:2–3, p. 262
4:3, p. 29
4:11–12, p. 264
4:26, p. 264
5:2, pp. 32, 133,
  219, 224, 227,
  242
5:3, p. 219
8:17, p. 135
15:3, p. 33
18:10, p. 48
18:12, p. 157
26:1–3, p. 218
26:20, p. 277
27:8–9, p. 181

27:14, p. 182
27:24, p. 227
27:24–25, p. 182
27:25–26, p. 227
27:26, p. 25
28:3, p. 182

Alma
5:14, p. 227
5:15, p. 130
5:26, pp. 96, 226
5:45–46, pp. 130–
  131, 224–225
7:11–12, p. 25
7:14, p. 46
7:21, p. 85
11:21–22, p. 95
11:26–39, p. 219
11:39, p. 21
11:41, p. 107
11:44, pp. 16–17
12:7–8, p. 219
12:9, p. 155
12:9–11, p. 188
13:11, p. 267
13:11–12, p. 267
14:6, p. 27
15:3, p. 27
18:23, p. 219
18:39–43, p. 217
19:6, pp. 217, 218
22:7, p. 219
22:14, p. 67
24:10, p. 67
24:11, p. 67
24:15, p. 67
24:30, p. 109
26:12, p. 302
30:6, p. 97
30:12, p. 97
30:13, p. 97
30:42, pp. 97, 98
30:43, p. 97
31:5, p. 202
32:21, p. 133
32:40, p. 130
33:22, p. 107
34:32, pp. 89, 160
34:33, p. 89
34:35, pp. 26, 28
34:36, p. 85
34:37–38, p. 84
36:5–24, p. 224
36:24, pp. 182–183
37:8, p. 149
38:6–8, p. 224

39:5–6, p. 101
40:3, p. 154
41:10–11, pp. 113,
  252
45:17–19, p. 171

Helaman
3:29–30, p. 83
3:35, p. 266
4:24, p. 85
5:30, p. 167
6:26–27, p. 102
7:9, p. 54
10:5, p. 234
10:5–7, p. 277
14:17, p. 107

3 Nephi
8:1, p. 74
9:15, p. 21
9:20, p. 288
11:3, p. 167
11:27, p. 17
11:36, p. 17
12:1, p. 24
12:5, p. 295
12:48, p. 296
13:5–8, p. 111
13:9–13, p. 112
13:22, p. 205
14:13–14, p. 92
17:13–14, p. 112
17:15–17, p. 113
17:21–24, p. 116
17:25, p. 112
18:19–21, p. 112
18:22–23, p. 112
18:23, p. 112
18:24, p. 205
18:36–37, p. 46
19:5–9, pp.
  121–122
19:6, p. 112
19:8, p. 112
19:15–18, p. 116
19:22, p. 117
19:24, p. 117
27:2, p. 112
27:7, p. 112
27:7–10, p. 156
27:19, p. 267
27:19–20, p. 268
27:28, p. 112
28:39, p. 27
29:8, p. 110
76:5, p. 112

4 Nephi
1:2, p. 242
1:3, p. 242
1:15, p. 242

Mormon
7:7, p. 17
9:3–4, p. 85
9:13, p. 107
9:14, p. 108
9:22–24, p. 244

Ether
4:11, pp. 125–126
4:18, p. 244
12:4, p. 272
12:19, p. 130
12:19–21, p. 238
12:32, p. 272
13:10, p. 267

Moroni
2:2, pp. 24n5, 46
3:4, p. 157
4:3, pp. 65, 87, 160
6:9, p. 156
7:12–19, p. 35
7:13, p. 153
7:16, p. 38
7:16–19, p. 217
7:18–19, pp. 41–42
7:27, p. 261
7:27–28, p. 114
7:36, p. 187
7:37, p. 249
7:40–41, p. 272
7:44, pp. 294–295
7:45, pp. 255, 293
10, pp. 245–246
10:4–5, p. 147
10:5, pp. 126, 147
10:7–8, p. 249
10:17, pp. 35, 247
10:22, p. 272
10:32–33, p. 296

**DOCTRINE
AND
COVENANTS**
1:24, p. 159
1:30, p. 58
1:38, p. 241
5:34, p. 153
6:9, p. 66
6:13, p. 267
6:14–15, p. 169
6:22, p. 169

6:23, p. 170
8:1–3, p. 171
8:2–3, p. 287
10:21, p. 299
11:7, p. 130
11:9, p. 66
11:12, pp. 148–149, 297
11:13–14, p. 126
14:7, p. 267
18:18, p. 148
18:32, p. 157
18:34–36, pp. 133–134, 179
19:20, p. 28
19:21, p. 66
19:23, p. 293
19:31, pp. 66, 189
20, pp. 197, 258, 260
20:9–11, p. 258
20:17–28, p. 258
20:27–28, p. 17
20:30–31, p. 258
20:31, p. 265
20:41, p. 46
20:43, p. 46
20:45, p. 156
20:60, p. 157
20:68, p. 46
20:77, pp. 65, 160
21:5, p. 241
25:8, p. 46
25:12, p. 61
29:30–31, p. 22
31:3–4, pp. 188–189
33:14, p. 258
33:14–15, pp. 24–25
33:15, p. 46
35:6, p. 46
36:2, p. 155
38:27, p. 32
39:6, pp. 155, 189
39:10, pp. 45–46
39:23, p. 46
42:6, p. 196
42:11, pp. 76–77
42:12–14, p. 197
42:14, p. 197
42:17, pp. 16, 118, 188, 277
42:22–23, p. 91
42:61, p. 155

45:3–5, p. 114
46, pp. 246, 248
46:2, pp. 156–157
46:7, p. 248
46:8, p. 247
46:8–9, p. 248
46:11, p. 247
46:13, p. 126
46:27, pp. 72, 249
46:30, p. 118
49:14, p. 46
50:10, p. 198
50:13–14, p. 198
50:17–20, p. 198
50:18, p. 198
50:24, p. 217
50:28, p. 74
50:29–30, p. 118
50:43, pp. 30, 54
52:10, p. 46
53:3, p. 46
59:4, p. 237
59:9, pp. 56, 263
59:21, p. 264
59:23, pp. 169, 274, 276
63:9, p. 251
63:16, p. 92
63:64, p. 190
64:5, p. 110
64:6–7, p. 99
64:29, p. 142
64:33, p. 178
67:10, p. 160
68:25, pp. 38, 46
68:28–29, p. 38
71:1, p. 189
76, pp. 1, 173
76:8–9, p. 175
76:11–12, p. 161
76:12, p. 162
76:22–24, p. 33
76:31, p. 100n18
76:31–33, p. 103
76:36–39, p. 107
76:43–44, p. 108
76:45–48, p. 108
76:52, p. 46
76:56, p. 273
76:69, pp. 259–260
76:107, p. 28
82:3, pp. 96, 109
82:10, pp. 238, 274
84:20, p. 111
84:33–38, p. 273

84:45–48, pp. 43, 217
84:46–48, p. 35
84:85, p. 189
84:109–10, p. 234
85:6, p. 167
88, p. 107
88:4–5, p. 282n18
88:6, p. 28
88:6–13, p. 34
88:13, p. 22
88:29–32, p. 107
88:32, p. 107
88:33, p. 68
88:35, p. 108
88:66, p. 179
88:67, p. 205
88:68, pp. 160, 175
88:73, p. 231
88:102, p. 108
88:106, p. 28
90:3–5, pp. 95–96
90:5, p. 180
90:24, p. 219
93:4, p. 33
93:6–18, p. 21
93:12, p. 61
93:13, p. 62
93:19–20, p. 62
93:24, p. 219
93:40, p. 38
93:43, p. 38
97:3, p. 178
101:16, pp. 119, 126, 170
101:54, p. 57
107:23, pp. 57, 126–127
107:34, p. 57
109:14–15, pp. 271n1, 282n18
110, p. 10
110:1–2, p. 162
112:20, p. 241
121–23, p. 287
121:26–28, p. 137
121:35, p. 90
121:37, p. 92
121:41–46, pp. 295–296
128:1, p. 287
130:18–19, p. 155
130:22, pp. 13, 14
130:23, p. 15
131:5, p. 277

132:7, p. 277
132:8, p. 74
132:19–20, p. 273
132:27, p. 102
132:49, p. 277
133:50, p. 28
136:4, p. 110
137:1, p. 161
138, p. 162
138:1–11, p. 162
138:33, p. 46

PEARL OF GREAT PRICE

Moses
1:9–11, p. 161
1:14, p. 161
1:32–33, p. 22
1:32–35, p. 33
1:39, pp. 20, 141, 255
1:42, p. 190
4:2, pp. 28–29
4:32, p. 190
5:1–9, p. 11
5:18–31, p. 103
5:22–24, pp. 105–106
6:36, pp. 57, 160
6:51–68, p. 11
6:57, pp. 43–44
6:58–59, p. 213
6:60, pp. 263, 267
6:61, pp. 16, 118, 155, 277
7:30, p. 22
7:35, p. 26
7:42–44, p. 113
7:47, p. 33
7:48, p. 113
7:59, p. 118

Abraham
1:2, p. 233

Joseph Smith–History
1:16–17, p. 161
1:20, p. 161
1:41, p. 36

Articles of Faith
1:6, p. 160
1:9, p. 192

SUBJECT INDEX

Actions: that offend Holy Ghost, 88–99; when lacking knowledge, 146–47

Adam and Eve, 11

Adoption, 214–15

Agency, 93, 233–34

Agents of God, 142, 194–95

Alma the Elder, 47–48, 157, 181, 182

Alma the Younger, 130–31, 181–82, 187, 223, 224–25

Ammon, 217

Amulek, 95

Angels, tongue of, 145, 187. *See also* Teaching

Apostles, loyalty and love for, 241

Ashton, Marvin J., 248–49

Atonement, 20, 28–29

Attitudes, that offend Holy Ghost, 88–99

Aunt Gladys, 185–87

Ballard, M. Russell, 85–86

Baptism(s): of Jesus Christ, 15, 145; by water and by Holy Ghost, 24–25, 44–46, 52–53; in waters of Mormon, 157

Beck, Julie B., 175

Bednar, David A., 227, 263, 282, 294

Belief, and rebirth, 217–22

Benjamin, King, 262–63, 266

Benson, Ezra Taft, 11–12n2, 173, 197–98, 225–26, 270, 276

Bible, knowledge of truthfulness of, 127–29

Birth, natural and spiritual, 252–53. *See also* Rebirth

Bishop(s): discernment of, 71–72; selection of new, 290–91

Blasphemy, 100–101n19, 104

Blessings, of Church membership, 141–44

Body/Bodies: of members of Godhead, 13; as temple of Holy Ghost, 86–87

Book of Mormon: attacks on, 131; gaining testimony of, 147

Boundaries, pushing, 63–65

Brother of Jared, 238

Bushman, Richard L., 86

Bytheway, John, 87

Cain, 102–3, 105–6

Calling and election made sure, 276, 277–78, 280–81

Cannon, George Q., 76

Caussé, Gérald, 32

Celestial kingdom, 161–62, 259–60

Certitude, 240

Change of heart, 105, 214. *See also* Conversion; Rebirth; Spiritual birth

Charity, 255, 269

Chastity, 39–40, 101. *See also* Sexual impurity

Children: raising, 38; treatment of, 116; wayward, 182–83; counsel for, 283

Christofferson, D. Todd, 240–41, 259, 267, 282n18

Church attendance, 60–61, 234–36, 248

Church of Jesus Christ of Latter-day Saints, The: unique characteristics of, 1–2; beliefs of, regarding beginning of Holy Ghost's ministry, 9–12; need for, 55–58; purpose of, 58; harmony of revelation with teachings of, 75; unchanging truths in, 135–36; blessings of membership in, 141–44; work of, 155–58; apathy toward, 236; opposition to, 298–300

Clark, J. Reuben, 136

Clark, Kim B., 230–31, 302–3

Clayton, William, 14, 278

Comforter, 278–81

Commandments, perspective on, 236–37

Common sense, 172

Companionship of Holy Ghost, 284–86, 295–96; loss of, 3–4, 15, 28; maintaining, 62–67, 283; and sensitivity of Holy Ghost, 85–86; actions and attitudes affecting, 88–99; feeling, 286–89; recognizing, 289–93; meekness and, 293–95

Confirmation, 44–46

Conscience, 29, 37–40, 42, 219–20, 289

Consecration, 233

Conversion, 200, 228–43. See also Change of heart; Rebirth; Spiritual birth

Cornelius, 50–51

Counsel, ignoring wise, 93–97

Covey, Stephen R., 4, 38–40, 41, 144

Covill, James, 45–46

Cowdery, Oliver, 169–71

Craig, Michelle D., 153

Creation, 21–22

Cyprian, 46–47, 240

Darkness, journey from, to light, 216–17

Dead, redemption of, 162

Death: sins unto, 99–100, 102–8; life after, 301–2

Deceased family members, nearness of, 163–64

Deception, 83

Decision making, 146–47

Degrees of glory, 103, 107, 161, 173, 259–60

Deny the faith, 91–92

Depression, 286–87

Desires, education of, 40

Dew, Sheri L., 120–21

Discernment, 71–72, 83; through Light of Christ, 35; and prophetic direction, 72–74; using, 74–76; and patience with spiritual growth, 76–77; emotion and, 77–80; through scriptures, 80–82; and knowledge of truth of all things, 147–50; gift of, 249; of truth from falsehood, 284

Distraction, and presence of Holy Ghost, 90–91

Divine guidance. See Revelation

Diving nature, partaking of, 255–56

Doctrine: determining source of, 74–76; and substance in teaching, 199–205; spiritual gifts and purity of, 248; themes in Restoration scripture, 258

"Doctrine of Christ," 144–45

Dominion, unrighteous, 92–93

Doubt, 220, 275

Dove, Holy Ghost descends in shape of, 15

Dreams: discernment and, 71–72; divine guidance through, 160–66. See also Vision(s)

Earnest payment, Holy Ghost as, 272–76

Eastern Orthodox Church, 24

Edge, living on, 63–65

Education, of desires, 40

Elijah, 166–67, 168

Emotion: spirituality and, 77–80; testimony and, 133. See also Feelings

Enduring to the end, 280

Enos, 239, 261–62

Enticings of Holy Ghost, 150–54

Ephesian disciples, 52–53

Eternal life, being sealed up to, 276, 277–78, 280–81

Eternal marriage, 277

Eyring, Henry B., 57, 97, 149–50, 253–54, 284–85

Faith: revelation and strengthening of, 75; and knowledge of spiritual things, 127–32; transformed into sure knowledge, 238–40; justification by, through grace, 258–65; centered in Christ, 272–73

False spirits. *See* Discernment

Family: unrighteous dominion in, 93; nearness of deceased members of, 163–64

Faust, James E., 202

Fear, 92

Feelings: spirituality and, 77–80; divine guidance through, 170–74; trusting, 298–99. *See also* Emotion

Final Judgment, 232

Fire, baptism by, 44–46

First Vision, 135, 160–61

Forgetfulness, in mortality, 141

Forgiveness, 29–30, 100–101n19, 258–65. *See also* Repentance

Fraternity brothers, listen to consciences, 38–40

Fruit of the Spirit, 252–55

Gentiles, gift of Holy Ghost poured out upon, 49–51

Gift of Holy Ghost, 46–48, 67–68, 122, 193–96, 221–22, 284

Gifts of the Spirit. *See* Spiritual gifts

Gladys, Aunt, 185–87

God: revelation as gift from, 4; and Creation, 21–22; and Light of Christ, 34, 41; great teachers as servants of, 37; worshipping, 60–61, 62; prayer as communion with, 116–21; existence of, 124–25; agents of, 142, 194–95; generosity of, 144; divine guidance through personal appearance of, 159–60; voice of, 167; and spiritual change, 211–12; turning life over to, 233–34; partaking of divine nature of, 255–56; remembering greatness of, 264; timing of, 288. *See also* Godhead; Kingdom of God

Godhead: everlasting covenant between members of, 9; natures of members of, 13; unity of, 16–18; work of redemption undertaken by, 20, 32; Holy Ghost's roll in, 194. *See also* God; Holy Ghost; Jesus Christ

Gospel, principles and ordinances of, 214–15, 265

Grace, 41n13, 61–62, 258–69

Great commission, 244

Guilt, 86

Hafen, Bruce, 132, 133, 203, 262

Hafen, Marie, 132, 133, 203

Hales, Robert D., 60, 216, 288

Hanks, Marion D., 254, 304

Heart: change of, 105, 214, softened, 218; as barometer for righteousness, 254

Helam, 157

Higbee, Elias, 1

Hinckley, Gordon B., 83, 114–15, 168, 240

Holland, Jeffrey R., 178, 202, 254–55

Holmes, Oliver Wendell, 203

Holy Ghost: identity of, viii; ministry of, viii; mission of, viii, 18–19; significance of, 1–5; praying to have, 2–3, 59; sent by Jesus Christ, 3, 22–25, 54; loss of, 3–4; beginning of ministry of, 9–12; Personage of, 12–18; may not tarry with individuals, 15; worshipping, 17–18; influence of, 18, 43–44, 47–48; powers of, 18; baptism by, 24–25, 44–46; Jesus Christ and fulness of, 25–27; departs from Jesus Christ, 28; heeding promptings of, 43, 94–95, 152–53; conferral of, 46, 52–53; gift of, 46–48, 67–68, 122, 193–96, 221–22, 284; function of, 54, 68; receiving, 58–67; maintaining presence of, 62–67; quenching, 84; sensitivity of, 85–86; body as temple of, 86–87; actions and attitudes that offend, 88–99; sinning against, 99–100, 104; denial of, 101–2; as mediator in prayer, 118, 119–20; knowledge through, 125–32, 137, 147–50; revelation through, 142; speaking by power of, 145; enticings of, 150–54; still small voice of, 166–69; as messenger of God and Jesus Christ, 194; teaching with, 196–99; customized counsel from, 242; fruit of, 252–55; as

sealer, 271, 272–76; as God's earnest payment, 272–76; omnipotence of, 277; as Comforter, 278–80; fulness of, 282n18; living worthy of companionship of, 283; comings and goings of, 285–86; recognizing promptings of, 289–93; trust in, 297–306. *See also* Companionship of Holy Ghost; Godhead
Hope, 272–73, 276
Humility, 264, 293, 294
Hunter, Howard W., 79, 93, 295
Hyde, Orson, 265–66
Hymns, 61
Hypocrisy, 98–99

Impurity, 91–92
Insecurity, 275–76
Institute of Religion, 93–95
Intellect, 198–99

Jacob, 239
Jared, brother of, 238
Jehovah, 13–14, 33. *See also* Jesus Christ
Jesus Christ: mission and ministry of, vii–viii; sends Holy Ghost, 3, 22–25, 54, 278–79; baptism of, 15, 145; and Creation, 21–22; baptizes by water and Holy Ghost, 24; dual inheritance and sinlessness of, 25–27; and fulness of Spirit, 25–27; suffers loss of Spirit, 28; life in, 28–32; being in, 30–32; seeking to emulate, 61–62; blasphemy against, 104; put to open shame, 105; teachings on prayer, 111–16; Nephites pray to, 116–17; knowledge regarding, 126–28; generosity of, 144; spiritual development of, 148; appears in Kirtland Temple, 162; and stewardship over sacred matters, 189–91; following example of, 193; taking upon name of, 193; and spiritual eclipse in teaching, 205–7; change through, 211, 243; rebirth through, 212–15; partaking of power of, 217; becoming like, 232, 269–70; issues great commission, 244; as Lord, 246; pure love of, 255; salvation through, 257–58; justification by

faith through grace of, 258–65; faith and hope centered in, 272–73; overcoming world through, 276; as Second Comforter, 278–81; denial of, 281. *See also* Godhead; Jehovah; Light of Christ
Joel, 36
John the Baptist, 9, 52–53
Joy, following forgiveness, 29
Judas Iscariot, 106
Judgment, 17
Justification, 258–65, 277

Keller, Flo Beth, 47
Keller, Roger, 47
Kimball, Heber C., 12–13, 104, 212, 221, 278
Kimball, Spencer W., 180, 187
Kingdom of God, 55–56, 212–15
Kirtland Temple, 162, 271n1, 282n18
Knowledge, 123, 137–38; of Holy Ghost, 16; denying, 97–99; sure, 123–27; of spiritual things, 125–27; through Holy Ghost, 127–32, 137, 246; through revelation, 131–32; and reason and reality, 132–37; action in face of lacking, 146–47; of truth of all things, 147–50; growing in, 203; cost of, 204–5; and rebirth, 217–22; faith transformed into, 238–40
Korihor, 97–98

Lamoni, 217
Language, used in revelation, 159n1
Laub, George, 13
Lawrence, Larry L., 242
Lee, Harold B., 81–82, 154, 164–65, 174–75, 228–29, 241, 251–52, 292–93
Lehi's dream, 216–17
Lewis, C. S., 234, 261, 269, 291–92
Life, in Jesus Christ, 28–32. *See also* Eternal life, being sealed up to
Life after death, 301–2
Light, journey from darkness to, 216–17
Light of Christ, 33, 40–42; Joseph Fielding Smith on, 14; natural and redemptive functions of, 33–36; poured out upon all flesh, 36–37; as

conscience, 37–40, 289; searching diligently in, 42; and sensitivity of Holy Ghost, 85; enticings of, 151; and spiritual gifts, 247
Lund, Gerald N., 260–61
Lustfulness, 91–92

Madsen, Truman G., 121n11
Marriage, 277
Marsh, Thomas B., 241
Maxwell, Neal A.: on following First Presidency, 96; on hypocrisy, 98–99; on prayer and Holy Ghost, 120; on faith in scriptures, 130; on Restoration, 136–37; on generosity of God, 144; on Holy Ghost teaching through memory, 149; on submission of will, 234; on meekness, 294; on gift of Holy Ghost, 295
McConkie, Brenda, 304
McConkie, Bruce R.: on Personage of Holy Ghost, 12; on presence of Godhead, 14–15; on perfection of Jesus Christ, 26–27; on Light of Christ, 35–36; on remission of sin, 46n3; on gift of Holy Ghost, 48; on sins unto death, 99–100; on Judas as son of perdition, 106; on Nephites' praying to Christ, 117; on Alma the Younger, 181–82n7; on teaching with Holy Ghost, 198–99; on scripture, 237–38; on spiritual gifts, 256; on calling and election made sure, 280–81; on companionship of Holy Ghost, 288–89
McConkie, Joseph Fielding, 142, 203–4, 304
McConkie, Oscar Sr., 41
McKay, David O., 158, 274, 292–93
Media, 63, 87, 88–89
Meekness, 293–95
Memory, quickening of, 149–50
Miller, Adam, 31–32
Millet, Shauna, 206, 273
Missionaries, 31, 43–44, 80–81, 147, 150, 177–78, 184–87, 188–89
Missionary work, 244–45
Modesty, false, 275
Monson, Thomas S., 175

Montgomery, John W., 134–35
Morality, 39–40
Mormon Gnostics, 76–77
Mortality, forgetfulness in, 141
Moses, 10–11, 171
Mosiah, sons of, 181–82
Mouw, Richard J., 142
Music, 61, 63, 87
Mysteries, 154–55

Natural birth, 252–53
Needy, caring for, 264–65
Neibaur, Alexander, 80
Nelson, Russell M., vii–viii, 4, 58, 149, 236, 305
Neuhaus, Richard John, 20, 256
Nibley, Hugh, 131–32
Nicene Creed, 23–24
Nicodemus, 212–13

Oaks, Dallin H., 63, 90, 132, 232, 290
Obedience, 260–61. See also Works
Old Testament: manifestations of Holy Ghost in, 10–12; institute class on, 94–95
Olive Leaf revelation, 34, 107–8
Ordinance(s): versus sacrament, 110–11; first, 214–15
Others: treatment of, 253–54; caring for, 264–65

Packer, Boyd K.: on doctrine's effect on behavior, viii; on forcing spiritual things, 77; on withdrawal of Spirit, 85–86; on noisiness of world, 170; on common sense and promptings, 172; on voice of Holy Ghost, 173–74; on temple ordinances, 191; on turning agency over to Lord, 233; on knowing difference between thoughts and promptings, 289
Palmer, Parker J., 205
Parables, 189–90
Patience, 40, 76–77
Paul, 30, 45, 52–53, 183
Peace: following forgiveness, 29; as product of revelation, 76; divine guidance through, 169–70; in mortality, 276

Peaceable things, 154–55

Pearce, Virginia H., 207–8

Pentecost, 10, 36

People, Holy Ghost works through, 176, 181–87, 192; words of prophets, 176–81; and stewardship over sacred matters, 188–91

Perdition, 102–3; sons of, 100, 105–8

Persecution, 105n28

Peter, 49–52, 113–14, 229–30

Peterson, Elmer L., 293–94

Plan of salvation, 18–19, 20

Poor, caring for, 264–65

Potter, Amasa, 247

Pratt, Orson, 55–56, 214

Pratt, Parley P., 34–35, 53–54, 164n6, 219

Prayer(s), 110–11, 121–22; to have Spirit, 2–3, 59; answers to, 90–91, 299; as sacrament, 110–11; Christ's teachings on, 111–16; offered by President Hinckley, 114–15; as communion with Deity, 116–21; unanswered, 146–47; for spiritual gifts, 247; trusting, 298–99

Preoccupation, and presence of Holy Ghost, 90–91

Priesthood: and conferral of Holy Ghost, 52–53; restoration of, 162

Prophets: function of, 57; discernment and, 72–74; heeding counsel of, 95–97; following, 137–38; Holy Ghost works through words of, 176–81; loyalty and love for, 241

Rasband, Ronald A., 153, 168–69

Reality, and knowledge, 132–37

Reason, 132–37, 172

Rebirth, 211–12, 227; through Jesus Christ, 212–15; and journey from darkness to light, 216–17; belief and knowledge following, 217–22; as process, 222–26; gaining testimony as, 228; hope in Christ through, 272. See also Change of heart; Conversion; Spiritual birth

Redemption: work of, undertaken by Godhead, 20, 32; Creation's role in, 21–22; and gift of Holy Ghost, 22–25; and Christ's fulness of Spirit, 25–27; and Spirit's departure from Christ, 28; and life in Christ, 28–32; of dead, 162. See also Salvation

Religion, modern-day participation in, 123

Repentance, 3–4, 65–67, 88–89, 99–100, 182–83. See also Forgiveness

Restoration, 136–37

Resurrection, 16–17, 106–8, 127–28, 134–35

Revelation: as gift, 4; individual and institutional, 60, 180; determining source of, 74–76; knowledge through, 131–32; through scriptures, 133–34; through Holy Ghost, 142; means of, 159, 174–75; through personal appearance of God, 159–60; language used in, 159n1; through visions or dreams, 160–66; Joseph Smith on receiving, 163; through still, small voice, 166–69; through peace, 169–70; through thoughts and feelings, 170–74; timing of, 288

Rigdon, Sidney, 103, 107, 161

Righteousness, 232, 267

Roberts, B. H., 37, 41, 202–3, 268

Romney, Marion G., 191, 276

Sacrament: partaking of, 65, 110; versus ordinance, 110–11; remission of sins through, 263

Sacred matters, stewardship over, 188–91

Salvation: through Jesus Christ, 257–58; and justification by faith through grace, 258–65; and sanctification by grace and works, 265–69; Holy Ghost as earnest payment on, 272–76; present, 274–75. See also Redemption

Sanctification, 259, 265–69

Satan, 64, 100

Saul. See Paul

Scott, Richard G., 90–91, 153–54, 164, 288

Scriptures: discernment through, 80–82; in realm of faith, 130; revelation through, 133–34; Holy Ghost

works through words of, 176–79;
and increasing spirituality, 180–81;
likening, to ourselves, 237–38;
doctrinal themes in Restoration, 258
Scripture study, 59–60
Sealer, Holy Ghost as, 271, 272–76
Secular teachings, and spiritual
knowledge, 127–32
Self-examination, 231–42
Self-pity, 294
Seminary devotionals, 78
Sermon on the Mount, 24
Serving others, 253–54, 264–65
Sexual impurity, 91–92, 101. See also
Chastity
Sherem, 97–98, 238–39
Sign seeking, 250–52
Simon, 52
Simplicity, in teaching, 202–3
Sinlessness, of Jesus Christ, 25–27
Sins: forgiveness for, 29–30; remission
of, 45–46; unto death, 99–100,
102–8; unpardonable, 101–2, 103–4,
106–8, 281; ongoing cleansing
from, 263–64; removal of effects of,
265–69. See also Justification
Smith, George A., 159n1
Smith, George Albert, 23n4, 64–65,
164, 256
Smith, Hyrum, 297
Smith, Joseph: on unique characteristics
of Church, 1–2; on gift of Holy
Ghost, 5, 51; on everlasting covenant
between members of Godhead, 9;
on unchanging nature of gospel,
12; on nature of Holy Ghost, 13,
14; on presence of Holy Ghost, 15;
on Creation, 21–22; on perfection
of Jesus Christ, 27; on baptism of
fire and water, 45, 52–53; on music
and Holy Ghost, 61; on revelation,
74, 142; spiritual discernment of,
80; on forgiveness for blasphemy,
100–101n19; on unpardonable sin,
103; and vision of degrees of glory,
103, 107, 161, 173; on persecution
of faithful, 105n28; on sons of
perdition, 107, 108; and First Vision,
135, 160–61; on role of Holy Ghost,

157; and vision of celestial kingdom,
161–62; on receiving revelation, 163,
171–72, 174; on following Holy
Ghost, 172–73; on protecting sacred
matters, 190, 191; cost of learning
of, 204–5; on credit for powerful
teaching, 207; on rebirth, 214,
215; on knowledge of Jesus as Lord,
246; on spiritual gifts, 247, 248;
on justification, 265; on learning
gospel principles, 265; and calling
and election made sure, 277–78; on
Second Comforter, 279–80; Brigham
Young's vision of, 303–4
Smith, Joseph F.: on disciples of Jesus
Christ, 22–23; on Light of Christ, 85;
on unpardonable sin, 103; on Judas
as son of perdition, 106; and vision of
redemption of dead, 162; on nearness
of deceased family members, 163–64;
on bearing testimony, 200; on sign
seeking, 251; on companionship of
Holy Ghost, 288
Smith, Joseph Fielding, 14, 36–37, 104,
105, 155–56, 281
Smith, Lucy Mack, 80
Snow, Lorenzo, 221–22
Sonne, Alma, 81, 150
Sons of Mosiah, 181–82
Sons of perdition, 100, 105–8
Sorority sisters, listen to consciences,
38–40
"Spirit of the Lord," 13–14
Spirits, trying, 72–73. See also
Discernment
Spiritual birth, 252–53. See also Change
of heart; Conversion; Rebirth
Spiritual eclipse, 205–7
Spiritual experiences: forcing, 77;
emotion and, 77–78; recording, 113
Spiritual gifts, 244–45, 255–56;
teachings on, 245–50; seeking signs
versus, 250–52; and fruit of the
Spirit, 252–55
Spiritual growth, 76–77, 231–42
Spirituality, 77–80, 158, 180–81
Spiritual priorities, 282
Spirit world, nearness of, 163–64
Stephens, Carole M., 237

Stewardship, and determining source of revelation, 74
Still small voice, 166–69
Stott, John, 225
Strive, 85
Sweet, Northrup, 24–25

Talmage, James E., 14
Taylor, John, 172–73, 180, 220, 305
Teacher(s): as servants of God, 37; law of, 197–98
Teaching, 193, 207–8; and gift of Holy Ghost, 193–96; with Holy Ghost, 196–99; substance in, 199–205; avoiding spiritual eclipse in, 205–7
Temple: body as, 86–87; and opponents to Church, 131; sacred nature of ordinances and practices within, 190–91
Temptation, 64–65
Tertullian, 46
Testimony: experience and reason in, 133; bearing, 200; power of, 208; as miracle and rebirth, 228; conversion and, 228–31; and self-examination, 231–42
Thayer, Ezra, 24–25
Thoughts: controlling, 63; divine guidance through, 170–74; versus promptings, 289; trusting, 298–99
Time, unwise use of, 88–90
Tongues, gift of, 248
Tracting, 177–78
Treatment of others, 253–54
Trials, 240–41
Trust, in Holy Ghost, 297–306
Truth: denying knowledge of, 97–99; unchanging, 135–36; knowing, of all things, 147–50; discernment of, 284
Trying spirits, 72–73
Tyler, Daniel, 215

Uchtdorf, Dieter F., 42, 121
Unanswered prayer, 146–47
Ungodliness, 62–63

Unpardonable sin, 101–2, 103–4, 106–8, 281
Unrighteous dominion, 92–93

Van Buren, Martin, 1
Veil of forgetfulness, 141
Video games, 88–89
Vision(s): of degrees of glory, 103, 107, 161, 173, 259–60; divine guidance through, 160–66; of celestial kingdom, 161–62; of redemption of dead, 162; of Joseph Smith, 303–4. *See also* Dreams

Waiting, 40
Wayward children, 182–83
Weaknesses, 196–97, 241–42
Wells, John, 292–93
Western Church, 23–24
Wickedness, 112–13
Widtsoe, John A., 204–5
Will, submission of, 233–34
Wise counsel, ignoring, 93–97
Witherington, Ben III, 253
Woodruff, Wilford, 4, 76, 168n10
Works, 260–61, 265–69
World, overcoming, 276
Worship, 62. *See also* Church attendance
Worthiness: to receive revelation, 74–75; for presence of Holy Ghost, 85–86
Wright, N. T., 77, 253n9

Young, Brigham: on living up to privilege of Holy Ghost, 4; on dove at Christ's baptism, 15; on sin, 27; on withdrawal of Spirit from Christ, 28; on discernment through Holy Ghost, 83; on following our best judgment, 146; on degrees of glory, 173; on Spirit of revelation, 180; on protecting sacred matters, 191; on power of testimony, 208; on salvation, 274–76; Joseph Smith appears to, 303
Young, Joseph, 61

Zeezrom, 95